CONFLICT
POWER
AND
GAMES

The Experimental Study of Interpersonal Relations

James T. Tedeschi *SUNY/Albany*
Barry R. Schlenker *University of Florida*
Thomas V. Bonoma *IJR/Chicago*

ALDINE PUBLISHING COMPANY/CHICAGO

ABOUT THE AUTHORS

James T. Tedeschi is Professor and Director of the Social Psychology
Program of the State University of New York at Albany. Barry R.
Schlenker is Assistant Professor of Psychology at the University of Florida,
Gainesville. Thomas V. Bonoma is a Principal Investigator at the Institute
for Juvenile Research in Chicago.

First published 1973 by
Aldine Publishing Company
529 South Wabash Avenue
Chicago, Illinois 60605

ISBN 0-202-25018-0
Library of Congress Catalog Number 72-97246

Printed in the United States of America

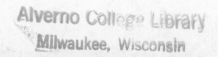

For Peg, Pat, and Maggie

Contents

Preface

Often in the history of science a particular tool or method of inquiry has had important effects on the development of significant theories. Galileo's invention of the telescope had strong impact on astronomy, physics, and atmospheric science; Leeuwenhoek's perfection of the microscope precipitated a state-change in microbiological theory; Skinner's invention of the operant box has been significant in the evolution of a novel approach to behavioral technology. In each case the scientist knew what it was that he wanted to study, was forced into the role of inventor because of limitations in existing technique, and subsequently made discoveries that immensely complicated his original theoretical perspective. Given that the grand strategy of scientific inquiry is the development of explanatory systems (i.e., theories) for natural phenomena, the empirical tactics devised to manipulate, control, observe, and measure events or processes of interest often require as much ingenuity and imagination as theory development itself.

The technological revolution that has occurred in the social sciences in the last decade or so has made available a set of research tools and data manipulation techniques that permit the study of a number of complex social processes heretofore inaccessible or not amenable to our observational powers. One important set of tools takes the generic title *experimental games,* which are characterized by the interactive protagonists' pursuit of relatively well-defined goals whose achievement is dependent on the others' behaviors. Generally the situation is so structured that certain rules govern participant behavior. Within these constraints the social psychological processes of conflict, influence, power, bargaining, and coalition formation can be studied. This book will attempt to explicate a theory of social influence that coherently organizes the existing empirical evidence obtained from researches performed with experimental games.

While the authors have made a concerted effort to avoid the more esoteric and technical jargon that some game researchers use, a rather explicit and complex vocabulary often was unavoidable in the exposition of a scientific theory. For this reason a glossary of terms appears at the end of the book. Although the reader needs no particular knowledge to follow the development of theoretical structures, it is presumed that the reader is serious, does not mind following an occasional complex chain of reasoning or the patient examination of evidence, and will accept that the authors often consider theoretically least important what may be the most interesting applied aspects of the enterprise. However, for those who seek relevance, the final chapter contains some teasers.

In order to transfer our thoughts and conversations from these ephemeral forms to words on paper, initial drafts of the chapters were divided among the authors. Hence, certain chapters bear individual structural marks. Each author thoroughly reviewed all of the chapters, so the end product often differed considerably from the initial gropings. In the end it became quite difficult to determine where an idea or phrase originated or what happened to it on the way to its present form. The present product represents a truly collaborative effort.

Many people have contributed to this book. Our laboratory and offices have always been filled with students who have suggested a research design, theoretical innovation, or equipment modification that has allowed us to escape from some cul-de-sac. The list is almost innumerable, but we would like to thank the following individuals for their unstinting efforts in our behalf: Lauren Ayers, Robert C. Brown, Jr., Thomas Faley, James Gahagan, Bob Helm, Joann Horai, Thomas Kane, Donald Lewis, Svenn Lindskold, Peter Nacci, Patricia Schlenker, R. Bob Smith III, Richard Stapleton, and Peg Tedeschi. Comments on the draft manuscript were generously given by Robert Becker, Daniel Ceranski, Harold Miller, and Leroy Pelton. Unnamed others must be content with the knowledge that but for some act on their part this book would not be possible.

It is usual to acknowledge the help of the secretary who typed the manuscript. Perhaps it is enough to say that without Terry Stapleton this book would still be in preparation. She typed parts of our manuscript that we could not decipher, kept track of the countless references, corrected our errors, and essentially got the book done. We challenge anyone to a secretarial duel.

The authors have received generous support from several sources during the preparation of the book. Tedeschi has been supported by grant #GS–27059 from the National Science Foundation, Schlenker by a predoctoral fellowship from the National Science Foundation, and Bonoma by a grant from the U.S. Arms Control and Disarmament Agency (National Research Council) .

1

Social Interaction and
Experimental Games

In *Games People Play,* Eric Berne skillfully presented a series of amusing anecdotes to illustrate how people manipulate each other in order to achieve their own ends in social interactions. Notwithstanding that many of Berne's examples are of pathological behavior, the person's purpose in such games in both normal and abnormal interactions is to maneuver another person into a vulnerable position or to elicit from him behavior that will benefit the manipulator.

For example, a young man may want to entice his current female companion to visit his apartment, ostensibly to view his etchings. The desire to show his etchings is, of course, used merely as a pretense for his real and possibly more graphic intentions. The young lady, for her part, may be quite aware of the young man's aspirations but for reasons of her own may visit the apartment. Although she may plan to frustrate any serious sexual advances, she may at the same time want to maintain enough interest to continue the liaison through the next evening's dinner date. Each individual attempts to fathom the other's behaviors, and employs deception to achieve a preplanned and expected outcome. Further, each is probably aware of the other's plan, and each devises counterplans and tactics based on this awareness. It is this calculated failure to fully communicate each other's intentions, the unwillingness to accept at face value the statements and proposals made, and the interconnectedness of social outcomes that gives the interaction the character of a game.

Most formal treatments of experimental games or game theory explicitly disassociate themselves from the loose anecdotes that Berne skillfully employs. The technical treatment of games, which for several not unrelated reasons differs from the nontechnical, refers to very specific types of

1

highly structured interactions and excludes most of the ambiguous situations to which Berne refers.

Berne's interest in games is applied and is directed toward clinical practice. In contrast, the scientist's first concern is in the development of theory, and he devises tools and laboratory techniques in order to assess the plausibility of his theories. Within the last 15 years social psychologists have employed various types of experimental games for research purposes, but as might be expected, the games the scientist uses are much more antiseptic than those illustrated by the full clinical paintbrush in *Games People Play*.

Here we will attempt to build a bridge between the technical and nontechnical approaches. We will be concerned with the more formal and technical aspects of games and how they are used for purposes of developing and testing scientific theory, but we will also examine the strategies that people use in attempting to manipulate others, including the application of force, deception, and impression management. Experimental games can be and have been used imaginatively in order to explore how people attempt to influence one another and how they respond to attempted influence or manipulation from others. The emphasis throughout this book will be on the development and empirical evaluation of a scientific theory of social influence and power in situations where the interests of the interacting parties are in conflict. In this context experimental games have provided many of the concepts and the preponderance of evidence that have helped to unravel many of the complexities of social behavior.

Formal Definition of a Game

A game may be defined as a situation in which the outcomes of two or more persons in interaction are conjoint and the persons are not certain which outcome will occur. To say that the actors' outcomes are conjoint means that the actors' actions (or inaction) are articulated with respect to the rewards or punishments each receives. For example, if two automobiles converge at an intersection at about the same time, what each individual does will have consequences for the other. If neither stops, both will most likely be involved in an accident; if both stop, neither will get through the intersection. A rule has been developed to help motorists coordinate their behaviors so that both can safely pass through the intersection: go when an arbitrary signal shows green; stop when red.

Some writers would add to our definition by stating that a game is a contest conducted under prescribed rules (e.g., Rapoport, 1960; Vinacke, 1969). The function of rules for many theorists is to narrow the range of response alternatives available to the players, thereby restricting the number of outcomes likely to occur. Such restrictions simplify the

problem of explanation and make predictions somewhat easier. In analyzing a game of tic-tac-toe, for example, if one specifies all the possible
moves allowable under the rules then the best moves available to the
players can be prescribed. Similarly, the rules of warfare preclude the use
of biological and chemical weapons, thereby restricting the available tactics that can be employed.

Unfortunately, people do not always obey the rules. One of the players
in tic-tac-toe might attempt to move twice during one turn or claim victory
by drawing a line through three cells that do not make a straight line.
Since social psychology must attempt to explain behavior as it actually
occurs and is little interested in providing prescriptions for how to behave, it cannot afford the luxury of assuming that persons will make life
easy by always behaving according to rules that would limit the possibilities of interaction. It would be just as foolish for the Pentagon to devise
contingency plans under the assumption that all possible future belliger-
ents will obey the international conventions on the acceptable moves in
warfare.

One of the more important problems in social psychology is to state
how a person defines the social situation for himself. What rules should
apply in most specific circumstances is not unambiguously interpretable
either by the actor or by the psychologist who tries to understand the situation in a post facto manner.

Most often games can be viewed as contests in which one person seeks
his own advantage at the expense of the other. Yet in some, albeit few,
situations the interests of persons in interaction are perfectly coincident,
and each can obtain his most preferred outcome. Some difficulty may
arise between the persons even in these cases. The players may not perceive
their common interests, or if they do they might not be able to coordinate
their behaviors so that the mutually desirable outcomes can be brought
about. Suppose that a combat patrol split into two groups, and one found
that an enemy machine gun nest stood between them and their military
objective. The first task would be to communicate the danger to the other
half of the company and then to coordinate their behaviors so as to best
accomplish the task of destroying the enemy. This example points out the
possibility that persons can be involved in games within games. The two
halves of the combat patrol are involved in one game in relation to each
other, and the entire combat patrol is pitted against the enemy in a second, larger game (metagame).

Interconnection of Outcomes

Social psychology has often been defined as the study of the individual's reactions to social stimuli (Shaw & Constanzo, 1970). Stimuli that
other persons or groups present have been assumed to be no different in

principle from the properties of physical objects: both presumably act on sense receptors and elicit particular responses from the individual. Of course, if the focus is the physiology of the sense receptor even social stimuli could be reduced to their physical properties. If such equivalence is assumed, then the application of principles from individual psychology to social interactions would be straightforward. However, if some properties of social stimuli are not ultimately reducible to physics, social psychological theory would require additional or unique concepts for the kinds of phenomena it seeks to understand.

Fritz Heider (1958) has provided a brilliant intuitive analysis of the perception of persons within the context of social interactions. He noted that social stimuli differ from physical stimuli in important ways. Persons

> are usually perceived as action centers and as such can do something to us. They can benefit or harm us intentionally, and we can benefit or harm them. Persons have abilities, wishes and sentiments; they can act purposefully, and can perceive or watch us. They are systems having an awareness of their surroundings and their conduct refers to this environment, an environment that sometimes includes ourselves [p. 21].

The crux of the matter is that the perception of social stimuli involves the encoding and decoding of benevolent or malevolent intentions, and that this process is clearly different from a simple mechanistic reception of physical stimuli.

Similar conclusions are echoed from alternative orientations in social science, where the contemporary trend is to study problems from an interdisciplinary perspective. This approach represents an attempt to examine all of the antecedent conditions for social behavior, including psychological, sociological, economic, and political factors, and is itself the scientist's analytic response to cries for relevance. The interdisciplinary movement has shifted the focus of analysis away from the individual's isolated responses and has placed it on the interaction of persons in social systems.

The theory of games (von Neumann & Morgenstern, 1944), an offspring of economic and mathematical thought, has also played an important role in the emerging reconceptualization of social psychology. The social problems approach has provided observational grounds, while game theory has presented logical reasons for the choice of a social rather than an individual unit of analysis. Two key concepts of all of these views are (1) *interaction* and (2) *the interconnectedness of outcomes*.

Interaction is that state of affairs in which people emit behaviors in the presence of others (Thibaut & Kelley, 1959). Such social behaviors almost always produce or have associated with them certain consequences both for the individual making them and for the other person (s) in interaction with him. Simply making eye contact with or smiling at another may elicit cooperative behavior, which, in turn, could mediate rewards for both persons. In modern, developed societies most of our rewards and punishments are mediated by other persons, groups, or institutions. We depend on the grocer for food, the medical center for health care, an organization for our livelihood, the patrolman for safety, friends for affection, and kin for security, and they depend on us for their livelihood, affection, and security. Hence, interaction usually implies some form of exchange of values.

Homans (1961) has applied principles of behavioral exchange to social interactions. As might be guessed, behavioral exchange is a direct analogy to economic processes of exchange. Just as a buyer and seller effect an exchange, such as money for commodities, two persons might exchange behaviors or sentiments, as when an individual grants esteem, status, or attraction to another person in exchange for that person's expert assistance in solving a problem. The example alerts us to a distinction between material, extrinsic or exogeneous rewards and intrinsic or endogenous rewards. Any behavior an individual emits may have several associated outcomes. Homans refers to outcomes or payoffs as gains and costs. He postulates that individuals act in a manner calculated to maximize their profits in social interactions, where a profit is the total gains minus the total costs associated with a given behavior.

Typically the individual cannot accurately assess the gains and costs likely to occur in social interactions. Even the intrinsic satisfactions associated with the individual's own behaviors may turn sour if the other person somehow does the wrong thing. For example, a person may derive intrinsic satisfaction from helping others; so if the recipient reciprocates favor for favor, both intrinsic and extrinsic satisfaction derive from the profitable interaction. However, the recipient may ignore or even resent the benevolent gesture as patronizing and may verbally abuse the favor doer, thereby increasing the costs, perhaps spoiling the intrinsic satisfaction (gain) of the behavior, and hence leaving the favor doer with a net loss for the interaction. The consequences of interaction can be difficult to foresee because they depend as much on the behavior of others as on oneself.

The interconnectedness of outcomes for various possible interactions of two or more persons can be represented in matrix form. If all possible behaviors of each person are listed and the outcomes associated with all pairs of possible articulated behaviors are indicated, a matrix may be constructed. However, the behaviors listed should be both *mutually exclusive* and *exhaustive;* that is, each behavior (or set of behaviors) represents an alternative for the actor, he cannot choose more than one behavior at a time, one alternative must be chosen, and no other alternatives exist.

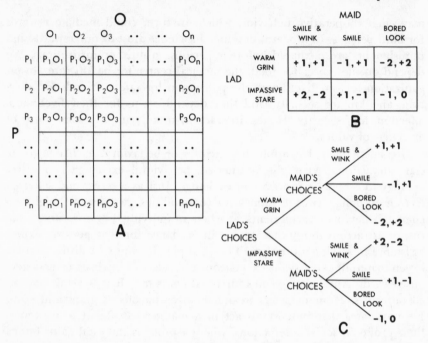

FIGURE 1.1 *Matrix representations of interdependence. (A) A generalized out-come or payoff matrix. (B) A handsome lad is introduced to a pretty maid (from Jones & Gerard, 1967). (C) A game tree analysis of the handsome lad and pretty maid example.*

Figure 1.1a represents the possible interactions of two individuals, P and O. The behavioral alternatives of P (P_1, P_2, P_3 . . . P_n) are listed on the left side of the figure, and the alternatives of O (O_1, O_2, O_3 . . . O_n) are listed on the top. The profits (either net gains or net costs) are represented numerically in the cells of the matrix (P_1O_1 . . . P_nO_n). Each outcome represents what would happen if the two parties per-formed the associated responses. Thus if P makes response P_1, any of the outcomes listed in the first row of the matrix could occur, depending on what O did. If O were then to make response O_3, the outcomes formed by the intersection of their behaviors (in this case P_1O_3) would accrue to each. The use of an outcome matrix in the analysis of behavior has been heuristically described by Thibaut and Kelley (1959) .[1]

A more concrete example of interaction and interconnected outcomes as represented in matrix form is a situation described by Jones and Ge-rard (1967) in which a handsome lad meets a pretty maid. Suppose for purposes of simplicity that the lad has available only two response

1. The question of how numerical values can be assigned to these outcomes can be quite complex and will be discussed further in Chapters 2, 3, and 8. For now we will arbitrarily assign numbers to matrices.

choices: he may either smile warmly or emit a passive stare (see Figure 1.1*b*). Further suppose that the maid can choose among three response alternatives: a smile and a wink, a smile only, or a bored look. An arbitrary numerical value is assigned the payoff to each party for each set of interconnected outcomes, and the payoff of the row player (the lad) is reported first in each cell, the payoff to the column player (the maid) second in each cell.

If the lad initiated the interaction by smiling at the maid, he would value the maid's smile and wink (+1) more than a reciprocal smile (−1), which might indicate only a courteous acknowledgement of his friendly hello. The lad would definitely not want his smile to be met with only a bored look from the maid (−2). If the lad receives a smile and wink in response to his own impassive stare, the maid must certainly be indicating her liking for him, a flattering outcome (+2), but even a smile in response to a passive stare would be a rather good outcome (+1). If the impassive stare is met with a bored look, the lad has gotten no response from the pretty maid, a disappointing outcome (−1).

A similar account could be made of the maid's estimates of her outcomes, which are dependent on the handsome lad's responses as well as her own. Her best outcome (+2) occurs when the lad indicates his interest by smiling even when she has given only a bored look, while her worse outcome (−2) would be associated with giving the lad a smile and a wink and receiving only a passive stare in return.

It should be noted that the value of the same response (say, from the maid) may be different depending on what the lad does. In other words, the meaning (and hence the value) of the maid's smile is different depending on whether it is elicited by the lad's own smile or is volunteered by the maid in the face of the lad's impassive stare. Similarly, the costs associated with a response are dependent on what the other person does. If the lad's smile is met with a bored look, he has unsuccessfully stuck his neck out and therefore incurs greater costs (−2) than if he had given the maid only an impassive stare (−1).

Another pictorial device for representing interactions is shown in Figure 1.1*c*. The lad–maid interaction is depicted in extensive form, also referred to as a game tree. The two major limbs of the large V represent the lad's two behavioral alternatives, and the three branches off each limb represent the maid's behavioral alternatives. The outcomes associated with each pair of choices are indicated by the payoffs placed next to each branch. Again, the first number represents the lad's outcome, the second number the maid's outcome. If we drew the game tree from the maid's point of view three major limbs would sprout from the origin, each with two branches stemming from it; then the maid's outcomes would be presented first and the lad's second.

Both the matrix and extensive forms of representation help to make explicit the essential features of the situation. If all possible behaviors and outcomes were accurately represented, then the job of predicting behaviors would be much simplified. Actually, our ability to specify all possible behaviors and to precisely calculate outcomes is quite poor and can almost never be done in real life.

The value of laboratory games, as we shall see, is that both behavioral alternatives and payoffs can be identified and measured. In these controlled situations the predictions of various theories about the ways in which certain variables affect social interactions can be rather precisely tested. The explanatory power of the emerging theory may later be applied in the analysis of real-world social problems. The reader is cautioned that constructed laboratory games are *not* assumed to represent complete analogs of real-world social interactions. The authors recognize the extreme simplicity of laboratory games and use them exclusively for experimental purposes. Questions pertaining to the validity of experimental games will be discussed more extensively in Chapter 7.

A distinction can be drawn between outcomes that accrue to interacting persons as a consequence of their *simultaneous* responses and those that are a consequence of *alternating* responses. In many types of situations, as in the lad and maid example, each person must make a choice of a behavioral alternative in ignorance of what the other will do, and these choices must be made simultaneously. The matrix is the typical way of representing simultaneous responding. The extensive form of the game tree typically represents alternating responses, in which one party makes a move (performs a response), the second person, knowing the response of the first, makes his move, and then the first player makes his second move with knowledge of the preceding moves, and so on until the terminal outcomes for each party are attained.

When simultaneous choices are made, knowing the intentions of the other person beforehand obviously would be important in choosing one's own behavior. For this reason much social interaction consists of attempts to probe the other person to ascertain (1) how he views his response alternatives and (2) the values he assigns to outcomes. Probes are information-gathering activities that may be used to predict what others will do. If an actor could accurately predict the behavior of others, he presumably could increase his own profits by choosing astutely among his own behavioral alternatives.

When a situation is characterized by alternating or successive responding, principles of behavioral exchange become particularly relevant (Blau, 1964; Homans, 1958, 1961; Nord, 1969). The temporal pattern of articulated responses suggests further social psychological processes based on economic analogies, such as investment and credit in which a person might make a sacrifice (incur a cost) as an investment in gaining some larger profit. A chess player, for example, might sacrifice a knight in order to capture a queen, or a person may do a favor for another in hope of incurring a debt that can be cashed in at a later date. The possibility of developing strategies and tactics over time increases the complexity of interaction and immensely complicates the social psychologist's task of explaining social behavior.

The recognition that individuals are future-oriented and base present decisions on likely outcomes of behavior suggests that the perceived pattern of outcomes will have an important impact on the behaviors of both persons. Schelling (1960) has classified types of games in terms of the correlation that exists between the parties' outcomes. He distinguishes among situations of *pure conflict, pure coordination,* and *mixed motive.*

A pure conflict game is one in which the outcomes associated with interaction are perfectly and negatively correlated, as in Figure 1.2a. Suppose that we invented a game in which P and O could choose one of two colors, green or red. Both must choose simultaneously. If both choose green, P wins $5 and O loses $5. If both choose red, P wins $10 and O loses $10. If P chooses green and O chooses red, P loses $10 and O wins $10. Finally, if P chooses red and O chooses green, P loses $15 and O wins $15. Notice that whenever one player wins, the other player must lose. Further, the amount won always equals the amount lost so that the sum of the two entries in any one cell equals zero. That is why pure conflict games are called *zero-sum games.*

Only rarely is pure conflict found in the real world. Even in parlor games and wars between nations, common interests can almost always be found between the two parties. For example, a poker game usually carries a gentleman's agreement that no one will cheat. In wars both sides typically (tacitly) agree to limit the violence or the type of weapons that will be employed. During the Korean conflict the United States and China maintained a tacit agreement: the United States did not bomb north of the Yalu, and the Chinese did not attempt to prevent the use of port facilities in South Korea. Agreements or rules such as those given in the examples indicate that not all of the possible outcomes are negatively correlated and that some area of agreement and coordination of interests is present.

When outcomes are perfectly and positively correlated, the situation is referred to as one of pure coordination. In the game presented in Figure 1.2b, P and O are given a choice between two response alternatives, green and red. It can be seen that the best outcome for both persons occurs when the parties choose opposite colors; when one chooses red and the other green they both win $10. The problem for the two persons in a simultaneous choice situation is to coordinate their behaviors so that both can receive their most preferred outcomes. Instances of such pure coor-

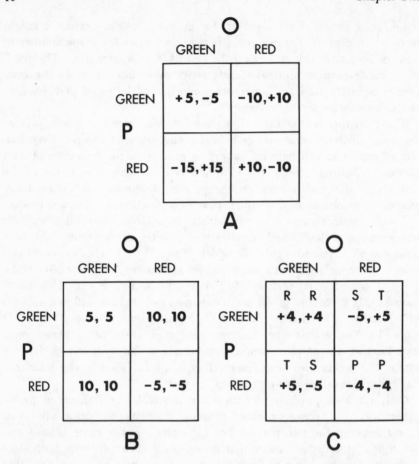

FIGURE 1.2.   *Three types of interdependence. (A) Pure conflict situation. (B) Pure coordination situation. (C) Mixed-motive situation.*

dination are found among members of the same athletic team, where the independent behaviors of a number of teammates are articulated in carrying out sparkling offensive or defensive plays.

Schelling (1960) illustrated the problem of a pure coordination interaction by the example of two people cut off during a telephone conversation that both want to continue. If both call back immediately, both will find the line busy (i.e., both lose). If neither calls back, both lose. The problem centers about getting it together. One must call while the other waits. Few situations are entirely free of conflict, and it would not be too difficult to uncover covert areas of disagreement between persons even when their interaction appears on the surface to be one of pure coordination. Although members of a team may cooperate to win a game, they may be jealous of one another or find themselves competing for the same position.

Most interactions lead to conjoint outcomes that are not perfectly correlated. Typically, in dyadic interactions both individuals stand to profit if they coordinate their responses in a given manner; one can gain at the expense of the other; or both can lose as they attempt to exploit each other. Such a mixed-motive interaction is shown in Figure 1.2c. In a simultaneous choice situation where both P and O must choose either green or red, both can win $4 if both choose green, and both can lose $4 if both choose red. Of course, both persons might settle for mutual cooperation and a profit of $4. Yet both obviously would prefer $5 to $4 and are therefore tempted to choose red in the hope the other will choose green.

This form of interaction is described as mixed motive not because the parties lack clear objectives but because of the ambivalence of their relationship (Schelling, 1960). Their interests are partially coincident and partially in conflict. The two persons may perceive each other as opponents one moment but an instant later may view each other as partners. In both mixed-motive and pure coordination situations the outcomes found in the cells of the payoff matrix do not sum to zero and hence are referred to as *nonzero-sum games.*

The structure of conflict in mixed-motive interactions can be further indicated by the *relationships* among the payoffs in Figure 1.2c. If we name the payoffs so that mutual rewards are labeled R and mutual punishments P, the most preferred payoff is called temptation (T) and the least preferred sucker (S), then it becomes clear that varying the magnitude of R, T, S, or P can increase or decrease the degree of conflict that exists between the two persons (Rapoport & Chammah, 1965).

Suppose that the value of T is increased from 5 to 25 while all the other payoffs are held constant ($R = 4$, $S = -5$, and $P = -4$). Both persons in the interaction should be sorely tempted to try to obtain the 25 points for himself, which would require that each make the red choice; consequently each would lose 4 points. It should be expected that such increases in the temptation payoff would reduce the chances that the two persons could effect a compromise by cooperating (choosing green) and sharing mutual rewards (R payoffs).

Reducing the value of the P payoff should also increase the conflict between the two parties, since they will have less to lose when they seek but fail to gain the temptation payoff because the other person also chooses red. Suppose that the value of P is zero. Then the persons can try for the temptation payoff, and even when they fail they will lose nothing, though, of course, they could have won 4 points had both chosen green. Reduction of conflict, as indicated by increasing cooperation between the two persons, should result when the values of R and S are increased. Rapoport (1964) has empirically demonstrated these relationships.

Changes in the absolute magnitude of the values used in the payoff matrix apparently do not affect the response choices of persons who play experimental games (Jones, Steele, Gahagan, & Tedeschi, 1968). What does make a difference is the relationship between the values of outcomes associated with cooperative choices and those associated with competitive choices. Steele and Tedeschi (1967) investigated several hundred possible formulas for predicting behavior in two-person, two-choice, mixed-motive games and found that the degree of competitiveness was most directly related to the log $\left(\dfrac{T-S}{R-P}\right)$. Matrix changes that increase the value of this equation will decrease the degree of cooperation of subjects who play the game. Thus in laboratory situations the experimenter can artificially manipulate the degree of conflict between persons.

The structure of outcomes associated with the mutual response choices of persons in interaction may also indicate the type and amount of power that each has over the other. Thibaut and Kelley (1959) have suggested that an index of interpersonal power can be measured by the extent to which one person can affect the range of outcomes the other receives. The wider the range of outcomes one person can mediate for another, the greater the power of the first over the second.

Thibaut and Kelley have distinguished between two types of interpersonal control—*fate control* and *behavior control.* Fate control is characteristic of a situation in which one party has unilateral control of the other's outcomes; the controlling party can determine the outcomes the dependent party receives irrespective of the dependent one's behavior. In Figure 1.3*a*, *P* has fate control over *O* because *P* can either choose green and give *O* one point or choose red and give *O* four points. What *O* does has no effect on his own outcomes. However, *O* also has fate control over *P*, since *O* can choose to give *P* either 10 points or nothing. In such instances of mutual fate control each party has an incentive to give the other the larger of the possible outcomes in order to induce reciprocity. In our example the range of outcomes through which *P* can move *O* is 3 (i.e., 4 − 1 = 3), while the range of outcomes *O* controls is 10 (i.e., 10 − 0 = 10). Thus *O* is more powerful than *P*, although both have absolute control over the other's outcomes.

Whenever by varying his own behavior *P* can make it desirable for *O*′ to similarly vary his behavior, we have an interaction characterized by behavior control. As can be seen in Figure 1.3*b*, if *P* makes the green choice, *O* should want to make the red choice in order to receive four points; conversely, if *P* makes the red choice, *O* should want to make the green choice in order to receive four points. Assuming that *P* wants *O* to make his green choice (thereby maximizing the payoffs to *P*), *P* should choose red every time; then *O* can maximize his own profit only by choosing green. Thus *P* can control *O*'s behavioral choice, but, as indicated, *O* also has behavior control over *P*. Figure 1.3*c* depicts a situation in which *P* has fate control over *O*, while *O* has behavior control over *P*.

The above analysis shows clearly why numerous social scientists have concluded that the structure of an interaction is quite important for determining what each party actually will do. If we can discover that a situation is one of pure coordination, pure conflict, or mixed motive, or that it is characterized by fate control, behavior control, or some mix of the two, we can make better predictions about social behavior. Then, too, if two persons in interaction believe that they are in a pure conflict situation when actually they are in a mixed-motive situation it becomes possible to convince both parties that some mutual behaviors are in the interests of both, and conflict resolution becomes more likely.

In the post-World War II period the United States and the Soviet Union have often perceived their relationship as one characterized by pure conflict: any gain by the one party surely implied a loss for the other.

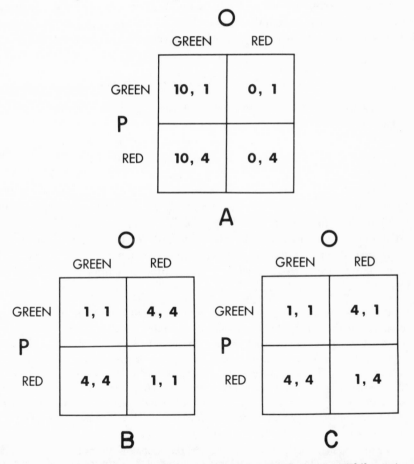

FIGURE 1.3. *Types of interpersonal control (modified from Thibaut & Kelley, 1959). (A) Mutual fate control. (B) Mutual behavior control. (C) Fate control of P over O and behavior control of O over P.*

Fortunately these two superpowers have now reexamined their perceptions and interests, and currently seem to view their relationship as a mixed-motive one. It can be hoped that neither side will be so tempted to seek competitive advantage that mutual cooperation and mutual benefits cannot be gained.

Although most real-world situations are mixed motive in character, people are not always aware of the degree of conflict present between them. As Kuhn (1963) has noted, the phenomenology of conflict is often muted or absent because "custom or habit have decreed the terms, the costs are too small to argue about, or sympathy has transformed the motives [p. 340]." That outcomes are interconnected and, further, usually are mixed motive in form gives each individual a rational motive for attempting influence to control the behaviors, attitudes, and values of others, since such control directly affects his own outcomes. Even the individual who wants to remain above the fray must resort to the use of influence, if only to protect himself from the initiatives of others.

Some Popular Types of Mixed-Motive Games

The most used experimental game is referred to as the prisoner's dilemma game (PDG). The strict definition of the PDG is that it is a two-person, two-choice, mixed-motive (nonzero-sum) game that meets certain rules with regard to the structure of payoffs. The rules are: $T > R > P > S$, and $2R > (T + S) > 2P$.[2] The matrices shown in Figures 1.2c and 1.4a satisfy the formal definition of a PDG. In Figure 1.2c, for example, the values of T, R, P, and S are 5, 4, -4, and -5, respectively (satisfying the first rule), and $2R = 8$, $(T + S) = 0$ and $2P = -8$ (satisfying the second rule). Further, each player must choose strategies simultaneously and in ignorance of what the other person does, and neither can communicate with the other. The essential dilemma of the PDG is described by Luce and Raiffa (1957).

> Two suspects are taken into custody and separated. The District Attorney is certain that they are guilty of a specified crime, but he does not have adequate evidence to convict them at a trial. He points out to each prisoner that he has two alternatives: to confess to the crime the police are sure they have done, or not to confess. If they both do not confess, then the D.A. states he will book them on some very minor trumped-up charge such as petty larceny and illegal possession of a weapon, and they would both receive minor punishments; if they both confess, they will be prosecuted, but he will recommend less than the

2. For the nonmathematically oriented reader, the symbol $>$ means *greater than*, and the two inequalities can be read as follows: the value of T is greater than R, which is greater than P, which is, in turn, greater than S; and 2 times R is greater than the sum of T and S, which is greater than 2 times P.

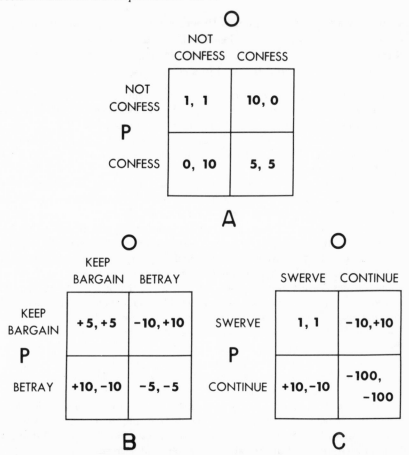

FIGURE 1.4. *Mixed-motive games. (A) The prisoner's dilemma, with the outcomes given in years in prison (all numbers are negative payoffs). (B) Tosca and Scarpia, PDG. (C) Chicken matrix.*

most severe sentence; but if one confesses and the other does not, then the confessor will receive lenient treatment for turning state's evidence, whereas the latter will get "the book" slapped at him [p. 95].

Figure 1.4a depicts some numerical outcomes corresponding to the alternatives the DA has posed for the two prisoners. *P* must consider whether he will or will not confess. If *O* does not confess it is clearly to *P*'s advantage to confess, since he will then receive no punishment (rather than one year in jail should he not confess). If *O* confesses it is again in *P*'s interests to confess, for then he will receive only 5 years in jail rather than the 10 years he would receive by not confessing. Thus, irrespective of what *O* may do it is in *P*'s best interests to confess. *O* should follow the same logic and also confess. However, if each chooses his own best strategy and confesses, then both will spend five years in jail and are worse off than if they had trusted each other and not confessed.

Rapoport (1962, p. 113) has vividly described the temptations and the possibilities of lust and betrayal in a classic case.

> In Puccini's opera *Tosca* the chief of police Scarpia has condemned Tosca's lover Cavaradossi to death but offers to save him in exchange for Tosca's favors. Tosca consents, the agreement being that Cavaradossi will go through a pretended execution. Scarpia and Tosca double-cross each other. She stabs him as he is about to embrace her, and he has not given the order to the firing squad to use blank cartridges.
>
> The problem is to decide whether or not it was to the best advantage of each party to double-cross the other. Again, we must assign numerical values to the outcome, taking into account what each outcome is worth to Tosca and to Scarpia. The values, although arbitrary, present the situation reasonably [see Figure 1.4b]. If the bargain is kept, Tosca's satisfaction of getting her lover back is marred by her surrender to the chief of police. Scarpia's satisfaction in possessing Tosca will be marred by having to reprieve a hated rival. If Tosca double-crosses Scarpia and gets away with it, she will win most (+10) and he will lose most (−10), and vice-versa. When both double-cross each other, both lose, but not so much as each would have lost had he or she been the sucker. For example, the dying Scarpia (we assume) derives some satisfaction from the thought of what is going to happen just before the final curtain, when Tosca rushes to her fallen lover and finds him riddled with bullets.
>
> Let us now arrive at a decision from Tosca's point of view: whether to keep the bargain or to kill Scarpia. Tosca has no illusion about Scarpia's integrity. But she is not sure of what he will do, so she considers both possibilities. If he keeps the bargain, I am better off double-crossing him, since I will get Cavaradossi without Scarpia if I do and Cavaradossi with Scarpia if I don't. If he double-crosses me, I am certainly better off double-crossing him. It stands to reason that I should kill him whatever he does.
>
> Scarpia reasons in exactly the same way: If she keeps the bargain, I am better off double-crossing her, since I will get rid of Cavaradossi if I do and have to put up with him if I don't. If she double-crosses me, I certainly should see to it that I am avenged. The execution, therefore, must go on.
>
> The result is the denouement we know. Tosca and Scarpia both get −5. If they had trusted each other and had kept the trust, each would have got +5.

The PDG is a particularly interesting situation also because it throws the economic concept of individual rationality into question. If a person does what is most rational for himself he does worse than if he had done what was best for *both* himself and the other person. When the PDG is iterated many times for the same players the choice of the nondominant response makes more social sense, since such unilateral cooperative initiatives may establish interpersonal trust and a resolution of the dilemma in the interests of both parties.

One could introduce explicit communications into the PDG—not allowed under the formal definition of the game—which might enhance trust, coordination, and hence mutual cooperation. For example, an experimenter may provide subjects (i.e., players) with notes that promise that the sender will cooperate on the next play of the game. This addition to the basic PDG does not escape the basic dilemma unless some type of commitment or enforcement procedure accompanies the ability to communicate. As Rapoport (1964) has observed, the addition of communications to the PDG just produces another game transposed on top of the original game. Each person has the choice of either keeping his promise (trustworthy and cooperative behavior) or breaking it (betrayal and exploitative behavior). It can be shown that breaking the promise is the best response. Hence when the game is played only once, Rapoport (1964, p. 51) suggests "that there is only one good reason to make the cooperative choice, namely in order to remain at peace with one's conscience."

Another type of mixed-motive game used frequently in laboratory experiments is "chicken." The basic difference between the PDG and "chicken" is that in "chicken" the P payoff is less than the sucker payoff. Shubik (1968) has described a real-world form of the chicken game.

> . . . consider two leather-jacketed California high school dropouts, each armed with a souped-up old car, driving toward each other on a superhighway, each with one pair of the wheels of his car on the line in the middle of the road. The first one to veer from the collision course is deemed to be "Chicken" (presumably a derisive term) and loses the game. Of course, if neither veers, they crash and may both lose their lives but maintain their honor [p. 85]."

If we assign arbitrary values to each of the outcomes, the matrix shown in Figure 1.4c represents the adolescent game just described. It should be clear that the only way one adolescent can win is by convincing the other that under no conditions will he veer from the collision course. If this commitment is believed, then the only rational alternative left to the other person is to swerve and avoid the inevitable collision. Kahn (1965) suggests that a player might insist that the game be played at night, show up quite drunk and wearing dark glasses, refrain from turning on the car lights, and when under way throw the steering wheel out the window. These tactics might communicate that the actor is quite irrational, but in these conditions apparent irrationality is the most rational strategy to use if one wants to win (Schelling, 1966). More than one policy analyst has observed these dynamics in international relations.

Many other types of games are used experimentally. Rapoport and Guyer (1966) and Harris (1969) have classified all games with a 2 x 2 matrix form and have indicated which psychological processes are most likely to be associated with each type of game. It is beyond the purposes of this book to exhaustively review all forms of experimental games, but it will be worthwhile to indicate the range of simplicity–complexity that can be involved in game research.

Simple and Complex Games

Games as research tools have varied from the use of highly barren, antiseptic, and artificial situations, such as the presentation to two subjects of the choice between two switches, a four-celled payoff matrix and no communications, to an imaginative and rich environment in which subjects can communicate with each other and engage in complex influence strategies.

The simplest of all social situations is aptly referred to as the "minimal social situation," and was first explored experimentally by Sidowski, Wycoff, and Tabory (1956). In their study two subjects were met in a waiting room and escorted to separate rooms, where they were seated and hooked up to a shock apparatus. Each was given two buttons and told to push either of them in any way they wanted and as often as they wanted. Each subject's goal was to maximize the number of points he received on a cumulative counter and to avoid electric shock. Presumably, from the subject's point of view, some unknown connection existed between pushing the buttons and receiving points or shock.

Unknown to the subjects, the outcomes each received were totally controlled by the button choices of the other. If P pressed his left button O received a shock no matter what he was doing; if P pushed his right button O received a point no matter what he might be doing. O's choices similarly rewarded or punished P. The situation, presented in matrix form in Figure 1.5a, shows that each person has fate control over the other. It was found that when the shocks were strong the subjects soon learned to press the button that rewarded the other person and not press the button that delivered shock. When the shock was weak the participants did not learn such coordination. Apparently social behavior of a cooperative nature can be obtained from persons who do not even know of the social aspects of their predicament!

The minimal social situation eliminates all social cues. Thus if the experimenter does not inform the subjects, they are not aware that they are in interaction, and they search for solutions purely on the basis of a trial-and-error sort of activity just as they would in an individual learning experiment. Kelley, Thibaut, Radloff, and Mundy (1962) have hypothesized that subjects adopt a "win–stick, lose–shift" principle in coordinating their activities in the minimal social situation; that is, a person will tend repeat a response that results in positive outcomes and will change to the alternative response after a negative outcome. If both people follow this rule while responding simultaneously, they must eventually wind up in a mutually satisfactory cell of the payoff matrix.

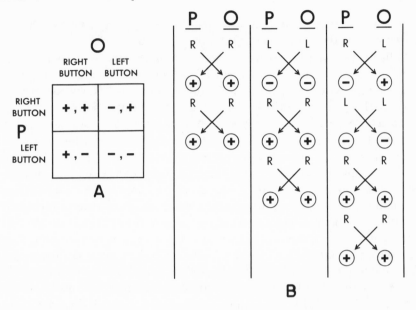

FIGURE 1.5. *The minimal social situation. (A) Outcome matrix for the minimal social situation. (B) The win-stick, lose-shift rule.*

Achievement of rewards in the minimal social situation is illustrated in Figure 1.5*b,* which shows all starting combinations of left and right switch choices for *P* and *O.* In the left-hand column of the figure both *P* and *O* begin responding by pushing their right button, which gives each the point reward. Since both have been rewarded each sticks to that choice and pushes the right button on the next trial, and again the result is mutual rewards. Their behavior should soon stabilize in this mutually beneficial pattern of responding, which does not appear immediately but does tend to work out over time.

In the middle column a different *P* and *O* begin the game by pushing the left buttons, which results in the delivery of mutual electric shocks. Since this outcome is hardly desirable for either player, each will shift to his alternative behavior on the next trial and push the right button. Mutual choices of the right button produce mutual rewards and as the consequence, and *P* and *O* will stick with this pattern.

In the pattern of responding represented in the last column of Figure 1.5*b,* another *P* and *O* begin by making opposite choices: *P* pushes his right button, while *O* pushes his left button. The result of this choice pattern is the delivery of a reward to *O;* therefore, *O* sticks to the choice of the left button on the next trial. As a result of the first trial *P* receives a shock; therefore, *P* shifts to the choice of his left button on the next occasion. The pattern of choices on the second trial produces the delivery of shock to both players, causing both to switch choices and push the right button on the third trial. *P* and *O* should stick with right button choices after receiving the mutual rewards following the third trial.

Kelley et al. hypothesized that when persons are allowed to make their responses in alternation the win–stick, lose–shift rule should not produce such simple coordination because of timing problems. They found support for their reasoning that mutually accommodative solutions were easier to achieve when responding was simultaneous rather than alternating.

The PDG provides a social interaction much more enriched than the minimal social situation because it seems intuitively to provide a close analogy to many real-world situations that involve such complex processes as trust and suspicion. However, some psychologists view the PDG as a situation too abstract and unrealistic to be useful in determining anything about human behavior. These critics cite the restricted number of alternatives and the low stakes (typically involving trivial outcomes, such as points, play money, or very small sums of real money) as support for the contention that little knowledge can be gained from an apparently sterile situation. We will have more to say about this view in Chapter 7.

Some social scientists have attempted to enrich games by building into them a greater correspondence to the real world. For example, Deutsch and Krauss (1960, 1962) constructed a realistic trucking game in which two subjects in the roles of owners of trucking companies (Acme and Bolt) must transport products from their starting places over a stretch of road to their final destinations. On each trial of the game each player receives a fixed sum of money from which the costs of delivery can be subtracted. Costs are a direct function of time spent on route; therefore, profits are maximized by making the trip in as short a time as possible. Each trucker has a choice of two routes to his destination: a short route that maximizes speed of delivery but contains a one-lane stretch of road through which only one truck at a time may pass, and a longer alternate route that takes much more time to traverse but has no comparable impasse. The situation is depicted in Figure 1.6.

On any one trip a trucker can profit only by taking the one-lane short route. The longer route results in a slight loss of money for the trucker who takes it. However, if both players attempt to profit and take the short route they will meet head-on on the one-lane road, and both will lose money because of the time lost through confrontation and backing up. The only way both players can make a long-run profit is to coordinate their responses over trials and alternate in taking the one-lane route. Any other strategy would result in one person's attempting to exploit the other for his own advantage. Naturally, if both players adopt exploitative strategies they both suffer. The mixed-motive character of the game should be apparent. To complicate matters further, one or both players

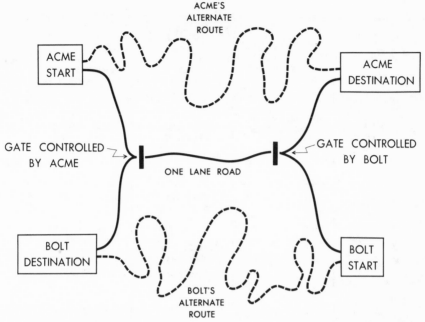

FIGURE 1.6 *Subjects' road map in the trucking game.* (From Deutsch and Krauss, *Jour. Ab. Soc. Psych.* 61: 183.)

can be provided with gates to block the other from using the one-lane route.

Deutsch and Krauss actually provided their subjects with maps and a complicated control panel to guide the movement of their trucks and the gates, but elaborate apparatus is not essential. In fact, Gallo (1966a) reduced the basic moves of the trucking game to three and gave subjects a matrix representation of the game, a modified version of which appears in Figure 1.7. The 3 x 3 matrix represents the basic moves of the original situation: take the short route, take the longer route, or wait at the start until the other player is through the short route and then head out. Each person received payoffs that depended on the cell of the matrix entered and were determined by carefully studying the payoffs of the original study. For example, if on the first move one player took the short route while the other took the alternate route, the first made 26 cents and the second lost 16 cents. Payoffs for each cell of the matrix were similarly determined, with reductions in payoffs each time the players made choices that resulted in an impasse. Gallo found that his matrix representation of the game produced results quite similar to those in the original version, down to the absolute amount of money players won.

The type of game an investigator uses depends on the social psychological process that most interests him. Experimental games, ranging from

BOLT

		SHORT ROUTE	WAIT	ALTERNATE ROUTE
A	SHORT ROUTE	TRUCKS BLOCKING ONE ANOTHER. CHOOSE AGAIN.	BOTH REACHED DESTINATION.	BOTH REACHED DESTINATION.
C M E	WAIT	BOTH REACHED DESTINATION.	TRUCKS BOTH WAITED, THEN MOVED OUT AT THE SAME TIME. ARE BLOCKING ONE ANOTHER. CHOOSE AGAIN.	BOTH REACHED DESTINATION.
	ALTERNATE ROUTE	BOTH REACHED DESTINATION.	BOTH REACHED DESTINATION.	BOTH REACHED DESTINATION.

FIGURE 1.7. *Matrix representation of trucking game* (after Gallo 1966a).

simple to complex, are continually being invented because existing ones do not capture some nuance or process that the investigator wants to study. Games experimenters play are serious attempts to develop and evaluate scientific theory; yet it must be remembered that analogies are not scientific generalizations, and that the results of game experiments should not be applied directly to the complex problems of the real world (see Chapter 7).

Game Theory

Many social scientists automatically associate experimental games with *game theory,* but we will be careful to dissociate the two. Game theory is an analysis of conflict-of-interests situations among players who interact according to certain rules. It "is probably the most elaborate mathematical theory that has been conceived and developed with an intended interpretation in the domain of the social sciences [Coombs, Dawes, & Tversky, 1970, p. 202]." The purpose of game theory, developed by John von Neumann and Oskar Morgenstern in their classic work, *Theory of Games and Economic Behavior* (1944), was to prescribe an optimal strategy for a person in a conflict-of-interests situation. A strategy is a "set of directions which tells a player what he is to do in every possible situation in which he may find himself while playing" a conflict-of-interests game (Rapoport, 1966, p. 40).

In games of pure conflict game theory prescribes that each person choose a strategy that will maximize his minimal or assured gain; in other words, he chooses that strategy that will give him his best outcomes in the worst possible conditions the other person can mete out. This strategy is called the maxmin (or minmax, depending on whether one is playing the rows or columns of the matrix). When both persons have such a strategy the cell of the payoff matrix that represents the intersections of these strategies is called the saddle point, or minimax. Two players will find themselves at the saddle point if both behave rationally. The saddle point in the PDG shown in Figure 1.2c is the *P, P* outcome. If a game does not have such a dominant strategy for both players, then some random mix of strategies is prescribed (see Rapoport, 1964).

Schelling (1960) has contended that game theory has yielded important insights into the strategy of pure conflict but has not yielded comparable insight into mixed-motive situations. The reason for this lack becomes apparent when one examines the nature of the PDG, where social or ethical tissues are eschewed in favor of dominant, rational individual strategies. In this regard Rapoport (1964) concluded that nonzero-sum games offer no solution that will intuitively satisfy everyone.

Game theory addresses itself to questions at one or more of three levels of theory. At the most abstract level game theory is a *formal theory* concerned with definitions and theorems. At this level of analysis game theory is an abstract mathematical collection of terms and their relationships and is devoid of any empirical or real-world meaning. Game theory is also a *normative* or *prescriptive theory* that offers advice to the strategist about how to go about selecting strategies in certain conditions. If an individual seeking strategic advice could provide a game theorist with his own and the other person's value preferences, the game theorist could provide an optimal strategy. It is assumed that the prescriptive advice of the game theorist represents the way individuals *should* behave given that they have perfect information and an infinite amount of time to analyze the situation. Finally, game theory can be viewed as a *descriptive theory* of the way individuals actually do behave. At this level the optimal strategies of game theory represent the ways individuals *would* behave given that they have perfect information and an infinite amount of time to analyze the situation.

For several reasons none of these forms of game theory will be used in our analyses. Formal theories may be of interest to mathematicians and to scientists who want to sharpen up some of their conceptual ideas and gain additional insights into intricate logical relationships, but unless formal game theory can be interpreted so as to yield testable hypotheses it is of little interest to the scientist. Nor is the scientist qua scientist interested in suggesting what values a person should apply to the kinds of decisions he makes. Even if an applied scientist were interested in giving strategic advice for many of life's difficult decisions, he would be in a bad position to do so, since he does not know how to complete and represent the matrices, nor does he know all of the responses and their worths to the individuals in the interaction. Thus the normative use of game theory is quite restricted. Finally, no one has successfully shown that game theory can accurately predict actual human behavior even in the context of very simple abstract games. Stochastic learning theories have fared much better in predicting simple game behavior (see Rapoport, 1964).

A scientist may use experimental games without having the slightest interest in game theory. The theory of social power and conflict expounded in this book has been generated by and has largely been evaluated in the context of experimental games. However, the focus is not on games per se but on several social-psychological phenomena that can be and have been studied primarily with the aid of experimental games. Game theory has no part at all in our analysis. Social conflict produces a condition in which social power and influence are obviously important factors in determining the course of interaction. In subsequent chapters we will first explore the simplest power relations in dyadic conflicts and ask what kinds of influence can be used and what causes the target to comply to the wishes or demands of the source of influence. Then we will question why a source attempts influence, whom he chooses as a target, and what influence modes he uses. The more complex processes of interpersonal bargaining and coalition formation will then be explored. The concepts and methods introduced in this and the next chapter will be continually applied in an attempt to understand and explain complex social interactions.

2

Components for a Theory of Conflict

The major goal of science is to foster understanding of real-world phenomena through the development of coherent theories. Scientific theories
must be evaluated by empirical data that reflect on the plausibility of the
causal relations specified through the interrelated hypotheses of the conceptual system. Often analogies drawn from theories in the physical or
biological sciences have been helpful in developing new theories in social
science. For example, the biological theory of evolution has its analogies
in cultural anthropology and economics. Similarly, the concepts and
methods derived from the theory of games and from economic theories of
exchange have had a significant and perhaps revolutionary impact on social psychology. Economic theory has caused the social psychologist to
focus on three rather neglected aspects of social behavior: (1) the *interdependence* of the actors in terms of mutual responses and joint outcomes during interaction; (2) the *decisions* actors continually make between alternative response choices; (3) evaluation of relationships and
outcomes in terms of *normative rules* of justice or fair play.

Two persons may appear to a third-party observer to be interacting
with each other when, in fact, each individual's behavior is regulated primarily by self-produced stimuli. Conversely, each person's choice of action may be almost completely dependent on the cues the other person
produces. Jones and Gerard (1967) have discriminated four types of interaction that are theoretically possible. The structure of interaction indicates the degree of interdependence that exists between the actors.

A *pseudocontingency* interaction is characterized by a situation in
which each individual responds primarily on the basis of his own previous responses or simply carries out a preestablished plan. Social stimuli

are only minimally involved in the sequence of behaviors that occur in a pseudocontingency interaction. Each individual behaves as if the other person were not there or else merely uses the other's behaviors to punctuate or time the actor's train of responses. Examples in Jones and Gerard include well-rehearsed plays, heated debates, and ritualistic performances, such as weddings or inaugurals, in which each individual responds on the basis of his own plans for the interaction and uses the other person's behavior, if at all, only to time his own next statement. This form of interaction appears artificial in that neither party's actions influence the other to deviate from a fixed objective; yet much role-related behavior in everyday life differs only in degree from this simple type of preplanned interaction.

Reactive contingency is a relationship in which each individual's response is determined almost solely by the immediately preceding response of the other person. Unlike the pseudocontingency pattern, which reflects an almost exclusive concern with self-produced stimuli in the prediction of social behavior, reactive contingency focuses on situational and interdependent determinants of social behavior. For example, a chess novice tends to move his pieces toward or away from the last piece moved by his opponent; he reacts to the other's move without the benefit of any long-range plan of his own. A panic flight of a crowd from a burning theater or an outbreak of fighting in a riot often reflects a contagion of behaviors in which each person's responses are affected primarily by the responses of those around him.

Asymmetrical contingency, a mixed version of the above two patterns, occurs whenever one person is guided almost exclusively by self-produced plans and tends to ignore the actions of the other whose behavior is largely guided by the behaviors of the first. An example is an encyclopedia salesman who may follow his preplanned script to the letter, slowly luring the customer toward purchase but maintaining the sequence of his pitch whatever the comments or questions of the potential customer, who may be quite susceptible to persuasion and therefore reacts to the salesman precisely as the salesman wants. This type of social interaction occurs whenever one individual has had a better opportunity than the other to work out the details of the social interaction beforehand.

The fourth type of interaction specified by Jones and Gerard is the most common and of greatest interest to most social psychologists. In a *mutual contingency* relationship each individual's responses during the interaction are determined partly by internal stimuli (e.g., plans and attitudes) and partly by the responses of the other in the situation (e.g., social stimuli, rewards, and punishments). Thus, in their initial meeting our handsome lad and pretty maid (Chapter 1) both may have preconceived intentions and expectations with regard to each other, but the functional implementation or modification of these plans is dependent on the social responses of each during their encounter. The maid may be willing to trade a smile and a wink for a smile from the lad, but if the lad fails to smile, the maid may fail to implement her plan. The mutual contingency relationship is characterized by an exchange paradigm in which each individual both contributes to and takes from the interaction.

The concept of social interdependence drawn from game theory and the economic notion of exchange emphasizes that social behavior must be treated as more than the sum of a number of individuals' responses to social stimuli; rather, *both* intraindividual components and the interdependence generated through interaction must be considered in any theory of social behavior. When desired goals are at least partially dependent on the actions of both parties, problems of coordination, cooperation, competition, conflict, and social influence become ubiquitous to social interactions.

Seldom are the goals of interdependent actors perfectly coordinated. Typically some give and take must occur in the situation. The degree of incompatibility of the goals of two or more actors defines the amount of conflict between them. More formally, Boulding (1962) defined conflict "as a situation of competition in which the parties are aware of the incompatibility of potential future positions and in which each party wishes to occupy a position that is incompatible with the wishes of the other [p. 5]."

Morton Deutsch (1969) has made a distinction between *competition* and *conflict*. He defined competition much as others have defined conflict: "an opposition in the goals of the interdependent parties such that the probability of goal attainment for one decreases as the probability for the other increases [p. 8]." Deutsch reserves the term *conflict* for incompatible *activities* rather than incompatible *goals;* thus conflict may occur even when there is no perceived or actual incompatibility of goals. For example, two parents may be in conflict about how to treat their son's ailment, but they may share concordant goals. This distinction between conflict and competition has important ramifications for conflict resolution strategies. Competition can be reduced only through attempts to modify the goals of one or both of the parties—a task often quite difficult to accomplish. When conflict is not based on underlying goal incompatibility the participants need only discover ways of coordinating their behaviors. Although we will occasionally make use of this distinction between conflict and competition, unless otherwise noted the terms will be used interchangeably.

The potential for conflict and competition is increased by two sets of environmental conditions: (1) when the amount or quantity of desired rewards or end states is in short supply and the parties to interaction want all or a large part of the available resources; (2) when the goal-directed behaviors of one party to the interaction are of a sort that precludes the other party's goal attainment. In these circumstances the individuals involved must decide whether to simply give up on the particular goal desired, to reach some mutual accommodation of interests, or to exert power and influence in an attempt to reach a solution to the reward distribution problem.

When the interaction is one of mutual contingency in which each actor's behavior is determined by both internal plans and the other's actions, each individual's problem becomes one of reward maximization within the social constraints imposed by the other's goals and desires. In such situations one individual's effort to maximize outcomes often leads to a minimization of the other individual's outcomes—a competitive situation. Alternatively, the problem may become one of coordinating and articulating responses so that the exchange between the individuals approaches some degree of fairness. In any case the concepts of power and influence become central to the discussion.

Knowing the structure of a dyadic relationship can sometimes allow the social psychologist to make rather good predictions about the behaviors that will take place in the interaction. However, within most dyadic interactions a great deal of flexibility and variability still is not determined by the situational structure. Although game and exchange considerations have caused social scientists to reconceptualize interactions and to consider the interdependencies and hence the influence relations between actors, game theory per se does not provide an adequate theory of social conflict. An adequate theory must both classify and analyze the intraindividual as well as the interdependent components that determine the ways in which parties to conflict go about making decisions to get their way in interactions.

One person's deliberate attempt to elicit behavioral compliance from another has interested political scientists, sociologists, and social psychologists for many years, but no adequate theory of power or influence has been developed. The many arguments about definitions and relationships are, however, suggestive of the components that any theory of influence must include. We now turn to some of the issues raised in analyzing the concept of power from which a classification of the types of social influence frequently used in interaction will be developed.

Analyses of Social Power

Schur (1969) defined power as the "ability to determine the behavior of others in accord with one's own wishes [p. 85]." MacIver (1964) similarly considered power to be the "capacity to control, regulate, or direct the behavior of persons or things [p. 77]." Hans Morgenthau (1969) has offered the most general definition of power, which he defined as coextensive with any behavioral changes in one person that can be at least partially attributed to the actions of another person. That other as the controlling person or the causative agent is considered the powerful individual. The breadth of these definitions is almost as encompassing as the entire area of social science and yields little precision in theory and no testable predictions about either the exercise of power or the compliance gained. Yet the definitions indicate that power and influence are considered as ubiquitous concepts relevant to all social interactions. No wonder that Karl Deutsch (1966) defined all of political science as the study of how compliance is gained.

Harsanyi (1962b) has attempted to bring some definitional precision to an analysis of the power phenomenon. He suggests that one party's compliance to the wishes of another constitutes the operational criterion for the successful exercise of power. In a condition of bilateral power where each individual has some influence over the other's behavior, the amount of power is defined as the probability that a powerful person will be able to get a preferred joint policy adopted when he favors one policy and another person favors a different policy.

Thus, for Harsanyi, power is defined by its effects (i.e., the probability of the other party's compliance), and it is measured by the likelihood that one individual can get his way with respect to the dyad's *joint* approach to an issue when the participants to interaction differ in their policy preferences. For example, a husband and wife may have conflicting preferences about how they will jointly spend their vacation time. The husband might want to go duck hunting, while the wife may want to visit her mother. Then the husband's power would be measured by the likelihood that they will go duck hunting rather than visit his mother-in-law. Power, according to Harsanyi, is a relevant factor in social interactions only where social conflict exists; that is, where two or more individuals have conflicting preferences and a decision must be made about whose preferences shall prevail.

Dahl (1957) has taken a similar approach by asserting that one person has power over the other to the degree that the first causes the second to do something he would not otherwise do. However, Dahl adds the restriction that the powerful person's actions must be *deliberately* undertaken to produce changes in the weaker person before we can speak meaningfully about power.

The requirement that there be intent to influence introduces the novel but complex empirical problem of determining the intentions and attributions of the participants *before* the presence or absence of power manipulations can be determined. However, even if this problem could be easily

solved, the means or processes through which power was achieved would
still be unidentified in both Dahl's and Harsanyi's formulations.[1] Parenthetically, Chein (1967) has combined Dahl's notion (i.e., no intent, no
power) with Harsanyi's contention (i.e., no resistance, no power) to pose
the paradox of Unconditional Omnipotence: an omnipotent person must
at the same time be powerless, for he can have neither occasion to want
anything nor any resistance to overcome!

In comparison with the above theorists, Bachrach and Baratz (1963)
have limited the domain of power to an event set of smaller size. They
argue that three relational characteristics are associated with the existence of social power: (1) there must be a conflict of interests or values
between two or more persons or groups; (2) one party must actually
comply to the other's demands; (3) the powerful party must possess the
capability to threaten and invoke sanctions in order to gain compliance to his demands. Thus power is the process of affecting the policies
of others with the help of threatened sanctions for noncompliance to the
policies demanded.

Since the use of threats implies intent in the source of influence to pro-
cure compliance from the target person, Bachrach and Baratz probably
agree with Dahl that power requires intent. Similarly, inclusion of the
conflict-of-interests requirement puts Bachrach and Baratz in agreement with Harsanyi that where no conflict exists, no power exists. However, Bachrach and Baratz restrict power to the successful use of threats
to obtain behavioral compliance to demands. They consider the actual
application of sanctions (i.e., punishments) for noncompliance to be a
property of force rather than power.

The meanings for the actors and the consequences of the application of
force differ from those in the successful exercise of power, though potential force is the basis for the effectiveness of threats. From an ahistorical
point of view punishment of a target person for noncompliance to a
threat may be considered a nonrational action on the part of the threatener, since the noncompliance has already occurred and subsequent punishment cannot erase it. Of course, the actual application of sanctions
does help to establish the credibility of the source's threats and may serve
to enhance or decrease his effective power in the future. The exercise of
force, therefore, is essentially future-oriented.

The distinction between threats and force has important implications
for international relations. As many of our strategic thinkers and deterrence theorists (Kahn, 1960; McDermott, 1971) are amply aware, the
imposition of a thermonuclear punishment in the form of cataclysmic war

1. Dahl and Harsanyi do discuss lists of several means of influence, but neither theorist
includes such means as differentially affecting his measure of social power.

can make sense only if some future benefit can be gained. Bertrand Russell (1961) has argued that as long as there is more than a minimal likelihood that total destruction would follow a thermonuclear war the very use of nuclear threats is irrational, since there can be no reason in either the present or the future for backing up such threats.

Although Bachrach and Baratz limit their discussion of social power to threats of punishment for noncompliance, it is clear that the source has available other influence modes by which to communicate his intentions or desires to a target person. Parsons (1963) has suggested three basic types of influence—inducement, persuasion, and activation of commitments—in addition to threats of punishment (which Parsons calls "deterrence").

Inducements rely on the carrot rather than the stick; that is, the source offers rewards to the target for compliant behaviors rather than threatening punishments for noncompliant behaviors. Persuasion is an attempt to restructure the goals or attitudes of the target through the use of propaganda, argument, or technical knowledge, and without the direct provision of any inducements or deterrents to the target for adopting the source's policies. A target complies to a persuasive appeal not because he anticipates rewards or fears punishments from the source of communications but because it appears to be the most reasonable thing to do in pursuing his self-interest. Finally, activation of commitments is the source's attempt to invoke normative or ethical standards in order to produce target reassessment of the behaviors that would be most appropriate to the situation at hand.

Parsons analytically separates the concepts of power and influence. He considers power to be a form of abstract currency, frequently referred to as legitimacy. Persons often obey or comply with the commands or requests of others in society without the invocation of threats, promises, force, or even persuasion. Indeed, commands often are given quickly and without justification or elaboration—for example, on a battlefield or in the middle of a surgical operation. The compliant or conforming individual does as requested because he feels he *ought* to do so (Heider, 1958). Legitimacy is vested in an office or socially prescribed role and not per se in the man who serves the office. The study of existing authority structures is essentially a sociological problem, but the establishment of legitimacy and its use for influence purposes is a social psychological process (McDermott, 1971).

The assumption that has been made either explicitly or implicitly in all the views of power and influence considered here is that one party in a dyadic relationship wants something from the other and as a consequence needs to control or modify the other's behaviors in order to attain his goals. The degree to which the interests of the two parties are divergent and the degree of resistance one party gives to the influence attempts of the other define the intensity of conflict that exists in the situation. Exchange theorists (Blau, 1964; Homans, 1961) explicitly assume that persons would not interact with one another unless some form of exchange could be effected or unless no alternative relationship would yield better outcomes. Even between the best of friends conflicts exist, and each uses the other to facilitate goal attainment (after all, what are friends for?) .

Power and influence should not be conceived as Machiavellian strategies that only corrupt characters use. Though a negative connotation is associated with the concept of power, as long as interdependence exists between persons but total agreement between them is lacking, they cannot avoid their dilemma. Naturally, the parties' characteristics and their longer-term relationships will partially determine the manner in which they find a solution.

From this cursory overview of some of the issues and concepts related to social power three basic sets of factors emerge as essential for any theory of social conflict: (1) a conflict situation in which individuals have at least partially conflicting preferences, desires, or intentions; (2) some communication modes by way of which influence or power is exercised; (3) the personal characteristics of the participants to conflict. The first two sets of components represent the theorists' recognition of the importance of structural factors for a *social* analysis of interpersonal power; the third set of components includes the intraindividualistic plans and characteristics of the unique participants to particular conflict situations in the prediction of social behavior.

For influence to be exercised some form of communication must occur in which the source makes known to the target his preferences, demands, or wishes. Even the most simple views of power posit the source's use of reinforcing or punishing events to provide the target with an incentive to carry out the source's wishes. Communications convey or transmit meanings from one party to another and may be explicit or tacit in nature. Thus, a slap in the face may have more meaning than a verbally shouted epitaph. The literature on power suggests that threats, force, promises, rewards, persuasion, and activation of commitments are communication modes that should be more thoroughly examined, perhaps more carefully operationalized, and incorporated into a theory of social conflict.

Communication Modes

The categorization of influence modes that will be adopted here derives from several considerations. First, influence is conceived as a causal relationship between the source's behavior and a target's behavior. Hence only those modes of influence used in direct interactions will be considered. Second, a distinction will be maintained between those modes of influence that communicate the source's intentions to directly and personally affect the target's outcomes by the source's control of reinforcements (e.g., threats) and those modes that are not directly attached to the source's personal control over rewards or punishments (e.g., persuasion). Dahl's insistence that the exercise of power implies intent on the part of the source alerts us to a third distinction. Although it is intuitively obvious that a target may imitate a source's behavior without the source's knowledge of the effect he is having, and a target may anticipate the source's unexpressed (or unconscious or nonexistent) wishes (cf. Freidrich, 1963), we will restrict our discussion to those influence attempts that the source consciously intends.

THREATS

Although consensus among social scientists could be gained for the view that communication modes are environmental stimuli that a source produces and a target reacts to, little agreement can be discerned about the nature of the stimuli or the target reactions of interest. For example, Singer (1958) has defined threat perception (by the target) as based on perceived intent and perceived capability of an opponent who allegedly plans some action detrimental to the target. Threat, then, is conceived as one person's act or behavior that has the effect of producing threat perception in a target person. If it is remembered that those who feel threatened can always find intentions, the question then becomes whether the source really intended to arouse threat perception. The lack of clear and objective criteria for determining whether intent actually exists and, if so, to what extent leaves the threat perception theorist without a clear and unambiguous definition of threats.

Nonverbal responses of an actor may be utilized to deliberately communicate a threat to a target. Facial expressions, connotations of communications, and many other behaviors (Goffman, 1959; Hall, 1959) yield subtle cues for an experienced and mature adult observer. Such cues frequently are used for tacit communications and imply the same content and form as do more explicit verbal communications. Our strategy will be to develop a theory with regard to explicit intentional communications and then later expand the theory to include the more ambiguous tacit communications.

A threat message may be noncontingent or contingent. A noncontingent threat takes the form, "I will do X," where X is an action, the withholding of an action, the production of a noxious stimulus, or the removal of a positive reinforcer, any of which can be perceived by a target as detrimental or punishing. The source simply communicates his punitive intentions to the target but does not delineate any actions the target can take to avoid the threatened punishment. A contingent threat does not merely convey an intent to do harm but centers the use of punishment to coerce another to further the threatener's goals. Thus the form of a contingent threat is: "If you don't do Y, I will do X."

Schelling (1966) suggests that contingent threats may be either deterrent or compellent in nature. Deterrent threats are communications that order the target not to do something. The United States has clearly indicated to the Soviet Union that an invasion of Western Europe would bring swift and devastating retaliation. Deterrent threats specify what the target should not do but do not require any positive action. Compellent threats require that the target perform specific actions. In 1971 the United States threatened its own allies with a surtax on all imports unless they increased the value of their currency in relation to the dollar. Deterrence forbids certain behaviors; compellence requires specific actions.

Fisher (1969) has analyzed the formulation of policy in international relations in terms of the specificity of threats. He suggests that even when contingent threats are communicated, threateners often do not clearly specify either the request or the consequences associated with their messages. Hence, although the target is aware that a threat has been communicated he may not be able to determine either what the source wants or what will happen to him if he does not obey the source's commands. A threat may be request-specific but punishment-nonspecific, as in: "If you cross that line I will do something that you will not like." Or a threat may be request-nonspecific and punishment-specific, as in: "If you don't make the correct response I will deliver an electric shock to your finger." Of course, a threat may be both request- and punishment-nonspecific. Whenever a source does not explicitly reveal his preferences or intentions, the threat message takes on a tacit character. The target must attempt to infer or decode what the source wants and what the source will do if he doesn't get what he wants.

Baldwin (1971) has pointed out that the degree of ambiguity conveyed in a threat message from a source to a target may not only vary as a result of semantic variables (such as choice of words), but may also be systematically manipulated by the interactive participants for their own ends. Thus a relatively impotent source of threats may intentionally transmit a consequences-nonspecific threat message simply because were the consequences clearly defined it would become obvious to the target that the threatener could not possibly punish noncompliant behavior.

PROMISES

Promises could be defined in a manner consistent with the perception definition of threats. For example, promise perception could be based on the target's hope of accruing gain for himself because he attributes benign intentions to the source. A promise would then be any actor's action that leads a perceiver to anticipate future mediated gains. The problems in relating perceptions of hope to an actor's intentions are just as formidable with promises as with threats. Hence it is easier to develop a theory around explicit promises and seek later to generalize the theory to tacit communications.

Like threat messages, promises can be either noncontingent or contingent. If the promise is noncontingent it constitutes a self-prediction purposefully communicated from the source to the target that at a specifiable future time the source will do something that the target prefers be done. A noncontingent promise takes the form, "I will do *Y*," where *Y* is an action, the withholding of an action, the production of a commodity, or the removal of noxious stimuli, any of which the target can consider beneficial. If the promise is contingent the source expresses an intention to reward particular target behaviors and implies thereby that other target behaviors not included in the promise message will not be rewarded, at least not by the source. The contingent promise takes the form, "If you do *A* (or not *A*), then I will do *B*," where *B* is a source's action beneficial to the target. Like threat messages, promises may be request-specific or nonspecific and may be reward-specific or nonspecific.

Contingent threats and promises share the identical if–then implicative form, but they formally differ in that though both may call for some target response, threats offer punishments and promises offer rewards as the basis for attempting influence. The source's perceptions of the target's values are important if the source's intentions and the target's perceptions are to correspond. If the source intends as rewarding what the target perceives as punishing, then an intended promise will be perceived as a threat. If the source intends as punishing what the target perceives as rewarding, then an intended threat translates as a promise. However, given the same cultural milieu it is likely that the direction of a value (i.e., positive or negative), if not the degree, will be grossly the same for both source and target.

Punishment and Reward

A typology of the kinds of rewards and punishments associated with promises and threats might be important because sources may possess or targets may be selectively responsive to different specific classes of reinforcers. Unfortunately, neither learning theory nor motivational research in psychology is of much help in developing such a typology. Our categories are based on only hunch or intuition and ought to be accepted as a kind of working hypothesis. A different set of intuitions can be found in Turner, Foa, and Foa (1971).

Punishments may take the form of *noxious stimulation, deprivation of*

existing resources, deprivation of expected gains, and *social punishments.*
The favorite punishment that psychologists administer to their animal
and human subjects in experiments has been noxious stimulation. Electric shock, which ranges from a tickle to a stiff jolt, is a form of punishment that varies along a continuum on which capital punishment by means
of an electric chair could be placed at one extreme. Noxious stimulation
may be threatened, and if target's noncompliance follows the influence
attempt the source can deliver it directly.

Alternatively, a threatener may choose to deprive the target of some of
the target's existing resources. Such costs (or fines) may be in the form
of points accumulated in a game, candy, money, or other valuables the
target possesses. Extreme forms of such costs may be associated with de-
priving the target of his automobile, bank account, or home (as in black-
mail attempts).

Expected gain deprivation is clearly different from either noxious
stimulation or the assignment of costs. Instead of administering noxious
stimuli or taking away some of his existing resources, the source may deprive the target of anticipated or earned gains. Thus points, candy, money, or other valuables that the target does not possess but expects to gain
may be denied him. Expected gain deprivation is an especially interesting
form of punishment because of the effects that frustrated expectations
have on social behaviors. This point is exemplified in current theories of
revolution (Brinton, 1952), which note that the disconfirmation of economic expectations is a major source of unrest and rebellion in nations.
Though the risk of volatile reactions is present, the temptation to use expected gain deprivation as the basis of threats is also high. A source may
first offer to a target a noncontingent gain, which he never intends to
provide, and then threaten to take it away (contingently). In this way a
source can perhaps wield power without actually possessing the basic resources at issue.

Finally, social punishments are related to the target's self-concept and
the image or impression that he wants to maintain in the eyes of others.
Impressions of dislike, name-calling, and social ostracism are rather clear
forms of social punishment. Disagreements and the use of key words such
as *wrong* may also act as negative reinforcers. Even such subtle cues as
postural slouching or the failure to smile may be taken as disapproval
(Bugental, Kaswan, & Love, 1970; Bugental, Love, & Gianetto, 1971;
Mehrabian, 1970).

The rewards offered for a target's compliance to promises can be similarly categorized. *Pleasure-giving rewards* include any stimuli directly
pleasurable or satisfying to the body, such as food, drink, or sexual stimulation. A source may offer an *increase in existing resources* by promising or providing candy, points, money, or other material commodities.

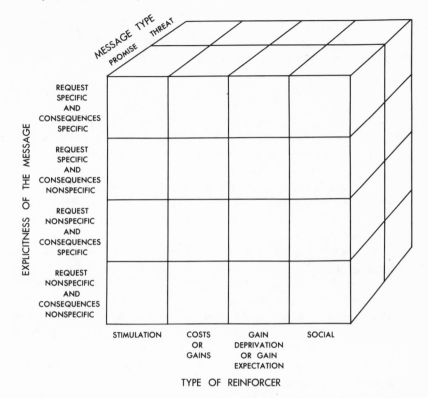

FIGURE 2.1. *Types of threats and promises, punishments and rewards.*

Confirmation of *expectations of gain* associated with promises is complementary to the use of expected gain deprivation with threats and includes
the promise and provision of pay raises or professional advancement at
intervals during a career. Typically, the confirmation of expectations is
timed so that the reinforcement is provided sooner than promised. Finally, *social rewards* in the form of approval, praise, conferred status or
medals of honor from one's peers or betters can also be offered in exchange for compliance to promises, and probably constitute the least expensive and most frequently used category of rewards available to potential influencers.

Figure 2.1 summarizes our discussion of the various forms of threats
and promises and the types of rewards and punishments that may be associated with them. There are two types of contingent messages—threats
and promises—four forms of each type of message, including the explic-
itness of the request and the specificity of the consequences, and four
kinds of rewards and punishments. Thus 32 different contingent threat
and promise messages can be analytically discriminated. Of course, there
are also 16 different kinds of noncontingent promises and threats (i.e.,

four kinds of rewards and punishments, two kinds of messages, and the specificity or ambiguity of the consequences communicated). Whether all of these possible distinctions are theoretically important is a matter for experimental determination.

When individuals, for whatever reason, do not want to use personally mediated reinforcements as a means to achieve their ends in social interaction, they may instead attempt to effectively use information to persuade or dissuade others. Information control can be effective if by means of screening out or censoring information it makes a particular decision by the target person a foregone conclusion (Bachrach & Baratz, 1963). The value of censorship is to prevent others from considering alternative choices or preferences. If no competing ideas or values exist, then the available values will dominate actions. Although this kind of gatekeeping of information may be effective as a mode of influence, more typically specific information is presented to targets to affect and change their decisions, preferences, and actions. The use of arguments, propaganda, or facts will be effective only if the information has value consequences for the target. Such value consequences may be either negative or positive. Thus at least two different modes of persuasion are suggested.

Psychologists sometimes have referred to fear-arousing communications or warnings as a significant aspect of the persuasion process. However, definitions of warnings, like those of threats and promises, have not been without ambiguity (e.g., Janis & Feshbach, 1953; Withey, 1964). We will define a warning as a communication that predicts that harmful consequences will befall the target if he continues to do what he is doing or refrains from an action or behavior that the source recommends.

A critical factor in distinguishing a warning from a threat is that the source of a warning does not control either directly or indirectly the contingency or reinforcing consequences specified in the message. Thus when the source merely describes to the target contingencies that are beyond the source's control and have outcomes that would be punishing to the target, the message constitutes a contingent warning to the target. A positive prediction of a contingency between a behavior that the source recommends and a favorable outcome (not controlled by the source) may be called a mendation. A racetrack tipster communicates a mendation. Usually a warning is an attempt to stop an individual from doing something the source does not like, and a mendation is an attempt to influence the target to do something the source prefers. However, warnings and mendations may be used for the opposite purposes or for both purposes simultaneously. Both types of persuasive communications may predict consequences that stem from nature (hurricanes) or from other human beings (robbery).

Warnings and mendations may be noncontingent or contingent, they may specify relevant behaviors and consequences, or they may leave one or both components to the contingency unspecified. The punishments or rewards associated with warnings and mendations could be classified in exactly the same manner as are threats and promises; Figure 2.1 could represent warnings and mendations just as well as threats and promises.

Warnings and mendations are psychologically more complicated for a target than are threats and promises. The target must take into account not only the intentions and capabilities of the source, but also whether the source in fact has any influence over the contingency he points out, whether the contingency is probable, and, if the contingency is probable, the magnitude of the consequences. In addition, a target may have to consider the intentions, capability, and influenceability of a possible third party who does control the contingency. Thus all of the factors involved in the perception of threats and promises plus other factors are involved in perceptions of warnings and mendations. From the source's point of view, though, warnings and mendations may be simpler than threats and promises, since no obligation or responsibility for the consequences involved rests with him, except perhaps for the responsibility associated with him as a monitor of events.

OTHER COMMUNICATIONS

Much human behavior is in the form of social reconnaissance. People attempt to discover the causal structure of the natural environment so that they can learn how to solve problems and achieve rewards. Social communications that appear to have no ostensible purpose, such as small talk, story-telling, and humor, have important functions as probing tools to discover other people's values, preferences, and likely response choices.

The alert actor can use this information for his own purposes. The same communications used for probing may simultaneously serve the purpose of revealing or disguising the actor's preferences, values, and response dispositions, and people may adopt extremely subtle communication strategies to manage the impressions that others have of them in the service of maximizing influence effectiveness. Impression management strategies (cf. Goffman, 1959) may be used to convey the source's alleged sincerity, honesty, benevolence, commitment, or any other factors associated with the four influence modes identified. We will not now concern ourselves with these allied probing and impression management communications but will consider them later in the context of actual conflict interactions.

Before progressing to the characteristics of the participants to conflict it would be wise to attempt an assessment of the communication typology we have constructed. Other typologies have been formed (e.g., French &

Raven, 1959), and other influence theorists have also identified lists of punishments and messages employed in social interaction. One crucial index of the merits of any theoretical scheme is whether or not it is amenable to operationalization. That is, can the conceptual modes of threats, promises, warnings, and mendations and their attendant rewards and punishments be translated to the level of precise measurement in rigorous experimentation?

Operationalizing Threats and Promises: The Modified Prisoner's Dilemma

Whether or not a target believes the threats a source makes is undoubtedly affected by numerous factors. One major factor is the degree to which a source's deeds have matched his words in the past. The truth or credibility of a threat can be operationally defined as the proportion of times a source backs up his threats by punishing the target on those occasions when the target fails to comply to the stipulated demands. If a threatener communicates, say, 15 identical threats to a particular target over a period of time, and the target complies 5 times, then the degree of credibility associated with the source's threat will depend on how often the source punishes the target on those 10 occasions when noncompliant responses occurred. If the source punished all 10 noncompliances his threats would be 100 percent credible; if he elected to punish none of the 10 noncompliances his threats would be 0 percent credible; if he punished 7 of the noncompliances his threats would be 70 percent credible.

Horai and Tedeschi (1969) modified the prisoner's dilemma game so that they could study the effects of threats of varying credibilities (10, 50, and 90 percent) and punishment magnitudes (low, medium, and high) on the behavioral compliance of target subjects. The prisoner's dilemma game, as noted, is a two-person nonzero-sum conflict interaction that presents each player with one of two choices on each trial—cooperative or competitive. Figure 1.2c depicts the generalized prisoner's dilemma matrix as well as the specific set of payoff values Horai and Tedeschi employed.

A robot player, who followed a strategy preformulated by the experimenter, and a subject faced game panels (shown in Figure 2.2). On the illumination of the *Go* light, the robot and the subject independently responded by pressing either the Choice 1 (cooperative) or the Choice 2 (competitive) button. After a short, automated, variable delay period for purposes of simulating decision behavior on the part of the robot, the cell of the payoff matrix corresponding to the joint strategy selections made on that trial was illuminated, and the point outcomes for both the subject

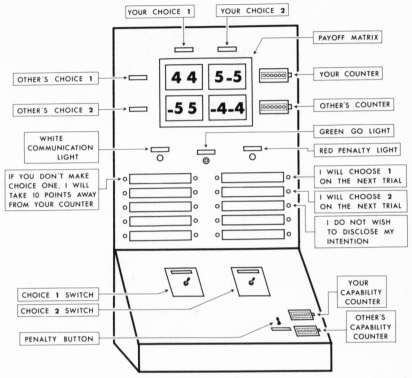

FIGURE 2.2. *Modified prisoner's dilemma game panel as seen from the subject's viewpoint.*

and the robot were tallied on the cumulative counters (upper right-hand side of the panel in Figure 2.2).

A threat message, posted on the left-hand, incoming, side of the subject's panel, specifically demanded: "If you do not make Choice 1 on the next trial, I will take *n* points away from your counter." The amount of punishment was varied in the Horai and Tedeschi study and across treatment conditions assumed the values of 5, 10, or 20 points; the robot intermittently and on a preplanned schedule sent the threat to the subject. The robot could illuminate the white *Communication* light on the subject's game panel, indicating to the subject that the communication circuit was open and the robot had the option of transmitting a message. Subjects were instructed that a small green light immediately adjacent to the message would light up if the message was sent to them.

Following the transmission of a threat, the *Go* light once again illuminated, indicating to both subject and robot that a strategy selection must be made. If the subject defied the threat by making Choice 2, the robot then had the option of deducting the stipulated amount of points from the subject's counter. The availability to the robot of this penalty option was made known to the subject by the illumination of the red *Penalty* light located on the upper left-hand side of the subject's panel (see Figure 2.2). Depending on the threat credibility assignment of the particular subject, the robot would or would not actually deduct the number of points stipulated in the message. For instance, if the credibility level was to be 50 percent, the robot punished the subject's noncompliances half of the time. The *Penalty* light was automatically extinguished after 10 seconds, and if the robot had chosen not to exercise his punitive power option by that time, the subject knew he would not be punished on that trial.

Several game trials then ensued before the next message was sent to the subject, and so on until the conclusion of the experiment. The results showed that compliance increased as a direct function of both threat credibility and punishment magnitude.

The alert reader will have noticed that the outcome accruing to a subject after he has received a threat is not simply a function of whether the robot will or will not punish him; it also depends on the strategy choice the robot makes on a threat-relevant trial. If a threatener generally makes the competitive game choice, the target subject should perceive himself as trapped in a least-of-evils situation. If the target complies, he is exploited by the threatener and loses five points in the game shown in Figure 1.2*c*. If the target defies an exploitative threatener both lose four points, but the target may suffer further punishment in the form of the negative side payoff. Conversely, if the threatener has generally made the cooperative choice on the message-relevant trial of the game, the target should perceive himself as faced with an approach–avoidance situation. If the target complies with the threatener's demands, both benefit by winning four points; if the target does not comply with the threatener's demands, the target will gain five points at the expense of the threatener, but the threatener may then levy the threatened punishment. Thus the threatener may be exploitative and seek a competitive advantage, or he may seek accommodation through the use of both the carrot and the stick.

An overview of the sequence of behaviors can best be presented in extensive form. As shown in Figure 2.3, the robot player *(P)* initially chooses to instigate either a threat game or a nonthreat game by either transmitting or not transmitting the threat message to the target *(W)* prior to a play of the prisoner's dilemma. *P* and *W* then make their game strategy choices (Choice 1 or Choice 2). If a threat game is being played *W*'s choices constitute behavioral compliance to or defiance of the threat message (Outcomes A–F); if a nonthreat game is being played *W*'s responses are simply cooperative or competitive in nature (Outcomes

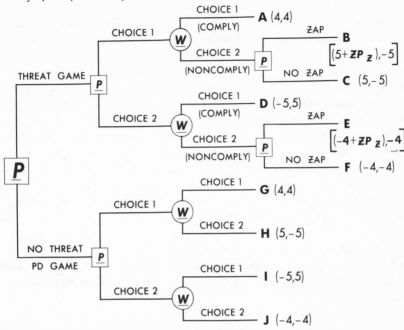

FIGURE 2.3. *Decision tree representation of threat and nonthreat trials in the modified prisoner's dilemma.*

G–J). If *W* does not comply by making the cooperative response in a threat game, *P* has the further option to punish *W* (i.e., to zap him). The exercise of punishments depends on the dictates of the credibility manipulation chosen for the experiment.

Of course, the degree of cooperativeness of the robot on nonmessage game trials may influence what happens on threat-relevant trials. To minimize decoding of the tacit meaning of nonmessage trial behavior, to provide a backdrop of conflict to the interaction, and to prevent subjects from discovering some plan the robot may possess, the many studies that will be reported in later chapters have had the robot respond on a 50 percent randomized schedule of cooperative and competitive responses on nonmessage game trials.

Many real-world conflicts are so complex that events are difficult to predict, but out of the ill-defined background of conflict explicit contingent threats are used and become salient aspects of the conflict situation. In a sense two separate games are constantly being played. One game is ill-defined, and strategy choices are partially coordinated but without specific communications about them (nonthreat game). The other game concerns specific threats and the use of force to lend credibility to the communications (threat game). The form of punishment used in most experiments has been the deprivation of existing resources (e.g., points, money, candy).

A robot source can also issue contingent promises during a prisoner's dilemma game (i.e., "If you make Choice 1 on the next trial, I will add n points to your counter"). The credibility can be manipulated by varying the proportion of times the robot does what he says he would do. The credibility of contingent promises, like contingent threats, is dependent not only on what the source does but also on what the target does. If the target person does not do as the promisor requests, then there is no occasion on which to provide the contingently promised rewards. Instead of punishing noncompliance, as with threats, the robot rewards compliance. The credibility of a contingent promise, therefore, should be a function only of those occasions when the target does comply to the source's requests. Hence the credibility of contingent promises may be operationally defined as the frequency of times the source does provide the reward over the total number of opportunities the source has to provide the promised rewards.

Promise credibilities can be manipulated by controlling the probability that the robot will reward compliant responses. In order to establish a set credibility level a criterion number of 10 successful promises, or those occasions on which the target subjects do as requested, may be established for all subjects.

Reward magnitudes can be established for the promise message just as punishment magnitudes were established for the threat message. The robot can deliver the reward by pushing what had been labeled the *Penalty* button but that can just as easily be identified as a *Reward* button. The reward can be given by pushing the *Reward* button when the red *Reward* option light is illuminated on the subject's game panel (see Figure 2.2). The result of this action would be the addition of the positive side payoff (reward) to the subject's counter.

In all other respects the threat paradigm as outlined above can be used for the study of promises. The criterion number of promises can be established, promise credibilities and reward magnitudes can be manipulated, the robot promisor can be accommodative or exploitative on promise-relevant trials, and so on.

It may have occurred to the reader that if the source can be simulated by the play of a robot so that systematic effects on target subjects can be studied, so can the target be simulated to observe the effects of his actions on subjects acting as the source of threats and/or promises. Target characteristics and behaviors, such as compliance, verbal ploys, cooperativeness on nonmessage interactions, and retaliation, can easily be manipulated as can certain situational factors, such as instructional sets, matrix values, and conflict intensity (for an extended discussion see Tedeschi, Bonoma, & Brown, 1971). Experiments studying the behavior of subjects as possessors of power will be systematically discussed in Chapter 4.

In conclusion, the conceptual analysis at the beginning of this chapter has been complemented by an empirical tool that allows unambiguous operationalization of threats and promises, their credibilities, and attendant rewards or punishments. We can now turn to an examination of the unique characteristics of the parties to conflict that may be expected to modify both the nature and outcome of their interaction.

Characteristics of the Parties to Conflict

THE SOURCE

A wide range of personal characteristics may be relevant to the exercise of influence. In a study of an American community, Dahl (1961) categorized as bases of influence a person's wealth, social standing, popularity, control over jobs and information, and access to the legal apparatus. Each of these influence bases assures that those who possess them achieve personal and worldly success, perhaps reflecting a basic American cultural orientation. Dahl's belief that potential influence is synonomous with control over resources concentrates attention on the source's potency and activism and assumes the target's passivity or lack of contribution to the influence process.

Although it may seem intuitively obvious from common observation that some people have more power than others (whatever is meant by power), theorists disagree about the bases of these power differentials. Lasswell and Kaplan (1950), in contrast to Dahl, have viewed political behavior and influence in terms of an exchange of resources or values between actors. They speculated that eight basic values can be subdivided into two groups of four. Those values that emphasize *deference or ascribed position* include power, respect, rectitude, and affection; those that deal with *welfare* include wealth, well-being, skill, and enlightenment.

Whenever a person has influence he enjoys a favorable position with respect to some value, and by his actions he can increase or decrease the value position of another individual. The amount and type of these values that one person controls for another serve as the basis of power and influence and are referred to as base values. Of course, influence is exercised to gain something of value from the target individual; the values the source gains from the target are referred to as scope values. According to the exchange theory of Lasswell and Kaplan, the source exchanges base values for the scope values that the target mediates.

The Lasswell and Kaplan influence theory had an immediate impact on a group of social psychologists at Yale University. Hovland, Janis, and Kelley (1953) postulated two source factors that determine the extent to which a target will accept a persuasive communication: the source's expertness and trustworthiness. A source was considered an expert to the degree that a target accepted the source's messages as containing valid content; trustworthiness referred to the target's perception that the source intended to communicate a valid message. A target would infer expertness if a source had special training or experience, education, history of success in problem solution, or from such general source attributes as age, role position, seniority, or social background. A source would be perceived as trustworthy to the extent that he was considered to be objective and to have no vested interest in influencing the target. Hovland et al. postulated that both expertness and trustworthiness contribute to the source's credibility and effectiveness in influencing the target.

At the end of the 1950s French and Raven (1959) devised a typology of the bases of social power that has had important effects on subsequent psychological research on the influence processes. They classified all influence as either socially dependent or independent of the source. The exercise of *informational influence,* a source-independent base of social power that may be described as a pure form of Parsons' category of persuasion, results in a change in the target's attitudes, values, and preferences. As Raven (1965) has noted, in informational influence "it is the content of the communication that is important, not the nature of the influencing agent [p. 372]." French and Raven discriminated five source-dependent bases of power: expert, legitimate, referent, reward, and coercive power.

According to French and Raven, the degree of expert power that a source has depends on the amount of knowledge or ability the target attributes to the source, the amount of knowledge the target perceives in himself, and the relevance of the knowledge to the object being judged or problem being solved. To distinguish expert power from informational influence, Raven (1965) has used the example of a student–teacher relation. If a student accepts a teacher's advice in applying a particular formula to solve a mathematics problem because he understands why the solution is applicable, informational influence has occurred; if the student accepts the formula on faith that the teacher should know best, then expert power is the basis of influence. The more expert a source is perceived to be, the more influential he should be.

Referent power stems from a target's wish to maintain similarity with and to be accepted and liked by the source person. Referent power is perhaps most clearly illustrated by the process of identification, and corresponds to an internalization of values, attitudes, and behaviors that constitute both compliance to influence attempts and an attempt to bring

the target's values into congruence with the source's values. The more attracted to a source the target is, the more influential the source should be.

Legitimacy may be said to have the property of requiredness (Asch,
1952; Köhler, 1938; Wertheimer, 1935). A person who complies to a
source because he feels he *ought* to is responding on the basis of legitimacy. Legitimate authority is distinguished from reward and coercive power
by the absence of immediate and explicit promises of rewards or threats
of punishments, and from informational influence in that people a
priori suspend their own judgments and accept that of the legitimate authority without having to be convinced of the accuracy of his view.

Authority relies on a set of symbols, myths, legends, documents, slo-
gans, and rules for its legitimacy, and rationalizes its requests on the basis
of such paraphernalia. Cartwright and Zander (1968) have aptly noted
that "it appears to be almost impossible to describe what happens in
groups without using terms which indicate the 'place' of members with
respect to one another [p. 486]." Numerous definitions of place or legitimacy have been offered in an attempt to integrate the notion of a hierarchy of obligations and rights associated with roles in groups. Authority
associated with a role position ordinarily is referred to as status. Status is
imbedded in the group and derives its effectiveness from members of the
group who enforce compliance to the requests of a high-status source
(Blau, 1964). Of course, the greater a source's perceived status, the
more influential he will be.

Reward and coercive power refer to promises and threats. It is assumed that the greater the magnitude of reward and punishment the
source possesses and the higher the probability of their use, the more influential the source will be. However, as we have defined promises and
threats they are communication modes rather than source characteristics
and, like French and Raven's category of informational influence, can be
considerably refined. Presumably the source's capability for carrying out
his promises or threats is based on his control over the requisite resources
so that he can give the promised rewards or carry out the threatened punishments. Even if the source is perceived as possessing the capability to
credibly employ promises and threats, he is likely to be disbelieved if he
is perceived as unwilling to spend his resources in the service of influence. Thus both the intentions and the capability of the source may be
considered as important factors in the influence process. Singer (1958;
1963) has specifically proposed a model of international relations within
which he defined threat perception as a function of both source capability
and source intentions.

Whenever the target perceives that the source has possession of material resources that can be used for influence purposes and has the intention or will to use them for such purposes, we will say that the source has

prestige. The higher the prestige of the source, the more influential he should be.

The characteristics of expertise or competence, attraction, status, and prestige correspond roughly with Dahl's power bases of control over information, popularity, access to the legal apparatus, and possession of wealth and control over jobs. These same four factors also correspond roughly with the Lasswell and Kaplan base values of respect, skill and enlightenment, affection, power and rectitude, and wealth. These analyses have strong intuitive appeal, and considerable evidence exists both for the independent effects of the basic four source characteristics and for consideration of each factor as independent of the others (cf. Tedeschi, Bonoma, & Schlenker, 1972).

One could, of course, construct long lists of source characteristics that might possibly affect how a target responds to influence communications. However, the history of psychology is replete with attempts to draw up lists of instincts and needs as bases for explaining human behavior, and psychologists have found that such lists are more a convenient method for renaming inadequately understood phenomena than a way of generating coherent theory. The number of discriminable source characteristics is probably quite large, and many of the names applied to these factors are overlapping or equivalent. It would be most parsimonious if a satisfactory list of source characteristics for use in building a theory of social influence could be compiled in an empirical rather than an intuitive manner. Fortunately such empirical techniques do exist and have been employed exactly for the purpose we have in mind.[2]

A basic technique that has been used to empirically derive a small set of source characteristics of primary importance for the social influence processes is called factor analysis. This statistical technique is based on the assumption that certain traits or attributes that are highly correlated with one another may actually form different aspects of a single, more general trait or attribute. For example, if we note that in small-group behavior dominance, friendliness, and talkativeness covary,[3] then we can meaningfully speak of a behavioral cluster called, perhaps, leadership.

As Carson (1969) describes it, factor analysis is a "rather complicated mathematical procedure by means of which a matrix of intercorrelated variables can be reduced to the minimum number of clusters necessary to account for the principal relationships existing among the variables. . . . Properly utilized, it is an excellent device for the reduction of complex domains to their principal dimensions or components [p. 96]." As with

2. The following summary of factor analysis is drawn from Carson's (1969) excellent discussion of the rationale behind that technique.

3. When dominance is high, friendliness and talkativeness are high also, and the converse.

any statistical technique, however, the worth of the results obtained with factor analysis can be no better than the amount and quality of the information processed. Thus while all the important source characteristics may not emerge in a single factor analytic study, we may find a common and overlapping set of such characteristics occurring regularly over several different investigations.

Carson (1969, pp. 98–103) has summarized a large number of factor analytic investigations that, although not directed toward social influence behaviors per se, attempted to account for the type and amount of general behavior produced in small group interactions. He points out that "the conclusion seems justified that major portions of the domain of interpersonal behavior can profitably and reasonably be conceived as involving variations on two independent, bipolar dimensions [p. 102]." The dimensions identified by the research Carson reviewed are labeled dominance–submission and love–hate. While the first is said to refer to controlling versus submissive behaviors, the second refers to behaviors that are either affiliative or disaffiliative in nature. Both Roger Brown (1965) and Timothy Leary (1957) have identified similar sets of two bipolar dimensions as important in the prediction of general forms of interpersonal behavior. Carter (1954) concludes from an early review of factor analytic studies that a third factor of competence or source expertise is necessary to explain small-group behavior.

Studies aimed more directly at the social influence processes have identified other important source characteristics. Marwell and Schmitt (1967) provided subjects with four situations within which various forms of influence could be used. Subjects were asked in job, family, sales, or roommate relationships to rate which technique they would use to gain another's compliance. Subjects could choose from 16 influence techniques, including threats, promises, warnings, mendations, aversive stimulation, social reinforcements, and activation of commitments messages.

Five basic factors emerged from the analysis. Rewarding and punishing activities, expertise, activation of commitments, and communications concerning the source's impressions of how good or bad the actor's behavior appears were the major higher order influence techniques identified. As can be seen, four of the factors refer to communications modes and one (expertise) to an attribute of the source of influence. If activation of commitment is equated with legitimate power, and rewarding and punishing activity with reward and coercive power, respectively, then Marwell and Schmitt's conclusion that they have provided empirical confirmation for French and Raven's (1959) typology power can be accepted.

In two separate studies Lemert (1963) asked college students in Canada and the United States to rate news sources on a set of bipolar adjectives such as good–bad and frank–reserved. The sources rated were newspapers and men in the public eye, such as Winston Churchill speaking on foreign policy. Sometimes the sources were identified with a topic and sometimes without a topic, though most of the communications were in the form of warnings, mendations, statements of fact, and activation of commitments.

These two factor analytic studies, along with a third, similar study by Berlo, Lemert, and Mertz (1966), found three principal factors—safety, qualification, and dynamism—representing all of the subjects' adjectival responses to all sources of communications. Safety apparently referred to the intentions the raters attributed to the source, and included such adjectives as good, gentle, fair, friendly, reasonable, unselfish. Dynamism included adjectives describing how active or powerful the source was, and included strong, emphatic, aggressive, forceful, and active. Qualification referred to the source's competence, and included expert, skilled, informed, educated, intelligent, experienced, and trained.

If we view safety as the target's attribution of intent to the source (benign or malevolent, accommodative or exploitative intent) and dynamism as perception of power, the two factors may be viewed as the components of what we have called prestige. Qualification is quite easily interpreted in terms of expertise. Lemert (1969) has found a sociability factor in addition to the other three factors, but only when the source was personally known or when a public source was not identified with any topic or message.

Studies similar to those that Lemert and his associates conducted have identified highly similar factor lists (Markham, 1965; McCroskey, 1966). In a review of such factor analytic studies Giffin (1967) concludes that five dimensions are relevant to a speaker's impact: expertness, reliability, intentions, dynamism, and personal attractiveness. In our terms these factors can be reinterpreted as expertness, credibility, the intentionality component of prestige, the capability component of prestige, and attraction, respectively.

Finally, Triandis, Vassiliou, and Thomanek (1966) described abstract persons by reference to male or female sex and the roles of physician, bank clerk, or unskilled worker, and asked subjects to scale how likely they would be to engage in various types of behaviors with such persons. They found that two basic factors termed status and interpersonal attraction were operating in terms of the rated preferences.

Although it might be argued that more source characteristics and communication modes exist than have been identified by the above factor analytic studies, apparently a minimum number of such characteristics accounts for much of the behavior variance in interpersonal influence interactions. These include expertise, prestige (i.e., the possession of power to reward or punish plus the intent to use that power), status, and interpersonal attraction. A theory of social influence might well try to determine what effects these source characteristics have on the successful use of the communication modes identified earlier. However, we have yet to consider the characteristics of the target of influence as they affect the influence process.

THE TARGET

Theorists have consistently qualified definitions of social power as the ability to implement one's will *despite resistance* (e.g., Harsanyi, 1962b; Weber, 1947). The successful exercise of power depends not only on the source's tactics, resources, and characteristics but also on the resources and characteristics of the person toward whom influence attempts are directed. Of course, it could be said that if a target person has more prestige, expertise, status, or attraction than the source of influence, the target could easily mount a defense against the source. Yet additional motivational and cognitive factors render a target person more or less resistant to influence.

Several specific motivational states have been identified with increased resistance to influence attempts. The target's needs give value to the source's resources as reinforcing agents and contribute to the target's overall susceptibility to influence. If the target person is very hungry and the source attempts to use motive-irrelevant praise as reinforcement, the target is likely to be quite unresponsive to such influence attempts. An aroused motive not only increases the prepotency of a reinforcing event but also broadens the class of stimuli that will be evaluated as reinforcing. If a person is relatively hungry he may eat a hamburger or a steak, but if he is starving he may also eat a dog, a horse, or even another human. Hence an increase in the strength of a motive (however established) decreases the person's resistance to the influence attempt of another person who offers a relevant reinforcement, *and* it increases the probability that the other person will possess a relevant reinforcer.

Research has indicated that a person's level of aspiration is used as a comparison for judging his own failures and successes (Lewin et al., 1944). Thibaut and Kelley (1959), drawing from level-of-aspiration theory, have postulated a relationship between influence and comparison level (CL). The CL is defined as the chronic or average level of reward that a person expects from any social interaction. The optimistic and self-confident individual should have a generally high CL, and a pessimistic and anxious person should have a generally low CL. In the way of outcomes the low CL person should be satisfied with much less than the high CL person. Thus the CL may be used to determine a rough index of the likelihood with which any individual will exert or resist influence.

While the concept of CL serves as a reference point for the value of outcomes in social interaction, Rotter's (1966) social learning theory in-

troduces a term to represent the generalized expectancy that one can produce intended effects. Thus CL represents a standard against which the
values of outcomes are compared, and Rotter's generalized expectancies
refer to the subjective probability of attaining outcomes.

Within Rotter's theory a person who has an orientation of *internal
control* tends to believe that he can determine his own outcomes and that
his abilities are such that he can affect and control his social and physical
environment in specific ways. A person who is high in *external control*
orientation has the general expectancy that his rewards and punishments
are not connected to his own actions but, rather, occur by chance, luck,
or fate. Rotter's theory makes it clear that generalized expectancies affect
behavior only when experience in a particular situation cannot be drawn
from the individual's background. Thus a specific expectancy would be
relevant to a son's reactions to his father, but a generalized expectancy
would mediate behavior to a stranger.

A theory of social conflict, power, and influence should include some
concepts that represent the target individual's values, trust of others, and
general manner of biasing the probabilities of receiving rewards and punishments. Knowledge of these individual characteristics should allow us
to predict more accurately how susceptible or resistant a target person
would be to particular influence attempts.

Conclusions

This chapter has identified and examined the basic factors and processes
that should be included in a theory of social conflict and influence. Interdependence of outcomes and at least partially opposed interests appear to
be ubiquitous in social relationships; hence conflict (of greater or lesser
degree) sets the problem for human interactions. The solutions for such
social problems often require the use of various modes of communications. These modes include threats, promises, warnings, and mendations,
all of which can be contingent or noncontingent, more or less explicit or
tacit, and may refer to specific types and magnitudes of reinforcements,
including sensory stimulation, rewards or costs, provision of gains or deprivation of expected gains, and social rewards or punishments. The credibility of threats and promises is a matter of matching words with deeds.
The effects of threats and promises on the course of conflict can be studied in the laboratory—for example, in a modified prisoner's dilemma
game. Source characteristics, including expertise, attraction, status, and
prestige, and target characteristics, such as motives, comparison level,
and generalized expectancies, also have important effects on social interactions.

3

Compliance to Social Influence

The major conclusion to be drawn from Chapter 2 is that we have elected to view the influence processes as an interaction involving a source's attempts to change or modify a target's behavior through the use of various communication modes and the attendant provision or prediction of different types of rewards or punishments. In this process it is assumed that the unique personal attributes or characteristics of both the source and target will have important facilitating or blocking effects on the outcomes of such influence attempts. Chapter 3 restricts and deepens our theoretical analysis of half of this influence paradigm: our concern here is with the ways in which source attributes and communication modes combine to produce a target person's decision of compliance or noncompliance following an influence attempt. The determinants of the source's behavior in selecting a target and mode of influence will be the focus of Chapter 4.

Economists have long been developing a theory of how individuals decide which goods to sell and for what price, or what goods to buy on the marketplace and for what price. Psychologists have broadened the purely economic analysis of such decisions to explain how people make decisions between choice alternatives in all phases of their lives. Since we are concerned with human interactions conceived of in terms of social exchange and in the context of some degree of social conflict, it makes sense to seek a marriage between the concepts of behavioral decision theory and the components of the influence relationships already identified. It will be necessary to develop an understanding of decision theory before the marriage can be consummated. Although the basic concepts and assumptions of decision theory are complex, we shall make our account as simple as possible (see Lee, 1971, for an excellent and complete discussion of decision theory).

Decision Theory

The concept of economic man was developed to enable economists to perfectly predict the choice behavior of an ideal man. Economic man was presumed to be perfectly informed about his available choice alternatives and the exact outcomes associated with each of his choices. That is, he knew not only every possible alternative open to him but also the precise consequences to which each alternative invariably led; in short, he was an omniscient man in a static and unchanging world. No unforeseen circumstances that could interfere with the analyst's predictions of behavior were admitted. The distinguishing characteristic of classical economic man was that in his marketplace activities he always made the most rational choice —a choice that maximized something (e.g., profits).

Classical economic theory could not make predictions about economic behavior unless it made the additional assumptions that the individual could state his preferences when given choices between various commodities or outcomes and that these preferences followed a rule of transitivity. The transitivity rule requires that the decision maker so rank order his value preferences that if he prefers commodity A to commodity B, and B to C, then when given a choice between A and C he will consistently choose A.

Given such simplifying assumptions as those of perfect information, knowledge that specific outcomes will certainly follow a given behavioral choice, transitivity in rank ordering preferences, and the motive to maximize outcomes, economic man's choice behavior should be perfectly consistent and easily predictable. Thus, if a decision maker is given a choice between one behavioral path that leads to an outcome valued at two dollars and a second behavioral path leading to a one-dollar outcome, it could be predicted with perfect confidence that the alternative that yields the most value will be invariably chosen.

The ideal economic man may have been perfectly informed and consistent in his preferences, but real men obviously appear at least partially ignorant about their choice alternatives and often seem inconsistent in their value preferences. Men simply do not ordinarily know all the alternatives available to them. A gambler, for example, might be ignorant of a different game or off-track betting parlor around the corner where he could get much better odds.

If real men are not perfectly knowledgeable about their choice alternatives it can still be assumed that they will maximize values in making decisions about the choice alternatives they *believe* they have. In experimental situations subjects can be perfectly informed by instructions about their choice alternatives and possible outcomes, thereby making the assumption about economic man true for our everyday man. Theories that make an assumption of perfect information can therefore be tested in the laboratory. In field settings the investigator is likely to have more difficulty in ignoring the perfect information assumption, artificially contriving a situation to make the assumption true, or fathoming what the decision maker believes his alternatives are.

Even if men do maximize values, are informed about their choice alternatives, and are able to order their preferences, the outcomes of choices are never completely certain but only more or less probable in the real world. For example, the weatherman's prediction of snow tomorrow is based on a 40 percent probability; the gambler knows that there is a 50 percent chance of winning a coin toss; the physician's prognosis is an 80 percent likelihood that an untreated disease will become an acute problem. When the connection of acts and consequences is probabilistic and the decision maker knows what the probabilities are, the decision is said to be *risky*.

In order to predict a decision maker's behavioral choices when outcomes are risky, the concept of *expected value* was developed. In deriving the expected value of a choice alternative it must be recognized that because of the probabilistic nature of the situation each choice usually has several mutually exclusive outcomes associated with it.

For example, if a gambler places a bet he has a certain probability of winning and a certain probability of losing. Each of these mutually exclusive outcomes has associated with it a particular value and a particular probability of occurrence. Given a decision between a gamble that would give him $1 if on a toss of a single die, any number but a 6 turns up or $20 if a 6 is thrown, which alternative would the gambler choose? The intelligent gambler immediately calculates the probabilities in favor of winning each bet. Assuming the die is fair,[1] taking the first bet would mean the gambler has a 5/6 chance of winning $1 and a 1/6 chance of winning nothing; taking the second bet would mean a 1/6 chance of winning $20 and a 5/6 chance of winning nothing. But which bet would be the best one?

One answer is that the gambler should choose the alternative that will maximize his expected value. *The expected value of an alternative is found by multiplying the value of each mutually exclusive outcome by its probability of occurrence and then adding these products.* In our example the expected value of the first bet is easily computed as:

$$(\text{5/6} \times \$1) + (\text{1/6} \times \$0) = (\$0.83) + (\$0.00) = \$0.83.$$

1. That is, unbiased; each face of an unbiased die has a 1/6 probability of occurring on each throw.

The second bet has an expected value of:

$$(\tfrac{1}{6} \times \$20) + (\tfrac{5}{6} \times \$0) = (\$3.40) + (\$0.00) = \$3.40.$$

If our gambler uses the choice criterion of maximizing his expected value, he will choose to bet on the second alternative, although his choice may yield him nothing, since there is, after all, a 5/6 chance that he will not win the $20. However, in the circumstances of decision under risk, and employing the maximization of expected value as the choice criterion, the $20 bet is the best alternative available to the gambler.

A complication arises for behavioral decision theory when choices between alternatives must be made and the probabilities of association between choices and outcomes are unknown. Such decisions are said to occur in conditions of *uncertainty*. The difference between risky and uncertain decisions can be illustrated by changing our $1 and $20 bet example to a game of Russian roulette in which the player is not sure just how many chambers of the six-shot revolver are loaded with live shells and how many with only brass casings. In many other situations a subjective estimation of the probability of occurrence of an event or outcome must be made on the basis of incomplete evidence, even though some evidence is available. Some other events occur so rarely that their probabilities of occurrence are difficult to objectively assess.

In conditions of uncertainty the decision maker must hazard a guess about the probability that a particular choice will lead to a particular outcome. When predictions about an individual's choice behavior must be based on the subjective probability of the occurrence of objective values, the choice criterion is referred to as *subjective expected value* (SEV), and the decision maker is presumed to act so as to maximize SEV. In this case as before two factors are involved (a value component and a probability component), and one can be more or less independently and objectively determined (i.e., value).

The usual research strategy has been to provide subjects with a series of choices, holding the values of the outcomes constant, and to infer from the actual choices an individual makes what the subjective probabilities must have been. Unfortunately, this approach has been rather unsuccessful in accounting for human choice behavior in conditions of uncertainty (see Edwards & Tversky, 1967; Simon & Stedry, 1969).

It is common knowledge that men are not consistent in the way they order their values; that is, their preference orderings are intransitive. For example, although a person may prefer steak to hamburger and hamburger to fish, on a given day he may choose fish in preference to either steak or hamburger. This behavior does not necessarily imply that the man is inconsistent. If our decision maker is a Catholic and is practicing voluntary abstinence in respect to religious tradition by choosing fish on Fridays, the condition in which his choice is made must be incorporated into our predictions about his behavioral choices. Thus our Catholic friend has in essence two separate preference lists of desired foods—one for Fridays only and one for the remaining days of the week. Each list is consistent internally, and if we know what day of the week it is we should be able to accurately predict his food preferences.

Inconsistencies of choice behavior may also be a function of temporary bodily states or motivational factors. If a person ate steak for all three meals each day for several weeks in succession, his preference for steak over either hamburger or fish might very well be changed through satiation or adaptation. After some period of time when steak has not been so readily and amply available, the person's initial preference for steak over either of the other two foods might be restored.

In addition to changing decision conditions and temporary motivational states, behavioral decision theory must also reflect that individuals largely learn their preferences. Hence what one person values highly another might not value. To the philatelist acquisition of a rare 1913 Ghanian elephant-head stamp may bring great joy; another individual who does not share such learned preferences for stamps may simply lick the object and place it on a postcard.

All of these considerations in unique and changing value preferences have led some decision theorists to develop the concept of utility. *Utility can be defined briefly as the subjective value of a commodity or outcome for a particular individual.* Although money can be given objective values, any particular amount of money may be worth more to one person than to another. For example, a dollar may be worth more to a beggar than to a millionaire. The beggar has so little money that each small increment is valuable to him, while the millionaire has so much that such a small amount has little worth or utility to him. Utility can therefore be understood (at least in cases that allow some objective assessment of the value of a commodity) as composed of two factors: the objective value of a commodity, and the subjective valuing process that derives from the quantity of that commodity the individual has consumed or possesses at the time a decision must be made or from previously learned preferences about the commodity.

One variety of behavioral decision theory uses the concept of subjective expected utility (SEU) as the choice criterion and assumes that individuals act so as to maximize their SEU. That is, in conditions of uncertainty individuals act to maximize the sum of the products of their subjective estimates that certain outcomes will occur and the utilities or subjective worths of those outcomes. The computational procedure for

determining the SEU of a choice is identical to that involved in the computation of EV; however, the probability and value components are subjective
rather than objective.

Each successive step in the development of behavioral decision theory,
culminating in the concept of SEU, has considered the choice situation
more from the subjective perspective of the individual. The decision maker is viewed as subjectively assessing both the probabilities and the values
of the outcomes associated with his choice alternatives. However, because
these components are subjective does not mean that they cannot be measured by being inferred from the subject's behavior or from other objective factors. The empirical problems in the measurement of both subjective probabilities and utilities are complex (see Lee, 1971; or Simon &
Stedry, 1969), but certain bypassing assumptions can be made in order
to allow tests of SEU hypotheses.

For example, often the problem of measuring utilities can be circum-
vented in research by simply assuming that a subject will prefer more of a
commodity to less of it (or vice versa). An experimental subject usually
can be expected to prefer more points, approval, or money to less of
these commodities or sentiments as long as we are not dealing with extreme values. Although individuals may evaluate the worth of a given
quantity of a commodity differently, all will probably desire and assign a
higher utility to more rather than less of the commodity involved. This consistency in valuing is sufficient for most experimental purposes; both the
beggar and the millionaire should prefer to receive $20 to $1, and both
should prefer a gamble of winning $20 with 1/6 probability of occur-
rence to a gamble of winning $1 with a 5/6 probability of occurrence.

For illustrative purposes the SEU choice criterion can be applied to an
analysis of subject's behavior in a prisoner's dilemma game. First suppose
that the values in the matrix for the game are the same as those shown in
Figure 1.2. Further suppose that a robot player is programmed to cooperate on 50 percent of the game trials, so that the objective probability
of the occurrence of the robot's selection of Choice 1 is 50 percent, and
of Choice 2, 50 percent.

Although we are interested in the subjects' SEU estimations for the alternatives of cooperation and competition, let's first compute the expected values based on the objective data and then see if these can be translated into SEU. If a subject makes the cooperative choice (Choice 1) he
may gain 4 points (given the robot's selection of Choice 1) with a probability of .5, or he may lose 5 points (if the robot competes and makes
Choice 2) with a probability of .5. Thus the EV for making the cooperative choice is calculated as:

$$(4 \times .5) + (-5 \times .5) = (+2) + (-2.5) = -0.5.$$

If a subject makes the competitive choice he may gain 5 points (the robot makes Choice 1) with a probability of .5, or he may lose 4 points (the robot makes Choice 2) with a probability of .5. Thus the EV for making the competitive choice is:

$$(5 \times .5) + (-4 \times .5) = (+2.5) + (-2) = 0.5.$$

These objectively calculated values would, of course, be modified for each individual as a function of the subjective factors discussed earlier, but in experiments it can be assumed that the average of the subjects' utilities and subjective probabilities should approximate the objective values and probabilities.[2] In the example above subjects should choose to select the competitive alternative rather consistently, since by so doing they maximize their SEU. Empirically it has been found that subjects do predominantly make competitive choices in the conditions of our example (Lindskold & Tedeschi, 1971a).

People may or may not have some type of cognitive calculator that produces a subjective expected utility for each of their behavioral alternatives. As a model for predicting behavior it seems reasonable to suppose that people actually do approximate SEU calculations in some way. The suggestion that decision theoretic concepts be applied to psychology in general and to the social influence processes in particular is not new (Berkowitz, 1969; Cartwright, 1959; March, 1955, 1968). In fact, restricted applications already have been attempted in a small number of cases (Gerard, 1965; Lanzetta & Kanareff, 1959; Miller, 1971). The integration of decision concepts and the source–communications–target model of the influence processes to be presented here simply represents a more general and incautious attempt to cement what appears to be a promising relationship for the explanation of human social behavior.

2. That this is so follows from the logic of experimentation. *Groups* of subjects are exposed to differing treatment manipulations in order to assure that any obtained effects are not due to the idosyncracies of one or a few individuals. Those readers familiar with analysis of variance in statistics may apply their knowledge here; the logic is similar. For the benefit of readers skilled in psychological measurement techniques we are assuming that we can measure utility on at least an ordinal scale for all subjects in a game situation, and that for most of our predictions this ordinal scale is sufficient. Thus, holding all other conditions constant, a subject will comply more when a threat has a high punishment magnitude than when it has a low punishment magnitude; the absolute quantities attached to the high and low punishment are immaterial to the prediction of the basic relationship between punishment magnitude and the choice of compliance or noncompliance. Given transitive orderings of preferences it can be assumed that the objective value and utility of these preferences are monotonically related; that is, an increase in objective value is paralleled by an increase in subjective utility. Given these assumptions the averaging of utilities across individuals does not seem to do much injustice to the facts that utility is an individual rather than a group concept and that normally a ratio scale is required to equate utilities across individuals.

SEU Theory and the Modes of Communication

When influence attempts are directed at him, the target individual has only two alternatives: to comply or to noncomply.[3] Among the types of communications that can be sent to a target are threats, promises, warnings, and mendations, each of which has associated with it both a utility (reward or punishment) and a probability component. The target must assess the probabilities and utilities associated with the contingencies proposed to him and then make his decision. Source and target characteristics are postulated as having the effect of causing the target to systematically bias the probabilities associated with the influence communications he receives. For example, a target who does not trust others may estimate the probability of receiving a promised reward as lower than would a trusting individual in the same objective circumstances.

The subjective expected gains or losses associated with each message type must be taken into account in determining the SEU for complying or noncomplying to an influence attempt. In a sense the subjective expected gains or losses associated with an influence communication are added on to the outcomes normally associated with a social interaction. They constitute side payoffs and comprise only part of the SEU for compliance and noncompliance. It is explicitly presumed that targets behave so as to maximize SEU during influence interactions.

THREATS AND PROMISES

The credibility of an influence communication is a function of the relationship between the message and subsequent events. The credibility of a contingent threat is defined as the cumulated probability that the source has punished the target for noncompliance to his demands. In weighing the SEU for complying to the threatener's demands against the SEU for noncompliance, both the credibility of the threat and the magnitude of the threatened punishment must be taken into account. Similarly, the target of contingent promises must make an estimate of the source's credibility given the source's record of fulfillment of previous promises, and before deciding on a course of action he must take into account the amount of reward the promisor has offered.

The success of an SEU theory of social influence in predicting the way people actually behave in an influence setting can be demonstrated by an analysis of experiments conducted within the modified prisoner's dilemma game paradigm described in Chapter 2. In the Horai and Tedeschi (1969) experiment the robot threatener periodically sent threats to the

---

3. The question of matters of degree of compliance will be ignored until the process of bargaining is considered in Chapter 5.

subjects. The robot was 10, 50, or 90 per cent credible in his use of threats, and the threatened punishment magnitudes were 5, 10, or 20 points. The robot threatener was always exploitative when sending a threat by making Choice 2 on all threat-relevant trials. In making their calculations of SEUs the target subjects had to consider the payoffs associated with the PDG choices as well as the superimposed threat payoffs (see Figure 2.3). Let's closely examine the decision criteria that subjects theoretically used in just two conditions of the experiment.

When the threat credibility was 10 percent and the punishment magnitude was 5 points, the subject after a few plays could estimate the SEU of complying or noncomplying by taking into account that he would be exploited with 100 percent probability and that he was being threatened with a punishment of 5 points, which would occur 10 percent of the times that he noncomplied. If a subject complied to a threat he would definitely be exploited (as summarized in Figure 2.3) and lose 5 points. The SEU for compliance would be approximated by:

$$(-5 \times 1.0) + (4 \times 0.0) = -5.$$

Calculation of the SEU for noncompliance must take into account the regular game costs plus the probability and utility of the negative side payoff threatened. That is, since he will be exploited he will definitely lose 4 points, plus he stands a 10 percent probability of losing the threatened 5 points as punishment. The SEU for noncompliance would be estimated as:

$$(-4 \times 1.0) + (5 \times 0.0) + (-5 \times 0.1) = (-4) + (0) + (-0.5) = -4.5.$$

Note that the effects of the threat merely add subjective expected costs to the outcomes that would normally accrue on that occasion. The target thus faces a least-of-evils choice in that he will lose no matter what he does; however, he would maximize his SEU by noncomplying.

When the robot threatened to take away 20 points and was 90 percent credible, similar calculations could be made. Since the threatener was always 100 percent exploitative, the SEU for complying to the threat is exactly the same as in the prior condition:

$$(-5 \times 1.0) + (4 \times 0.0) = -5.0.$$

The threat did not affect the SEU for complying, since punishment was threatened only for noncomplying and hence altered the SEU for only that choice. The SEU for noncompliance in this condition can be estimated as follows:

$$(-4 \times 1.0) + (5 \times 0.0) + (-20 \times 0.9) = -22.0.$$

Thus, according to SEU criteria, the target should defy the threatener in the 10 percent — 5 point condition but comply frequently in the 90 percent — 20 point condition.

The overall results of the experiment were consistent with SEU predictions. Subjects complied more frequently the greater the negative subjective expected utility (as estimated from expected value) associated with noncompliance to the threats. A review of the calculations indicates both intuitively and mathematically that subjects will comply more to threats the greater the negative utility of the threatened punishment and/or the greater the probability of punishment, holding all other factors constant. This relationship has proven highly reliable over a large number of studies (cf. Tedeschi, Bonoma, & Brown, 1971).

When a threatener is 100 percent accommodative SEUs for complying and noncomplying can be calculated in much the same manner. The only factors that change are the values associated with the PDG choices; the threat game outcomes are the same. Again assuming the matrix values of Figure 1.2, the target either can comply to the threatener's demands and share in the mutual rewards that the threatener's accommodative gestures offer or can noncomply and try to exploit the accommodative gestures while accepting a certain probability of being punished for his noncompliance. Bonoma and Tedeschi (1972b) found that when a threatener was accommodative, subjects complied more to the robot source's threats when the SEU for compliance exceeded the SEU for noncompliance. Given the same punishment magnitudes and threat credibilities, targets should be more compliant to an accommodative than to an exploitative threatener, since in the accommodative situation the source gives the target some benefits for complying. Schlenker, Bonoma, Tedeschi, and Pivnick (1970) confirmed this prediction.

If a promisor is totally accommodative in the context of a prisoner's dilemma he usually provides strong incentive for compliance to his requests. With the matrix values we have been using for the PDG, the target can gain only one point more for exploiting the promisor than could be gained by compliance, and if the target complies there is some additional probability that he can gain a positive side payoff. Suppose that an accommodative source is 50 percent credible in the use of his promises and that he offers an additional 5 points to the target for compliance. The SEU for compliance can be estimated from the following:

$$(4 \times 1.0) + (-5 \times 0.0) + (5 \times .5) = 6.5.$$

The SEU for noncompliance would be approximated by:

$$(5 \times 1.0) + (-4 \times 0.0) = 5.$$

Hence the target should comply relatively frequently to the source's requests.

A high level of compliance to the promises of an accommodative source has been empirically observed (Lindskold & Tedeschi, 1971a; Lindskold, Bonoma, Schlenker, & Tedeschi, 1972; Schlenker, Bonoma, Tedeschi, Lindskold, & Horai, 1971). However, if the accommodative promisor never fulfills his promises by providing the positive side payoff, compliance will be somewhat less than when he always does as he says he will (Horai, Haber, Tedeschi, & Smith, 1970).

An exploitative promisor does not provide the target with the opportunity to reap benefits by mere compliance. Rather, the target must depend on receiving the side payoff promised for his compliance or he will be a net loser for cooperating. In the context of a prisoner's dilemma game an exploitative promisor places the subject in a least-of-evils situation if both choices available to the target yield him losses. If the target complies he is exploited and loses points; if he does not do as the promisor requests and both make competitive choices, they both lose points. The target must weigh his alternatives and choose to minimize his losses in such a case.

Lindskold, Bonoma, Schlenker and Tedeschi (1972) found that when an exploitative promisor did not offer sufficient rewards (side payoffs) to compensate for the damage done by exploitation, little compliance was given to the robot's promises. However, when the reward was sufficient to more than compensate for whatever exploitation occurred, subjects were considerably more compliant. When subjects faced an accommodative promisor the magnitude of the promised side payoff had no effect on the subjects' frequency of compliance, since they already had sufficient reason to comply; the robot and subjects received mutual benefits when subjects complied, irrespective of whether the additional benefits were provided in the form of side payoffs.

The conditions of the prisoner's dilemma research reported above are quite restrictive. The target is rather powerless, has no retaliatory capability, cannot issue counterinfluence communications, and cannot escape from the situation. Few real-world situations are exactly like this, but evidence from other research supports the predictions made from an SEU theory of social influence. Zipf (1960) found that the subjective expected utility notion has phenomenological plausibility to experimental subjects. Using procedures very different from those considered here, she found a direct relationship between the magnitude of reward promised and subjects' written reports of subjective expected utility and consequent behavioral compliance. Even in the context of groups rather than dyadic interactions, the same function of SEU and compliance has been demonstrated.

Sampson and Kardush (1965) found that an evaluator's promises of rewards were more effective in improving group performance when the values of rewards were higher.

Further evidence for the subjective expected utility approach to influence comes from a number of nonlaboratory studies. Gibbs (1968) examined crime statistics from several states and found that the incidence of homicide was inversely related to both the magnitude of legal punishment actually adjudicated for convicted murderers and the probability that homicides were solved and carried through to criminal conviction. Although Gibbs concluded that the credibility component was more important than the negative utility associated with legal threats, Gray and Martin (1969) reanalyzed Gibbs' data and concluded that the SEU-like multiplicative function of probability and negative utility best accounted for the obtained findings. In a somewhat broader sociological analysis that also included several types of lesser crimes, Tittle (1969) reported that certainty of punishment was inversely related to the incidence of all crimes analyzed, whereas severity of punishment contributed only to the deterrence of homicide. Yet Chambliss (1966) found that the frequency of parking violations on a college campus was inversely related to both the severity and the certainty of punishment.

WARNINGS AND MENDATIONS

Analyses of the decision processes of target individuals as recipients of warnings or mendations follows very much the same rationale as that of threats and promises. Remember that a warning was defined as a source-to-target communication that predicts that harm will befall the target unless he changes his current behavioral direction, but the source does not mediate the harm. The target must calculate the SEU for continuing what he is doing (noncomplying to the warning) and the SEU for compliance to the warning. The subjective expected utility of noncompliance is the product of the cumulated probability that when the source has issued warnings in the past and the target did not heed them the predicted harm did occur, times the negative utility of the harm specified in the current warning. In addition, the target must calculate the expected gains from continuing his prewarning behavior. The subjective expected utility of compliance to the warning includes the costs of giving up the gains associated with the prewarning behavior.

A similar calculation of SEUs would follow the reception of a mendation. The credibility of the source of mendations and the utilities associated with compliance and noncompliance are the decision factors the target uses in making his behavioral choice. It is presumed that the target will choose the alternative that maximizes SEU.

In a decision-theoretic study of both warnings and mendations, Chu

(1966) employed persuasive communications that simultaneously varied the probability and the magnitude of harm associated with the danger of roundworms to health. He found that children were more willing to take remedial action (in the form of painful antiroundworm injections) as the subjective expected utility associated with noncompliance to the warnings became more negative. Chu also provided the children with mendations about the probability that such injections would successfully immunize them against the dreaded disease. The higher the probability stated for the mendations, the more willing were the children to take the injections.

Using a similar fear appeal, Dabbs and Leventhal (1966) found that the negative expected utility associated with warnings about tetanus was directly related to the willingness of college students to take preventive shots. However, as in the Chu study, both probability and utility were varied simultaneously, permitting no assessment of their independent contributions to SEU.

CONCLUSIONS

In general the evidence reviewed is supportive of the assumptions made by an SEU interpretation given to threats, promises, warnings, and mendations. The direct function of the negative subjective expected utility associated with noncompliance to threats and targets' behavioral compliance has been rather firmly established. When the threatener is accommodative and thus gives the target a positive incentive, the target will comply even more frequently. The gross frequency of compliance given to an accommodative promisor may not be affected by increments in the subjective expected utility of compliance if the mutual benefits gained through cooperation are already sufficient to induce such compliance, but when the promisor is exploitative then variations in the SEU of compliance to the promises could directly affect such behavioral compliance.

Although the evidence is consistent with the postulated direct relationship between negative subjective expected utility and the effectiveness of warnings, more evidence is necessary to confirm the multiplicative relationship between probability and utility. Taken together, the findings are consistent enough to encourage us to proceed in the development of a theory of social influence centered around an SEU interpretation of the choices posed by the communication modes the source uses.

Source Characteristics:
Authentication and Deauthentication

We have seen that an individual appears to make a decision about whether or not to comply to an influence attempt based on the relative difference between the SEUs associated with each choice. The SEU has been considered a function of the subjective probability and utility of each of the regular social interaction outcomes associated with a choice, plus the subjective probability of receiving side payoffs and the utility of the side payoffs. If the individual were not embedded in a social situation, the decision criteria we have described could be used to predict his behavior. The social relationship between the source and the target may act to *authenticate* or *deauthenticate* the probability estimates the target makes. Authentication refers to an upward systematic biasing or exaggeration of the probabilities of an event; deauthentication refers to a downward systematic biasing of the probabilities of an event. The direction of these systematic biases will depend on source characteristics and the type of influence message employed.

SOURCE ATTRACTION

If a target likes a source, the target is more likely to believe promises of reward and to disbelieve threats of punishment. This proposition derives from the intuitive hypothesis that the target will find it hard to believe that a friendly source will mediate harm. Alternatively, if the target dislikes the source, the target should be all too willing to expect punishment for noncompliance to threats and to disbelieve promises of reward. If reward mediation is a basis of attraction and the mediation of punishment is the basis of disattraction, then attraction for a person is based on the expectancies aroused by the conditions that form the affective relationship. Such expectancies cause the person to authenticate the promises and to deauthenticate the threats of a liked source. Conversely, the threats of a disliked source are authenticated, and the objective credibility of his promises are subject to the target's deauthentication revision.

The specific effect of source attraction on the decision criteria of a target depends on the positivity or negativity of their affective relationship as well as on the mode of communication employed in the service of influence. Figure 3.1, which represents an overview of the entire theory, shows that attraction is presumed to directly affect the target's estimates of SEU associated with the influence attempt.

Let's assume that the expected utility associated with compliance to a promise message can be calculated only on the basis of two factors: 50 percent credibility and an objective value of $10 offered as a reward— that is, an approximated SEU of $5. But if target likes the source, the theory stipulates that the probability component in the SEU computation will be subjectively overestimated, the individual will assign some subjective utility to the reward, and the resulting SEU associated with compliance is likely to be greater than $5. Correspondingly, if the target dislikes the promisor, the subjective probability estimate of the credibility of the promise will be deauthenticated (i.e., underestimated), yielding an SEU

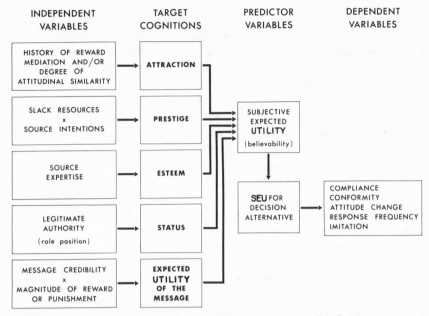

FIGURE 3.1. *Overview of the SEU theory of social influence.*

of somewhat less than $5. A target faced with objectively the same evidence with regard to the SEU of compliance to a given promise would comply more frequently to the requests of a liked source than to those of a disliked source. The reverse of these effects of attraction should occur if the source uses threats as the communication mode.

Schlenker, Bonoma, Tedeschi, Lindskold, and Horai (1972) carried out an experiment to test several of the above hypotheses. The study induced high or low attraction for the source by manipulating the degree of perceived attitudinal similarity (on questionnaires) between the subject and a confederate (robot), a technique that reliably induces a degree of positive or negative attraction (see Byrne, 1969). Subjects were targets of threats from the liked or disliked robot. The punishment magnitude of the threats was held constant, while the credibility was varied (10 percent or 90 percent).

If disattraction causes the subject to exaggerate the probability component of threats, more compliance should be given to the low credibility threat than the objective circumstances warrant. The high probability threats could hardly be exaggerated, though, since the probability was objectively very high. Results showed that targets who disliked the source complied as often to the low as to the high credibility threats, supporting the proposition that dislike does cause the target to authenticate (over-estimate) the objective probability of punishment, increasing negative SEU and subsequent compliance.

However, and contrary to SEU predictions, targets who liked the source usually did not underestimate the credibility of threats; such subjects were realistic in their appraisal of the situation and complied more often to the high than to the low probability threats. Dislike is apparently a form of power when threats are used as the mode of influence, but positive attraction is not a basis of power in a coercive relationship. Derivative from these findings is the proposal that when a source of threats does not have the resources or the intention of spending resources for punishing noncompliance he can still be effective in exercising influence if he can incur the target's dislike.

Almost all social-psychological theories of interpersonal attraction predict that the source's attractiveness will enhance the efficacy of his persuasive communications (Cartwright & Harary, 1956; Heider, 1958; Newcomb, 1953; Osgood & Tannenbaum, 1955). Persuasive communications, composed of tacit or explicit warnings and mendations, describe the causal texture of the environment for a target and usually include the source's recommended or remedial actions. The causal structure of the environment includes the motives and actions of third parties, who may be represented as the future agents of harm or benefits for the target.

Attraction for the source should directly mediate compliance to the recommendations of a persuasive communication, because the target should tend to overestimate the probability that the source's descriptions and/or predictions are correct. Such authentication derives from the target's belief that a liked source wants similar goals and assesses the intentions and capabilities of third parties in much the same way as the target would. Also, a liked source would tend to be perceived as having a concern for the target's best interests (cooperative) and to be sincere and honest in his description of reality (trustworthy), considerations not likely to obtain with a disliked source of persuasive communications. Evidence shows that the target does have suspicions about the intentions and the objectivity or accuracy of a disliked source (cf. Bramel, 1969; Hovland, Janis, & Kelley, 1953; Mills & Jellison, 1968).

The present theory postulates that a target will authenticate the warnings and mendations of a liked source but will deauthenticate the persuasive communications of a disliked source. Thus the target's SEU calculation for compliance to a persuasive message should be greater when the source is liked than when the source is disliked. Considerable evidence supports these postulated relationships (Abelson & Miller, 1967; Burnstein, Stotland, & Zander, 1961; Dabbs, 1964; Mills & Aronson, 1965; Wright, 1966). For example, Brock (1965) found that perceived similarity (and presumably positive liking) mediated compliance to a source's mendations. Salesmen-experimenters in the paint sections of a department store attempted to persuade customers to purchase a brand of paint that was either more or less expensive than the kind the customers originally requested. The persuasive communication indicated that the source had used the recommended paint on a similar or dissimilar job with excellent results. More customers purchased the paint recommended by the similar source, irrespective of the price change involved.

It should be noted that in Figure 3.1 the characteristics of the source and the probability and value components of messages are represented as independent variables. Each factor is perceived by the target, and they combine to produce SEU estimations, the predictor variable of the theory. The laws of combination of the independent variables—for example, the *joint* effects of low attraction and high status—are not specified by the theory; rather, they are left to empirical determination, a job that has hardly been begun. Each factor is treated independently of the others, as we have treated attraction separately from other source characteristics, and predictions are made for each type of influence message.

Every theory must be operationally anchored on the antecedent and consequent ends of its predictions; otherwise no empirical evaluation of the theory would be possible. Thus we are bound by our consideration of attraction to operationalize attraction, the communication mode (and its components, probability and utility), and the target's behavioral compliance. We have indicated that attraction can be operationalized by manipulating perceived similarity, by sociometric measurement of existing relationships between persons, by nurturant behaviors, or by other means. The expected value of threats and promises has been operationalized, particularly in the context of a prisoner's dilemma, but the probability component of warnings and mendations has not been satisfactorily operationalized.

Additional dependent variables, including conformity, imitation, and attitude change, represent extensions of the basic theory and will be considered in Chapter 8. As we move on to consider the effects of such source characteristics as status, expertise, and prestige, concern must be manifested for explicit conceptualization of these factors and the careful scrutiny of experimental operationalizations of source characteristics. Researchers have not always given sufficient consideration to these matters.

SOURCE STATUS

Perhaps the most conceptually ambiguous source characteristic, when the empirical literature is consulted, is status. Operational definitions have included source competence or expertise (Hollander, 1964), the degree of the source's control over those reinforcing events that are important for the target (Whiting, 1960), and target estimations of the capability the source possesses (Hurwitz, Zander, & Hymovitch, 1968). The factor analytic studies reviewed in Chapter 2 indicate that these are separable

source characteristics and may have independent effects on the social influence processes. Unfortunately, few experiments control only one characteristic. Most often all of these factors are combined in a single study
as if only one independent variable were being manipulated.

The definition of status offered here is restricted to the authority associated with a role position and is consistent with the French and Raven
(1959) concept of legitimate power. Of course, whether or not a source
deserves deference is a matter the target individual subjectively decides,
but presumably this subjective assessment is functionally related to objective factors associated with the source's role position and the social situation.

Status is embedded in a larger group and carries with it a set of rights
and obligations that produces a hierarchy in the group (Cartwright & Zander, 1968, p. 486). Unlike the more direct influence exerted in the form
of coercive power, legitimacy or status derives its effectiveness from the
group members who enforce compliance to the requests of the person
who occupies a privileged role position (Blau, 1964). The learning of the
hierarchical structures within groups and the acceptance of the status quo
are subject to long-term socialization processes and are too complex for
discussion here (see Tedeschi & Bonoma, 1972).

In the context of the laboratory, status is often taken where it exists,
such as in military hierarchies, or is induced by election procedures in ad
hoc groups or by the appointive powers of the experimenter, who himself
is a legitimate authority. Needless to say it is difficult to separate expertise from status, since a competent person in a society that allows mobility across class lines is likely to acquire status as a reward for his contribution to the group. Even so, expertise is not the basis of the deference a
high status source receives as a consequence of having status, as many an
army private will confirm.

It is postulated that high source status causes the target to authenticate
and low source status causes the target to deauthenticate every form of
influence communication. High source status authenticates the negative
SEU of noncompliance to threats and the SEU of compliance to promises
not only because the source is likely to have the support of others in the
group and to possess the requisite resources to back up his words but also
because he would have a *right* to punish or reward the target. It is not
only because a policeman possesses weapons that he is obeyed. The responsibilities of high authority are to provide orientation for the group, to
define the nature of social reality, and to organize the group for purposes
of effectively achieving group goals (Lasswell, 1966). Thus the target's
subjective estimates of the credibility of the source's persuasive communications are also likely to be biased by the source's status.

Often the orienting function of the high status source is embodied in a set of commands or instructions. Evan and Zelditch (1961) found that subjects more frequently displayed covert disobedience to the technical rules and commands of a supervisor when he was perceived as incompetent than when he was perceived as competent. They obtained direct evidence that the less competent supervisor was perceived as not having a right to occupy his office. When a particular status is earned by the alleged possession of special knowledge or experience and the person who holds the status position is perceived by those beneath him as not possessing the competence commensurate with his role position, then the legitimacy of his authority is undermined. That status and expertise could be varied with different effects supports the assumption of the present theory that expertise can be analytically separated from status.

Bickman (1971) has reported convincing evidence that individuals whom others assume to be of high status receive more compliance to their general requests than do individuals who do not possess these marks of authority in our society. A confederate of the experimenter approached subjects in a telephone booth at Grand Central Station and asked them if they had found a dime, which the confederate had left in the booth a few minutes earlier. When the confederate was dressed as befits a person of high status (i.e., suit and tie) 77 percent of the subjects returned the dime. However, when the confederate was dressed in work clothes and carried a lunchbox or folding ruler only 38 per cent of the experimental subjects returned the lost money.

Faley and Tedeschi (1971) investigated the effects of source status on a target's compliance to contingent threats in a prisoner's dilemma game. They used as the subject population ROTC cadets of different military ranks. Cadets, who themselves were either high or low in authority or role position, were targets of threats from a simulated source who was believed to be of either high or low status. The design also included the manipulation of the expected values associated with the messages; three levels of threat credibility and two levels of punishment magnitude were employed.

The results confirmed the theoretical predictions: (1) low status targets were more compliant when the source was of high (rather than low) status, and high status targets were defiant of threats from a low status source; (2) the higher the expected utility associated with noncompliance to the threats, the more compliance subjects gave to the threats. Status and expected utility were separate in their effects, neither contributing to nor in any way affecting the other.

A somewhat surprising finding was that high status targets were just as compliant to an equally high status source as were low status targets to the same high status source. This result challenges the purely hierarchical notion of the effects of status. Apparently, high status equals are likely to

yield to each other's demands, presumably out of respect for rank, because similar deference is expected when the influence relationship is reversed, or because neither wants to place the other in the punishing position. It is plausible that as long as they are equals in rank the higher the
authority positions of two individuals, the more compliance they will
tender to each other's requests or demands. If this result can be demonstrated reliably across other source dimensions, it suggests an interesting
modification of SEU theory in order to incorporate the inordinately high
degree of reciprocity in which social elites engage.

No study has examined the effects of source status on the use of promises, but a vast empirical literature purportedly examines the effects of
source status on the efficacy of persuasive communications. After reviewing the literature Rosnow and Robinson (1967) confidently asserted that
"the consistent finding thus far is that the more persuasive communicator
is the one whose expertise, experience or social role establishes him as a
credible source of information presented [p. 25]." Though such a conclusion would add substantial support to SEU theory, it is unfortunately
true that sifting through the research reveals that few studies have man-
aged to examine status as legitimate authority apart from other source attributes.

Field studies have indicated that strong and consistent correlations exist between role positions of authority in organizations and the persuasive
effectiveness of a source of influence. Bass and Wurster (1953a,b) found
that when supervisory personnel were drawn from different management
levels of a large oil refinery rank in the organization and observer's ratings of individual effectiveness in small, leaderless discussion groups
were highly and positively correlated ($+.88$). When the topic of discussion was relevant to company matters and the source's authority was legitimate, the correlation was higher than when the topic was extraneous
to the legitimate business of the corporation. Similarly, French and Snyder (1959) found that noncommissioned officers had more influence
than enlisted men, and Crockett (1955) noted that emergent leaders held
positions of authority in their organizations.

Besides enhancing the probability that the source will receive compliance to his persuasive communications, high status probably will provide
a protective armor, inhibiting counterinfluence attempts from a low status
individual, who presumably would assign low probability of success to
such behaviors. In a test of this hypothesis Thibaut and Riecken (1955)
had a confederate play the role of an air force reservist in a unit different
from that of subjects. Over a telephone the confederate provided verbose,
inexact, and self-contradictory instructions about the placement of military positions on a map. When subjects were provided with an opportunity to criticize the confederate's instructions they directed more criticism
against the lower status confederate. However, de-legitimization of an au-

thority removes inhibitions that others have toward him. Horwitz (1963) found that subjects were more hostile to the unilateral action of an authority who went against the expressed electoral wishes of the majority of the group than when the authority's actions were clearly legitimatized by group consensus.

Torrance (1954) found that source status does have a direct relationship to targets' compliance to a source's suggestions for problem solution (i.e., mendations). Triads of permanent or temporarily assembled air force bomber crews were asked to reach unanimous decisions for four ambiguous problems. Each triad was composed of a high status pilot, an intermediate status navigator, and a low status gunner. The navigator and gunner generally accepted the pilot's suggestions even when his answers to the problem were mainly incorrect. The hierarchical nature of status in the triad was manifested in that navigators, although not so effective as pilots, gained more compliance to their suggestions than did the lowly gunners.

Where research evidence exists it is consistent with the predictions in the SEU theory of social influence. High status as compared to low status does enhance the source's ability to gain behavioral compliance to his threats and persuasive communications and, in addition, inhibits the use of counterinfluence, criticism, and aggression against its possessor. These conclusions seem to hold not only in the laboratory but also in natural groups in real-life situations. When the theory is extended to other dependent variables, such as conformity and attitude change, more supportive evidence can be found for its predictions (see Chapter 8). Nonetheless, the scarcity of relevant research is surprising and suggests that our conclusions be accepted only tentatively. The lack of relevant research does not reflect a lack of interest in status as a source characteristic; rather, it is the result of failure to cleanly operationalize the status dimension.

SOURCE ESTEEM

Although our discussion of status indicated that the deference for another's authority (i.e., legitimacy) is an important factor in the social influence processes, Lasswell and Kaplan (1950) apparently reserved the term *respect* for the person and not the office. Homans (1961) has conceived of esteem as a target cognition that others approve and respect a source. Homans suggests that an individual will receive approval and respect in direct proportion to the quantity and value of help he provides for other people. Help is exchanged for the socially valuable reinforcer of approval, and it is clear that the more competent or expert an individual, the more his help should be worth, all else equal.

Thus the concept of esteem considerably overlaps and may be coextensive with the French and Raven category of expert power, which is a base of power derived from the source's ability to provide help or information because of special competence, education, or experience. We will treat competence or expertise as the denotative source characteristic, and esteem as the target's perception of it. The distinction represents the difference between a person's attributes and his reputation. In general, esteem is postulated to be a direct function of actual source competence.

Expertise has been theorized to be an effective base of influence because of a target's dependence on the source's superior task-relevant information or skills (Jones & Gerard, 1967; Thibaut & Kelley, 1959). Bandura (1969) has expressed the general consensus of social psychologists: "A competent or prestigious communicator is generally more influential than a less competent one because the former's behavioral recommendations, if executed, are more likely to result in favorable outcomes [p. 600]." The present theory merely formalizes this consensus and attaches the authentication effects of source expertise specifically to the various communication modes used in the social influence process. Whether the source employs threats, promises, warnings, or mendations, the target will bias his estimates of the source's credibility as a function of the source's esteem. When source esteem is high, credibility will be exaggerated, and when source esteem is low, credibility will be underestimated.

Although the postulated relationships are clearly confirmed by the conformity and attitude change literature, very few studies have investigated the effects of source esteem in gaining behavioral compliance from a target individual. Tedeschi (1971) exposed subjects to a scenario that involved an interaction between an experimenter and a confederate, who would serve as the subject's future opponent in a modified prisoner's dilemma. In all conditions the experimenter appeared to know the confederate.

In the high esteem conditions the experimenter asked the confederate if he was still taking karate lessons and if he had as yet obtained his black belt. The confederate replied that he possessed a black belt and in response to a direct question confessed that he had once used karate against another person, but only in self-defense. The high esteem scenario was designed to portray the confederate as an individual who was an expert in controlled violence but who used his expertise intelligently.

In the low esteem scenario the experimenter asked the confederate if he had really flunked out of a course he had been taking. The confederate answered that he had and joked about being glad that he had not purchased the textbook for the course. The low esteem manipulation was designed to portray the confederate as a rather incompetent individual whom others did not take seriously.

The subjects' judgments of the confederate were obtained before the experimental interaction and established that the subjects perceived the confederate as deserving more respect and as being more intelligent in the high esteem conditions. It is worth mentioning that differences in interpersonal attraction did not occur.

The confederate then assumed the role of source of threats, and the subjects were targets of his coercive influence attempts. The confederate's threats were either 0 percent or 100 percent credible. The experimental results showed that subjects threatened by the low esteem source complied in direct relation to the credibility of the threats, and subjects in the high esteem conditions complied frequently whatever the credibility of the threats. This pattern of results is exactly opposite to that found when source attraction was manipulated by Schlenker et al. (1969).

Apparently, high esteem, like low attraction, causes an authentication of the source's threats. Contrary to predictions from SEU theory, low esteem, like high attraction, frees the target from the biasing effect that results from a source orientation so that the objective credibilities and point values associated with the threats and the subjects' calculated SEU for noncompliance were essentially equivalent. Low attraction and high esteem, though, may have the effect of causing the target to orient himself toward the source with the consequence that source characteristics contribute to the target's SEU calculations.

Few firm conclusions can be reached on the basis of this single experiment. Perhaps the scenarios meant to induce differences in esteem for the source aroused other processes that prevented the isolation of the pure effects of that single source characteristic. It is possible, for example, that general academic expertise would not mediate the effects found in this study of esteem and coercion. After all, the scenario did refer to the highly esteemed source as an expert in controlled violence, a skill that was directly related to the use of coercion in this experiment (unlike another type of skill, such as knowledge of theoretical physics).

The present theory raises more questions than it answers about the function of source esteem in the influence process. For instance, do targets perceive that experts more than nonexperts would keep their promises or enforce their threats? Is there a social consensus, developed through the socialization process, that experts are more concerned with the truth than are nonexperts? Until these and other basic questions have been more thoroughly investigated, it is premature either to modify the existing theory or to claim that it is right. Remember, however, that such questions might not even be asked were it not for a theory to generate them. The value of a theory does not rest exclusively with its correctness but includes its heuristic consequences.

SOURCE PRESTIGE

The final source characteristic obtained in factor analytic studies and incorporated within the present theory is prestige. Source prestige is presumed to be a multiplicative function of capability and intentions, a hypothesis adopted from Singer (1963). Capability is defined as the amount of slack resources the source possesses, and may take the form of economic, political, material, or social resources. Capability and message credibility are assumed to be orthogonal factors (i.e., unrelated to each other). Credibility is established over time and may be quite high, while in the current situation the source may have lost his wealth and be perceived as credible but weak and impotent (low prestige). Although capability might be considered more important for those forms of influence that require the direct use of resources, such as threats and promises, it is postulated in the present theory that high prestige authenticates all forms of social influence and that low prestige deauthenticates these communication modes.

The intuitive basis for believing that capability increases the efficacy of persuasive communications derives from several considerations. First, the more capability a source possesses, the less sure the target can be that the source does not directly or indirectly control the events he describes or predicts. Thus when the president of the United States warns Russia that it must get out of Cuba or there may be a war tomorrow, the target quite probably perceives this prediction of events as a rather explicit threat, since the president's capability includes the power to commit United States forces to military actions. The same sort of phenomenon probably occurs with regard to the mendations of powerful or capable others. If J. P. Getty advises one to do something "and you might get rich," it is quite possible that Getty himself is promising to make you rich (since he possesses the resources to do so).

Second, the source's capability may lead a target to presume that the source has special stores of information, because it is commonly thought that when one has money one can buy information or special consultants. Regardless of the form of influence used, then, SEU theory posits that source capability will directly authenticate the credibility of the source's influence attempts and, as a consequence, will increase the influenceability of the target.

Smith and Leginski (1970) have demonstrated the effects of resource capability as a factor that affects the prestige of a threatener in a bargaining game. Subjects were provided with one of four amounts of resources to use for purposes of backing up their threats and punishing the other player. Half of the subjects could employ their resources precisely by grouping their units into smaller or larger punishment magnitudes; half were constrained to employ their resources in large-scale magnitudes in an imprecise, all-or-none fashion. The two players (no robot was used) were allowed to communicate bids and offers and explicit threats, and they could administer punishments to lend credibility to their threats. Consistent with SEU theory, subjects accepted compromise bids more often the greater the capability of their opponent, irrespective of the precision with which the opponent could utilize his capability.

Bennis et al. (1958) obtained correlational evidence in a field setting, confirming the direct effect of source capability on influence effectiveness. Interview data established that nurses in hospitals where desired and obtained resources were most congruent perceived their supervisors as more effective in gaining compliance to directives. Bass (1963) obtained similar results. He gave ROTC members in five-man groups weighted values in evaluating the performances of other subjects in reference to their candidacy for advanced ROTC. It was found that the greater the capability of the subject, the more influence he attempted and the more influence he successfully exerted over the others. That the capability must be relevant to the target individual's motivations was indicated by the evidence that subjects who were not interested in entering the advanced ROTC program were uninfluenced by the source's prestige.

A person's perceived power is composed of more than just his capability. Prestige also depends on the source's willingness to expend his resources in the service of his influence attempts. A good example of the relationship between capability and intentions can be drawn from international relations. Sweden and Japan are two rather wealthy countries that could take a more active and potent role in relations among nations, but each has concentrated on internal economic development rather than on military capability, and each has been rather restrained in developing the resources relevant for international influence. Japan, for example, is the third greatest economic power in the world but does not exercise anywhere near that degree of influence. The missing ingredient is not capability but the determination to use that capability for purposes of power.

As previously mentioned, intuitive analysis suggests that the relationship between capability and intent is multiplicative in nature (Singer, 1963). If the relationship were an additive one and either component equaled zero, considerable prestige could still exist. Yet whatever a person's intentions, if he just does not have the capability to back up his influence attempts his perceived power is quite likely to be low and his influence ignored. Alternatively, if an actor is actively engaged in costly activities directed toward acquiring resources that are good only for specific purposes, such as the expensive procurement of large thermonuclear weapons systems, then the perceiver is likely to infer malevolent intent on the basis of the capability the actor seeks. This example indicates that the type of resource an actor possesses has relevance to the attributions the perceiver makes. Some resources are so specialized that they can be employed only for malevolent or benevolent ends, making the attribution of intent problem trivial for the perceiver.

A target will examine the words the source uses, the amount of profits or costs the source can accrue as a function of using or not using his capability, and the commitment strategies used by the source. Each of these bases of interpersonal information will contribute to the attributions the target makes. When the source uses contingent threats or promises, the target will attempt to guess how willing the source is to incur the costs associated with administering punishments or mediating rewards. If capability exists but the target does not believe the source is willing to expend his resources, the threat or promise will be perceived as a bluff or ploy meant to seek exploitative advantage.

Schelling (1966) has suggested that compellent threats, which specify actions the target must perform in order to escape punishment, are likely to be perceived as more hostile, coercive, and manipulative than deterrent threats, which specify an action that a target must not perform if he is to escape punishment. If the target of compellent threats attributes more resolute intentions to the source as compared to a target of deterrent threats, then more prestige would be associated with the source of compellent threats, holding capability constant. Assuming that the subjective expected utility of the two kinds of threats were held constant, the effect of prestige would be to generate a higher negative SEU for noncompliance to compellent than to deterrent threats. More compliance could therefore be expected for compellent threats.

Schlenker, Bonoma, Tedeschi, and Pivnick (1970) confirmed these hypotheses. A robot sent explicit threats of punishment to subjects in a prisoner's dilemma game. The threat asked subjects either to make Choice 1 or not to make Choice 2 and therefore really asked subjects to comply by making Choice 1 in either case. Yet the wording of the threat had the consequences Schelling suggested. Targets were more compliant to the compellent threat, which demanded they make Choice 1. Further, subjects rated the source of compellent threats less favorably than the source of deterrent threats. If it can be assumed that the compellent threatener, who was perceived as evaluatively worse than the deterrent threatener, did have more resolute intentions attributed to him, then the effects of prestige mediated the difference in compliance achieved by the two differently programmed robots.

Promises, warnings, and mendations are not likely to be believed if the source is perceived as exploitative. Hovland, Janis, and Kelley (1953) defined trustworthiness as the target's perception that the communicator is accommodative in his intentions and is motivated to communicate valid statements about the causal structure of the social or physical environment. Conversely, an untrustworthy source would be someone who is perceived as insincere and dishonest and possesses exploitative intentions. It is commonly recognized that a biased source who has a vested interest in his own version of reality is not to be automatically believed when he uses persuasion. Much evidence exists to show that trustworthy sources do gain more compliance to their persuasive communications (cf. Mc-Guire, 1969).

If trustworthiness is equated with the attribution of accommodative intentions and untrustworthiness with the attribution of exploitative intentions, then it is clear from the existing evidence that trustworthiness adds to the effectiveness of the communicator and untrustworthiness detracts from the source's ability to gain compliance. This analysis suggests the the strength of the source's intentions when persuasion is used will be determined on a scale of exploitative (weak) to accommodative (strong) intentions. If the source is perceived as totally exploitative his intentions will take on a value close to zero, and when multiplied against capability will yield a perception of low prestige and little ability to influence. Thus, holding capability constant, a trustworthy source will have higher prestige than an untrustworthy one, and the trustworthy source will gain more compliance to his persuasive influence attempts than will the untrustworthy one (all else constant).

Similarly, an exploitative promisor could hardly expect the target to believe that a reward would reliably follow target's compliance. If the promisor would act exploitatively to secure great gains for himself at the expense of the target's gullibility, why wouldn't he lie and withhold the promised rewards? An accommodative promisor, though, seems more likely to keep his word, since his actions are both benign and consistent with the benefits he holds out to the target. Thus the effects of attributions made about a promisor's intentions are similar to those made about a persuader's intentions. Accommodativeness will enhance a promisor's prestige, but exploitativeness will lower the promisor's prestige; it could be predicted that the accommodative promisor would gain more compliance than the exploitive one. Horai, Haber, Tedeschi, and Smith (1970) found that an accommodative promisor gained more compliance from target subjects than did an exploitative one, irrespective of the promisor's credibility.

A study by Pepitone (1949) also may be reinterpreted as supporting the hypotheses of SEU theory. High school students were interviewed by a panel of three people allegedly from a university. The panel was said to possess tickets to a highly valued or a not highly valued sporting event. The interviewed persons whom the panel judged to have the most worthwhile opinions were to be given free tickets. The friendliness of panel members during the actual interviews was also a condition of this ingenious experiment. In one condition all the panel members were basically either friendly or neutral in affect, while in another condition one member was friendly, a second neutral, and the third hostile. Following an actual interview subjects were asked to estimate the amount of power (prestige) each interviewer possessed. SEU theory predicts that the promisor who has the most valuable resources (high capability) and is most friendly (strongly accommodative) should be perceived as possessing the greatest prestige. The results strongly support this prediction.

An early study in social psychology (Asch, 1948) indicated that prestige affects the persuasion process in the same way it affects threats and promises. Asch attributed the statement "I hold it that a little rebellion, now and then, is a good thing, and is as necessary in the political world as storms are in the physical" to either Thomas Jefferson (the actual author) or V. I. Lenin. It can be assumed that American college students would perceive Jefferson as trustworthy and accommodative (high prestige), and would perceive Lenin as untrustworthy and exploitative (low prestige). When the statement was attributed to Jefferson, students indicated they were more in agreement with it, but when it was attributed to Lenin, students disagreed with it. Many similar studies have revealed the consistent finding that high prestige mediates more compliance to persuasive communications than does low prestige.

When a source issues warnings or mendations that appear to be contrary to his own best interests, or where no apparent gains can be achieved by successfully persuading a target, the source should be perceived as both trustworthy and benevolent. Although no study of behavioral compliance has been done, several attitude change studies support this hypothesis.

Powell and Miller (1967) exposed subjects to tape-recorded persuasive messages advocating the donation of blood to the Red Cross (without pay) rather than the sale of blood to a private (paying) agency. The source was alleged to be anonymous, a disinterested physician, or a chairman of a blood donor recruiting team of the Red Cross. Posttest ratings indicated that subjects viewed the disinterested physician as more trustworthy and disinterested than the Red Cross chairman. Further, attitude change toward the advocated position was greater the higher the source's perceived trustworthiness (prestige). Mills and Jellison (1967) obtained a similar finding. Subjects were provided with a speech advocating passage of a bill that would triple tractor-trailer licensing fees. They were told that the speech had been presented to one or another of two audiences—a local union of railway men or a truck drivers' union. Subjects shifted their own opinions to agree with the persuasive communication when the source was perceived as making the (unpopular) speech to the truck drivers and had more to lose by expressing his views.

In short, SEU theory's rather complex predictions about the effects of source prestige on target compliance seem to be tentatively supported by the data. Direct effects of capability on target compliance have been found. The exploitative or accommodative behavior of threateners and promisors leads to different responses from target persons. Although the effects of both capability and intentions on measures of behavioral compliance have been found, no study to date has confirmed the postulated multiplicative relationship of the two components of prestige. Further experiments must be done to study the attribution process and to determine the combinatorial rules for capability and intent.

Target Characteristics

Relatively little is known about which target characteristics are related to readiness to behaviorally comply to another person's influence communications. Self-esteem appears to be related to influenceability when persuasion is the mode of influence and attitude change is the dependent variable (Janis & Field, 1959); low self-esteem persons are more persuasible than high self-esteem persons. But verbal agreement is not the same as behavioral compliance.

Cohen (1964) has suggested that high self-esteem individuals are realistic and cope well with whatever circumstances arise, while low self-esteem individuals are defensive, avoidant, and unrealistic in their approach to problems. This analysis would suggest that high self-esteem persons would be more self-confident and hence less dependent on the information others provide about the causal nature of their physical and social environments than would their more anxious and less confident low esteem counterparts. Conversely, when faced with a source of coercive or reward power it might be expected that high self-esteem individuals would be most likely to behave rationally—that is, to maximize outcomes on the basis of SEU considerations.

Lindskold and Tedeschi (1971b) separated subjects into high and low self-esteem groups by paper-and-pencil measures. The subjects were then intermittently sent either threats or promises from a robot source during the course of prisoner's dilemma play. Whether the source exercised coercive or reward power, the choice alternatives clearly made compliance to the source's demands the more rational choice. High self-esteem persons did comply to both threats and promises more frequently than did low self-esteem persons. Thus high self-esteem subjects were more realistic and coped with the circumstances better than did low self-esteem subjects.

Rotter (1971) has developed a theory of interpersonal trust and has constructed a scale to measure this personality characteristic. The personality variable of trust is conceptualized as the "expectancy that the word, promise, verbal or written statement of another individual or group can be relied upon [p. 444]." These expectancies are developed from specific histories of interactions and generalize to novel situations to guide behavior.

For example, an individual who comes from an environment where everyone fulfills their promises would tend to place confidence in the promises of relative strangers (high trust), whereas a person who often has been misled would tend to disbelieve the promises of strangers (low trust). Schlenker, Helm, and Tedeschi (1973) directly tested this hypothesis. Subjects were administered Rotter's Interpersonal Trust Scale and divided into high and low trust groups. They then received intermittent noncontingent promises from a robot source during the course of prisoner's dilemma play. As predicted, high trust subjects displayed greater reliance on the source's word by cooperating more frequently on the promise-relevant trials than did the low trust subjects.

Trust and self-esteem apparently can be interpreted as typical ways that people have of biasing the credibility of communications from others. In addition to characteristic ways of estimating probabilities, personality may also be conceived of as the way a person typically assigns utilities to sets of values. Thus a person who assigns preferences to social values may be high on need affiliation, and another who assigns great values to the pursuit of excellence may be high on need achievement. This interpretation indicates how important the study of personality is for the SEU theory of social influence. However, too little is known now to present any firm generalizations.

Conclusions

We have presented a theory of behavioral compliance that focuses on the decision criteria that target individuals use in responding to influence communications. The independent and denotative source-message factors of the theory include the source's role position, the source's attractiveness (broadly defined to include attitude similarity and need complementarity), the source's available resources and intentions, the source's degree of competence, and the credibility and value associated with the influence modes of threats, warnings, promises, and mendations. The target's perceptions of source characteristics are some function of these independent factors and include status, attraction, prestige, esteem, and the subjective expected utility of the messages transmitted. The target is assumed to estimate the SEUs associated with compliance and noncompliance and to make his behavioral choice based on maximizing outcomes. In general the evidence supports the basic hypotheses of the theory.

It should be noted here that a usual assumption of decision theory, that men are rational, is really the belief that given his own calculations (of

SEU) the individual will act so as to maximize his subjective expected utility. However, if irrationality is a subjective biasing reality, the theory suggests that source characteristics cause such irrational processing of information. In a single sentence we may say that the theory offered here is a rational model of irrational behavior.

The theory as presented makes several simplifying assumptions that are just not true, and that any predictive power is retained at all is both an indicator of the validity of the basic ideas and a stimulus for future modification. For example, we have treated source characteristics as attributes either possessed by the source or attributed to him by the target. In a social psychological theory it is all too clear that this is a restrictive individualistic assumption, and treating interpersonal attraction as a one-way feeling is astoundingly simplistic. Similarly, a close reading of the prestige section will bring to the mind of an alert reader the question of why we have not included the intentions or attribution problem as central to the entire theoretical formulation. Even more, the problem of measuring utility has been skirted rather than directly faced.

Our only defense for such assumptions is that we wanted to have a theory that was testable and manageable and stayed within the boundaries of current technological developments. Kuhn (1962) has argued that the scientist, unlike the engineer, need not choose problems on the basis of urgency and without regard to the tools available. The scientist tends to concentrate his attention on problems he has good reason to believe he will be able to solve. As knowledge is accumulated, the more intractable problems may become soluble. By making simplifying assumptions and skirting what appear to be insoluble technical problems associated with measuring SEU, much can be learned about the social influence processes. The theory presented can be expected to be subject to continual modification and change.

4

The Exercise of Power

The great bulk of social-psychological literature is comprised of analyses of the factors that produce behavioral compliance, attitude change, obedience to authority, conformity to social pressures, imitation of a model, and the like. A primary reason for this lopsidedness in favor of studying the influenced to the exclusion of the influential is simply that the target of influence is relatively easier to study than is his source counterpart. The target is essentially the recipient of more or less ready-packaged and concise messages describing some relation between his own actions and possible source moves; the target merely has to decide whether to comply with or to resist these messages. Hence the outcomes of target actions lead to data interpretable in binary form—the target complies or does not; his attitudes change or do not; he conforms or does not.

In contrast, the series of decisions the source makes prior to the target's awareness of any attempt at influence may be formidable indeed. The problem is not simply that the actions of a potential source are of broader latitude than those of the target; there are qualitatively different decision factors to consider. To study the source of influence a scheme must be constructed that at the very minimum accounts for *who* the source chooses to influence out of the multiplicity of potential targets available to him as well as *how* (i.e., by what particular mode) the influence is to be attempted. Additionally, it is to be expected that a variety of situational factors will enter into and complicate each of these basic questions.

The study of source behavior cannot be reduced to the single binary choice to exercise influence or not to do so but must include the factors *who* and *how*. The complexity of the question indicates why considerable difficulty has been encountered in conceptualizing the systematic study of the influential. Only two basic problems associated with the source of influence have been systematically studied—ingratiation and leadership. These problems will be examined as a prelude for proffering a somewhat novel theoretical approach dealing with those who exercise power.

Ingratiation

Deliberate and illicit strategies people employ for the purpose of increasing their attractiveness in the eyes of others and in the hope of thereby acquiring subsequent rewards are collectively referred to as ingratiation (Jones, 1964). The use of ingratiation involves such tactics as publicizing one's own good traits, complimenting others, and conforming to opinion statements of others in order to be perceived as similar and therefore likeable and intelligent. Persons like to be liked because experience teaches that friends provide help and rewards, but those who are disattracted tend to do neither and possibly even want to do harm (Bramel, 1969). Almost everyone uses ingratiatory tactics to some degree, such as flattering the boss, extolling the virtues of the neighbor's daughter, or complimenting a friend's wife on her purchase of an atrocious hat.

Ingratiation is one of the few modes of influence available to those who would otherwise have only little power. Their threats are not believed because their ability to impose costs on those they threaten is quite limited, like a jester threatening his king. Their ability to offer sufficient rewards in exchange for favors from others is restricted, since they have little of value to exchange. Their persuasion attempts are not effective, since those whom they attempt to influence do not consider them expert or competent. In short, ingratiation is one of the few alternatives left to those who lack the other bases of power, and the plight of the groveling junior executive becomes easier to understand. However, powerlessness makes the use of ingratiation tactics suspect, and hence very subtle techniques become necessary if the weak source is not to be unmasked in terms of his own real intentions and beliefs.

Although empirical study of ingratiatory tactics is still in its early stages, the experimental results obtained so far tend to be both intriguing and in line with common sense. Davis and Florquist (1965), for example, have provided empirical support for the sort of ingratiatory subtlety necessitated by powerlessness. They found that dependent subjects would agree with a supervisor experimenter only indirectly rather than by slavishly (and obviously) endorsing all of the supervisor's opinion statements.

While it is likely that individuals do attempt to build their attractiveness in the eyes of others through ingratiatory channels of opinion conformity, flattery, and proclamation of their own virtuous attributes, it is equally clear that these are not the only tactics the influential use to gain their ends. Manipulators run the gamut of social ploys in their machinations and may choose to control the flow of information to a target by lying or filtering out items that might alter the power relationship between themselves and others. Alternative behaviors include the formation of coalitions with other weak parties to combat the more powerful, and the direct mediation of favors designed to build up social debts that can be collected in the future. Manipulators use all of these tactics, and it would seem that a more comprehensive theory of the exercise of influence would afford them equal consideration.

Leadership

By definition the study of leadership is concerned with people who control and direct the actions of others.[1] Theorists working in the area of leadership only recently have begun to explicitly conceptualize their field in terms of social power and influence. The early study of leadership was very much affected by theories of history and by technological goals. On the one hand, some researchers followed Carlyle's view that all important historical forces were generated by great men, and they set out to find the invariant characteristics of those people labeled *leaders*. Practical men in industry and the military have long been concerned with finding criteria by which to identify good executives and officers. On the other hand, many researchers became disillusioned on learning that very few personal and physiognomic characteristics separated leaders from followers. These researchers leaned toward Tolstoy's view that all men are the pawns of historical forces, and they attempted to determine the role situational factors played in leadership behavior.

Several recent attempts to bring together personal and situational factors within a single theory (Fiedler, 1964, 1967) have received only mixed support (Graen, Alvares, Orris, & Martella, 1970). Fiedler's approach examines task-relevant factors, interpersonal relations within the group, and the power of the leader, and then attempts to correlate these with group outputs (e.g., morale, productivity, liking). The major difficulty with this approach is that the processes through which the outputs are achieved are completely ignored. A process-oriented theory seems necessary.

At the present time no process-oriented theories of leadership exist. Studies have proliferated but often have nothing in common except the word *leadership* in their titles (see Janda, 1960). Psychologists have

1. See Cartwright and Zander (1968) for an excellent discussion of the area of leadership.

studied leadership by using as dependent variables the gross frequency of talking by each participant during group meetings, the frequency of directed or persuasive communications, the amount of liking for group members, the degree of compliance given to other group members' influence attempts (the person who most resists influence is the greater leader), the amount of compliance each group member gains from others, and success in overturning a majority opinion when it is opposed to one's own opinions. It can be seen from the above list that little agreement exists about exactly what is meant by leadership, even in an operational sense.

The study of leadership has reached the point where all recognize that power and influence are involved, that the criteria for being a leader are ambiguous, and that leaders are difficult to separate from followers. The common elements stressed in most definitions of a leader are that he does exert influence, that other group members demonstrate a willingness to comply to his influence because of his legitimacy or authority, and that the group members perceive these influence attempts as being ultimately for the good of the group (Hollander & Julian, 1970). In sum, a source who exercises great influence in a group and is perceived as acting in the group's interests will be identified as a leader. A theory that provides answers for questions such as who will most frequently exercise influence and why, which target will be chosen to influence, and what mode of influence the source will choose to gain compliance from the target will probably be broad enough to subsume the problem area of leadership.

The Modes of Social Influence

As a starting point for analysis we will restrict attention to direct and intentional influence attempts in dyadic interactions. Of course, in indirect influence the source *(A)* may attempt to control a second party *(B)* in order to influence a specified target *(C)*. For example, a person who has a great deal of authority in an organization may issue to his direct subordinates commands that filter down throughout the organization and ultimately affect all of the employees, some of whom the person with authority may not know personally or by name. Also, we noted earlier that a target may imitate a source or that a target may anticipate a source's desires when the source is unaware of his influence. Although both of these phenomena are interesting problems for social psychology they will not be considered further here.

The influence modes that a source may employ in dyadic interactions can be classified in a 2 x 2 matrix, as shown in Figure 4.1. The modes are more fully discussed in Schlenker and Tedeschi (1971) and Tedeschi, Schlenker, and Lindskold (1972). The first distinction is between open and manipulatory modes of influence. As was seen in the discussion

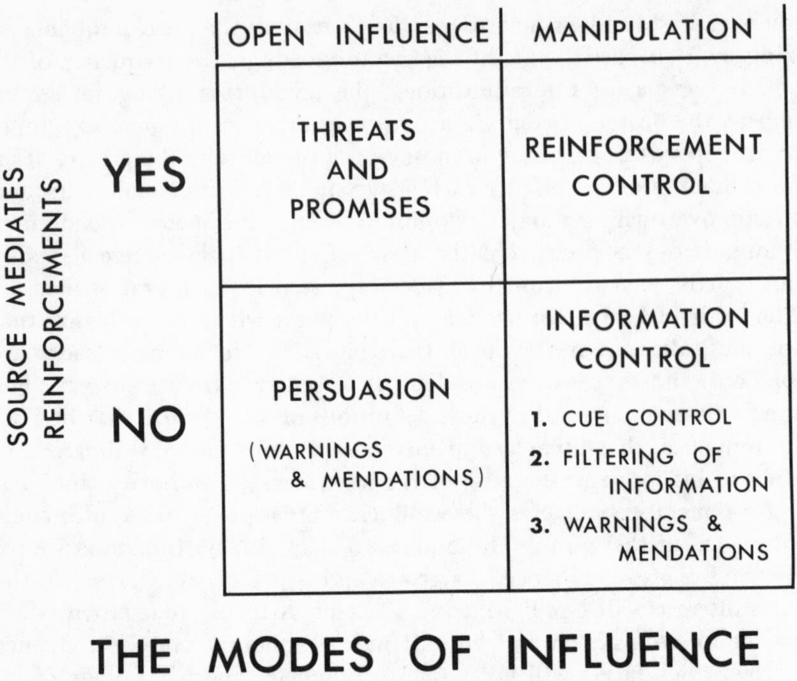

	OPEN INFLUENCE	MANIPULATION
YES	THREATS AND PROMISES	REINFORCEMENT CONTROL
NO	PERSUASION (WARNINGS & MENDATIONS)	INFORMATION CONTROL 1. CUE CONTROL 2. FILTERING OF INFORMATION 3. WARNINGS & MENDATIONS

SOURCE MEDIATES REINFORCEMENTS

THE MODES OF INFLUENCE

FIGURE 4.1. *Types of influence modes available to a potential source.*

of ingratiation, it is possible for a direct influence attempt to be made in a clandestine manner. Such manipulatory attempts may take many forms, but the identifying characteristic is that the source behaves as if the target were unaware that influence was being exerted or as if the target did not perceive the source's own interests in making the influence attempt. Naturally, some sources will be rather clumsy and obvious in their attempts at manipulation and may be semiaware that the target is not fooled by the tactics being used. Then the distinction between open, overt influence and covert, manipulatory influence must represent a continuum rather than separate categories. Open influence modes refer to those instances in which the source does not try to disguise his intent to influence the target.

The second distinction shown in Figure 4.1 is that between modes of influence in which the source directly mediates rewards and punishments for the target and modes in which some third party—another person, group, or nature—mediates the reinforcements. This distinction, typified by the difference between a threat and a warning, has received little attention in the social influence literature, but it may be quite important in theoretically integrating personal bases of power with modes of communication in answering the questions that pertain to the mode of communication a source will use when he chooses to seek influence. Let's examine these types of influence strategies in more detail.

OPEN INFLUENCE MODES

Threats and promises are influence modes in which the source controls and can mediate punishments and rewards to the target and does not attempt to hide his influence intentions. The communication of a threat or a promise may be either explicit or tacit. An explicit communication precisely states in language the contingencies involved. A tacit influence attempt is one that only implies but does not directly state what the target should or should not do; the possible contingent rewards or punishments are not spelled out in detail, although a clear understanding may be tacitly communicated. When a mother glares at her child over dinner, the child knows on the basis of previous experience that he had better eat his vegetables or he will go straight to bed.

The choice of using tacit or explicit communications will be determined partly by the situation. Often it is in the source's best interests to make his threats and promises as explicit as possible. Otherwise the target can rightly claim that he did not know just what the source wanted him to do. Roger Fisher (1969) has discussed the advantages of placing the target in a position where he simply must respond yes or no and has no room for interpretational ambiguity. However, sometimes the source does not need to make his threats and promises verbally explicit, as with the mother, child, and vegetables, because the target already has knowledge of the relevant contingencies. Occasionally the source himself is unsure of exactly what he wants the target to do, as so often happens in international affairs. The United States knows it doesn't like what China does but is not sure exactly what it wants her to do. Therefore, influence attempts often take a "stop that" form.

Tacit influence modes are also useful when the source does not want to fulfill a threat or deliver promised rewards. The source can always claim that the target misinterpreted the source's actions, no threat or promise really was made, and hence the source's credibility is not at stake in the interaction. Whether a threat or promise is explicit or tacit, there can be no question that the source's intent to exercise influence must be openly recognized both by himself, the target, and third-party observers.

The open use of warnings and mendations occurs when the source does not try to disguise his own interests in producing cognitive or behavioral changes in the target. However, the source does not control the punishments or rewards associated with these persuasive communications; rather, the outcomes are said to be controlled by other persons or by the causal texture of the environment. Advertising illustrates the open use of mendations when an audience is told that use of a particular toothpaste will gain the user friends, increase the frequency of dates, and ensure matrimony; as a side benefit tooth decay might also be arrested. Thus the source can often attempt to tie his own interests to those of the target so that their interests appear to correspond.

The open use of warnings and mendations possesses some clear advantages over the use of threats and promises. First, the veridicality of a warning or mendation is more difficult for the target to ascertain than is the truthfulness of a threat or promise. Consequently, the source's credibility is less endangered by the world's failure to conform to his predictions. While the source clearly controls the rewards and punishments associated with promises and threats and can be held accountable for not providing them when appropriate, the source of persuasive communications by definition does not control the state of the world (or other persons) and hence can more easily be excused for making an honest mistake, particularly when his own interests seem to be tied to his own stated views. Then, too, the source can always find reasons for the failure of his predictions. If the predicted consequences do not occur it may be because unforeseeable events occurred that changed the state of the world and negated his predictions. Hence the source's honesty or wisdom may remain relatively intact even after some of his warnings and mendations have been shown to be clearly wrong.

Another advantage of warnings or mendations is that they can predict contingent outcomes that are relevant to a more distant future than would be reasonable for threats or promises. The father of a son doing badly in school may warn that if grades are not improved the dream of medical school will be definitely out of the question. Although this warning ultimately may be wrong, the occurrence of the critical event is so remote that the father's credibility is not at stake in making the influence attempt.

Finally, the use of warnings and mendations does not endanger the social relationship between source and target so much as does the use of threats and promises. The punishment of noncompliance to demands or the failure to back up promises may help to produce enmity between friends. The effects of warnings and mendations on personal relationships is not likely to be detrimental, whatever the final outcomes of the specific influence attempts for either party.

MANIPULATORY INFLUENCE MODES

Rewards and punishments may be directly mediated to a target in a manner calculated to gain some advantage for the source as he attempts to disguise his manipulatory intentions from the target. This mode of influence will be called *reinforcement control.* For example, Jones's (1964) ingratiatory influence tactics include the use of enhancing evaluative statements about the target closely akin to the common meaning of the term *flattery.* The direct mediation of such verbal rewards, along with some small material favors, sets up the target for the time when the source attempts to cash in on his investment.

Punishments may be used in very subtle ways also. For example, a few nervous gestures, such as hand wringing or continual glances in other directions, are useful for conveying uneasiness or possible social disapproval to a boring or obnoxious character at a cocktail party, and they may have the desired effect of encouraging him to move on to talk with other guests. If the source's intentions were openly communicated an undesirable confrontation might result.

Many techniques are available to a manipulatory source who either does not possess or does not want to spend any of his own resources for the purpose of influence. *Information control* includes cue control, information filtering, and the manipulatory use of warnings and mendations.

Jones and Gerard (1967, p. 529) defined cue control as an "actor's provision of stimuli that elicit pre-established habit patterns in another." By systematic application of reinforcements during the learning process, trainers build up in their animal protégés a series of responses to discriminative stimuli. When, for example, the trainer raises both arms high above his head, the dolphin jumps out of the water and is promptly rewarded with a fish. After the habit has been thoroughly learned, anyone who provides the appropriate cue of raising both arms will be able to elicit jumping behavior. What is required is the knowledge of cue-response associations and possession of the ability to produce the cue. Such control over behavior is naturally subject to extinction if the response is frequently elicited and never rewarded. Thus knowledge of the target's habits can be a fruitful resource for manipulation purposes.

Certain types of manipulation may involve the concomitant and inseparable use of reinforcement control, cue control, and tacit promises. Psychologists have considered social approval to be a potent reward (cf. Bandura, 1969). Suppose that the source discovered a cue that reliably elicited a behavior from the target, and he directly reinforced the target by expressing social approval. Both of these tactics are manipulatory in nature, though one involves cue and the other reinforcement control. Similarly, in verbal conditioning studies it has been consistently found that by differentially reinforcing the emission of certain classes of words, such as attitude statements or plural nouns, with such social approval as *good,* subjects increase their frequency of emission of the critical words. The target, however, may interpret the source's behavior in terms of tacit contingent promises of the form, "when he provides the cue and I make

response X, then he socially approves of my behavior." Even though the
target responds on the basis of what he perceives as the open influence
mode of tacit contingent promises, the source may continue to behave as
if he were using manipulation.

Warnings and mendations also may be effective influence tactics in
manipulation. Hovland, Janis, and Kelley (1953) point out that a major
variable in determining a communicator's persuasiveness is his appearance of trustworthiness. Trustworthiness is the target's perception that the
source is accommodatively oriented and wants to communicate valid and
accurate statements about the nature of the social or physical environment. By concealing the gains he can accrue from the target's compliance, a source may give the impression that he is a trustworthy communicator and hence can manipulate the target's behavior.

Studies have reported that when a subject overhears a persuasive communication and does not know that the communication was, in fact, directed at him, greater attitude change results than when the same communication was openly directed at him (Brock & Becker, 1965; Walster &
Festinger, 1962). This phenomenon helps to explain why con men take
great pains to have prospective targets overhear communications that the
targets do not recognize as the start of a pattern of exploitation. Alternatively, the source may attempt to convince the target that source is trustworthy, honest, and accommodative and is really looking after the target's interests rather than his own. Several studies indicate that when a
source argues against his own apparent best interests, he gains greater
compliance than when the position he advocates coincides with his own
best interests (Mills & Jellison, 1967; Powell & Miller, 1967; Walster,
Aronson, & Abrahams, 1966).

The effect of the source's intentions on the impact of his influence attempts was indicated in a recent study by Schlenker, Schlenker, and Tedeschi (1972). They asked subjects to rate the amount of power possessed by hypothetical persons who were described in terms of various
combinations of adjectives. A threatener was rated as more powerful (a
potentially better influencer) when he was described as exploitative rather than accommodative. However, a source of persuasive communications was rated as likely to be more effective when he was described as
accommodative rather than exploitative. Depending on which form of influence is used, the source can maximize his effectiveness by displaying
the appropriate intentions to the target.

Finally, in the manipulatory use of warnings and mendations several
studies suggest the effectiveness of both tactics—the appearance of disin-
terestedness and the appearance of accommodativeness. It may often be
to the influencer's best advantage to try to convert warnings and mendations to their manipulatory form rather than use them in their open influence form. This lesson has not been lost on advertisers.

Decision Making by the Source of Influence

Given a classificatory scheme of influence modes, the concepts of decision theory can now be applied to provide the remainder of a theory to answer such questions as: What factors affect when influence will be exercised? What factors determine whether one person will attempt influence more frequently than another person? What factors affect the choice of a target of influence? What factors affect the choice of a mode of influence? How do situational factors affect the exercise of influence? In order to answer these questions it is necessary to examine the decision alternatives considered by a potential source of influence.

In a social setting a potential source of influence has numerous behavioral alternatives, each of which has a corresponding SEU. As we learned in Chapter 3, SEU is the sum of the products of the utility and subjective probability of occurrence of the various anticipated consequences of an action. The person may choose to influence someone or he may not. He may choose to influence person X or person Y or person Z. He may choose to use threats or promises or warnings or other means.

In almost all settings the decision to influence is inextricably bound to decisions about which target is chosen and which influence mode is used. That is, the SEU for using rather than refraining from using influence depends on what value each target possesses, how resistant each is likely to be to each mode of influence, the costs of influencing each, and so on. To make the problem scientifically manageable each of these decisions will be treated separately, presumably holding the other decisional factors constant. The major postulate of the theory is that a source will exercise influence whenever the SEU for using influence is greater than the SEU for not using influence. If several targets are available, if influence of any would yield an SEU higher than the choice not to exercise influence, and if only one can be chosen, that target who maximizes the source's SEU will be chosen.

The potential source is assumed to sift and sort through many alternatives before a decision is made. For example, when examining his decision alternatives between potential targets, X, Y, and Z, the person must generate an SEU for the alternative of influencing X if threats are used, another SEU for the alternative of influencing X if promises are used, and so on for all the influence modes and types of rewards and punishments available and for all the potential targets. Naturally no person could examine all of the logically possible alternatives, but within those alternatives the source does examine, the mode of influence and target chosen, if any, is postulated to be a function of maximizing SEU.

Suppose a young man goes stag to a dance. He becomes enthralled with a beautiful female who is obviously with a male companion. The stag male can choose between the alternative of merely looking from a distance, which provides some satisfaction, or trying to influence the lady to change male companions. If merely looking produces one unit of satisfaction that can be obtained with certainty, then the SEU of not exercising influence is 1: $(1 \times 1.0) = 1.0$. If the stag male attempts influence he might estimate that he has a 75 percent chance of succeeding, which would be worth 10 units of satisfaction to him, and a 25 percent chance of failing, which would leave him no worse off. In addition, he may feel certain that if he does succeed the lady's male companion will create a scene worth -10 units of satisfaction to our hero. The SEU for trying to lure the lady away from her companion would be comprised of the outcomes associated with successfully exercising influence $[(+10) + (-10)]$ times their subjective probabilities of occurrence, plus the utility of unsuccessfully exercising influence (0) times its probability of occurrence—that is, $(0 \times .75) + (0 \times .25) = 0$. The stag male should choose not to approach the beautiful lady, since he can gain more satisfaction watching her from afar.

A change in the value of any of four factors could increase SEU and cause the person to decide to attempt influence. (1) Increase the utility of the beautiful female from 10 to 20 units of satisfaction: $(20 - 10) \times .75 = 7.5$. (2) Increase the probability that the influence would be successful from .75 to 1.0, without changing the probability that a scene will occur: $(10 \times 1.0) + (-10 \times .75) = 2.5$. (3) Decrease the costs of influence by reducing the negative utility of the scene that might be provoked by the male companion from -10 to -5: $(10 \times .75) + (-5 \times .75) = 4.0$. (4) Decrease the probability of accruing costs from 75% to 50%: $(10 \times .75) + (-10 \times .50) = 2.5$. Each of these new SEU values is greater than the SEU $(+1.0)$ associated with the alternative of not attempting influence.

Exactly the same factors are involved when the person can choose between alternative targets. An SEU involving utility, subjective probability of success, the costs of influence, and the subjective probability of such costs will be generated for each potential target. The source should choose that target who maximizes SEU.

THE COSTS OF INFLUENCE

Two basic types of costs can be associated with influence attempts—*source-based costs* and *target-based costs*. Source-based costs are voluntarily incurred by the source. If a company decided to persuade people to buy its product it would have to hire an advertising concern and take out advertisements in newspapers or buy time on television. The costs of securing communication opportunities and the channels of communication must be considered before influence attempts are even made. Similarly, if a nation wants to acquire the capability of using high-magnitude international threats it must weigh the costs of developing nuclear capability against the possible gains in possessing such threat capability. For many nations the costs far outweigh the potential gains.

Another example of a cost that must be incurred just to be in the position of using certain types of influence modes is maintenance of adequate surveillance of the target of the attempt. A source who makes a threat must be in the position of knowing whether the target actually complied to the threat; otherwise the threat is useless. A source who makes a promise must know whether the target complied to the promise and deserves to be rewarded; the target might announce his compliance when, in fact, he noncomplied. Kelley and Ring (Kelley & Ring, 1961; Ring & Kelley, 1963) have discussed the need to maintain an adequate surveillance system when rewards and especially when punishments are made contingent on the performance of some criterion.

By purchasing channels of communication, by investing resources that later can be utilized for purposes of influence, and by developing an adequate surveillance system, the source must incur the costs irrespective of what any prospective target might do. In this sense the negative utility of source-based costs is 100 percent probable irrespective of whether a future target complies or noncomplies, or sometimes even if the source never finds a prospective target. As Gamson (1968) has noted, such costs are fixed and are spent to maintain readiness. Fixed costs "represent an overhead cost which can be distributed over a series of acts [p. 84]."

Harsanyi (1962b) was the first to stress source-based costs that are dependent on the target's reactions. These opportunity costs must be considered whenever a source attempts to exercise power. If, for example, the United States tries to impose its will on Indochina it might be successful but not without costs of men, matériel, and resources. Seldom can power be exercised without such costs. Whenever a target resists threats, the source is placed in a position of either putting up or shutting up.

Punishment of the target for noncompliance is usually costly in terms of time, effort, and resources. Since the threat has already failed and the costs of fulfilling the threat cannot recover the compliance foregone, the source is tempted to not punish the target. However, if the source anticipates future interactions with the target or is concerned with how others will view him, he will expend the necessary resources to maintain his credibility for future influence attempts. Similarly, if a target complies with a contingent promise of reward, the source is tempted to not provide the promised reward, since compliance has already been gained and the costs of giving the reward can no longer affect the prior behavior of the target. Again, the source will make good on his promise to the extent that he is concerned about his future credibility. To punish noncompliance to threats or to reward compliance to promises is a source-based but target-dependent cost that represents an investment in the future. Before influence attempt these costs are probable to the extent that the source considers the target likely to comply or noncomply.

Tedeschi, Horai, Lindskold, and Faley (1970) provided experimental support for the above analysis. Robot targets were programmed to defy the threats received from subject sources in the context of a prisoner's dilemma. The opportunity costs for exercising power were varied across conditions. Subjects were charged 0, 5, or 10 points for each use of the penalty option. Although subjects established high credibility for their threats in all conditions, fewer threats were sent when opportunity costs were highest. Apparently, subjects took into account the costs likely to be associated with exercising their power before deciding to send threats, but once threats were sent, subjects were committed to backing them up.

Target-based costs may take the form of resistance to influence, retaliation, or counterinfluence. The source can minimize target-based costs by the judicious choice of influence modes, because a target probably will not retaliate in response to a persuasive communication but is much more likely to respond to coercive influence with coercive countermeasures. However, the decision to impose these costs is strictly in the target's hands. The source could be expected to be in a much better position to accurately estimate the probable source-based costs associated with a potential influence attempt than to estimate target-based costs.

Tedeschi, Bonoma, and Novinson (1970) experimentally examined the differential effects of source-based opportunity costs versus target-based retaliatory capability. Within the context of a modified prisoner's dilemma game subjects were given intermittent opportunities to send threats to a simulated target and could administer penalties for noncompliance by subtracting 10 points from the target's counter. In one condition of the experiment subjects were charged a fixed cost of five points each time they exercised their punishment power; in a second condition the subject was told that the other player could retaliate when punished by subtracting five points from the subject's score. The simulated player was programmed to retaliate every time the subjects used their punishment power; therefore, in both conditions of the study subjects lost five points every time they used their penalty option.

Since the source-based cost was certain and, from the subject's point of view, the target-based cost was uncertain (though from the experimenter's point of view both types of costs were certain), it might be predicted that either fewer threats would be sent or fewer punishments would be administered in the source-based opportunity costs condition. That is, since the costs represented identical negative utilities but the subjective probabilities likely were different, the total subjective expected costs in the source-based costs condition should have been higher than in the target-based one. In accord with this reasoning the results revealed that subjects in the retaliation condition punished the target more for noncompliance than did subjects in the source-based costs condition. However, there was no effect of origin of costs on the sheer frequency with which subjects utilized threats.

The two studies we have examined that did vary the costs associated with the use of influence provided support for the hypotheses proffered. Further experimental work in this area is sure to follow.

Who Are the Wielders of Power?

A recurrent theme has been that all individuals, of necessity, use influence in their social interactions. However, some people seem to be more interested than others in wielding power, and some people's influence styles differ from others. A person's value preferences, his habitual manner of biasing the probabilities of receiving rewards or punishments, and other personal characteristics are important factors that affect how often he tries to influence others. Among his personal characteristics are his self-confidence, status, expertise, and prestige. Each of these factors will be examined for the types of effects they have on the source of influence.

SELF-CONFIDENCE

Chronic self-confidence may be defined as a generalized expectancy of success and is derived from an individual's past history of achievements. Individuals who have a history of successful problem solution and of receiving rewards are characterized by high self-confidence; those who have a history of failure and of receiving punishments are characterized by low self-confidence. An individual who is classified as chronically self-confident believes that he is competent across a variety of tasks, sets his goals at high but realistic levels, feels that by his behavior he controls his own reinforcements, and believes that he is deserving of the success and approval he receives. A person who lacks self-confidence would possess all the opposite beliefs. This conceptualization of personality borrows freely from many related ideas, including need achievement motivation (Atkinson, 1964), self-esteem (Coopersmith, 1967), internal–external control orientations (Rotter, 1966), level of aspiration (Lewin, Dembo, Festinger, & Sears, 1944), adaptation level (Helson, 1948), and comparison level (Thibaut & Kelley, 1959).

Given identical environmental conditions, individuals high in chronic self-confidence should estimate higher subjective probabilities of obtaining rewards and avoiding costs than individuals low in chronic self-confidence. Therefore, it is hypothesized that high self-confident sources should estimate higher probabilities that their influence attempts will be successful and estimate lower probabilities that resistance and counterinfluence will occur than will sources low in self-confidence. Hence, high self-confident sources should attempt influence more frequently than should sources who lack self-confidence.

Lindskold and Tedeschi (1971a) tested this prediction by dividing subjects into high and low self-confident groups, depending on how successful they believed they would be in the experiment, and then observed their behavior as sources of threats and noncontingent promises in a modified prisoner's dilemma. The results confirmed the hypothesis: high self-confident subjects directed more influence attempts at the robot target. Further, the low self-confident subjects displayed a strong preference for threats over promises, indicating lack of reliance on a mode of influence that did not provide a unilateral power advantage.

Several other studies have similarly supported the hypothesis that the use of influence is directly related to self-confidence (see Tedeschi, Schlenker, & Lindskold, 1972). However, no study has directly evaluated the basic assumption that self-confidence is functionally related to the biasing of the probabilities of success and costs in the influence process.

STATUS

The higher an individual's role position in an hierarchy, the more deference he and relevant others believe he deserves. It follows that the higher the person's status, the more he should expect others to comply to his influence attempts, especially when he uses legitimate modes of influence such as persuasion. His successes should increase his self-confidence, and as a consequence what has been said about self-confidence is applicable to status.

Status probably affects source estimations of the potential costs of influence in a manner somewhat different from self-confidence. This implication is drawn from Hollander's (1964) notion of idiosyncrasy credits, a bookkeeping notion that hypothesizes that persons earn credits from the group in proportion to their contributions to the group. The person can then spend accumulated idiosyncrasy credits in nonconforming or innovative behaviors; group members with fewer credits would be reprimanded for displaying the identical atypical behaviors. Simply put, a high status person has greater behavioral leeway than a low status person.

The implication is that persons who hold high status can more afford to fail at influence than can those of lower status. The law of diminishing returns suggests that the more of a commodity one possesses, the less each unit is worth, and applying this law to the value of idiosyncrasy credits, the more idiosyncrasy credits one has, the cheaper is the expenditure of each unit. Hence, not only should high status persons be quite confident but they also should perceive the utility of the costs of influence as relatively less than do low status persons. Rudraswamy's (1964) study, as well as several field studies, support the SEU prediction that high status individuals will attempt more influence than low status individuals. The available evidence gathered from studies of communication networks and group discussion tasks also support SEU theory (cf. Tedeschi, Schlenker, & Lindskold, 1972).

No studies known to the authors have investigated choice of influence modes among high and low status persons. However, several predictions might be made from the SEU theory. Blau (1964), Homans (1961), and Hollander (1964) have postulated that the approval of a high status person is worth more than the approval of a low status person. If this hypothesis is true—and it does have a certain face validity—it could be expected that high status persons would come to recognize the significance of their social approval and employ this very inexpensive and effective means of social control. Therefore, it might be predicted that over a wide range of activities high status sources would use manipulation with great frequency. If high status persons generally expect deference, persuasion would also be an inexpensive yet potent form of influence.

Low status persons ordinarily lack control over resources and do not possess expertise; they are therefore unlikely to succeed in using any of the open modes of influence—threats, promises, warnings, and mendations—unless, of course, they are interacting with someone of even lower status. Thus high status people would use a wider range of influence tactics than would low status people. Low status individuals should be more likely to try ingratiatory tactics as a means of manipulating higher status targets. Until the surprisingly small amount of experimental evidence bearing on the effects of status on the exercise of influence is considerably expanded, these speculations must be accepted for what they are—untested hypotheses.

SOURCE EXPERTISE

Expertise was defined in Chapter 3 as the amount of relevant information, knowledge, or skill one person possesses that other persons perceive as instrumental for goal attainment. The greater the demand for and the more scarce the information or skill the expert possesses, the more others should seek his help, and the more the expert could expect in exchange for his help. Not only is the expert's advice sought but his opinions also are often readily accepted as representing the true nature of reality. His history of success in influencing others should cause the expert to be rather self-confident in his interactions with others, at least as compared to a person who possesses little expertise.

Kelley and Thibaut (1969) assume that "the individual strives to determine the intrinsic attributes of the world around him [p. 6]." In the search for meaning the individual attempts to understand the causal structure of the world around him so that he can better plan his own activities and maximize his own satisfactions. The greater the instability of his attributions about the environment (i.e., the less expert he is), the more dependent he will be on others for information. The nonexpert is forced to withdraw from efforts to influence others in favor of efforts to attain stability, leaving the expert a ready-made power vacuum in interaction.

The expert's stock-in-trade is the possession of special information, and his preferred mode of influence should be the open and manipulatory forms of information control. However, these forms of influence are not likely to be successful in highly competitive conflict situations. It would therefore be predicted that in relatively cooperative interactions experts would estimate the probability of successful influence as relatively higher than would nonexperts, and the SEUs for the alternative of initiating influence would reflect the same relative difference.

In one of the few studies that did not confound the effects of expertise with both status and prestige, Lippitt, Polansky, Redl, and Rosen (1953) found that persons whom targets perceived as most expert were more assertive, resisted the influence attempts of others, and initiated more persuasive communications than did those perceived as less expert. Less direct confirmation for the hypothesized relationship between expertise and the frequency of attempting influence can be found in studies conducted in field situations and in problem-solving groups (cf. Tedeschi, Schlenker, & Lindskold, 1972).

SOURCE PRESTIGE

Resources indicative of prestige are those material and physical possessions that can be dangled before a target in an effort to secure his compliance. Money, weapons, control over the target's income, and even physical strength and prowess are examples of the material resources that can be used to reward or punish a target and reflect the source's prestige. Not all material resources are in a form usable as reinforcements, however. Money invested in a factory and equipment is not easily withdrawn to be used as a resource for influence. Numerous theorists (e.g., Dahl, 1961; Kuhn, 1963) have made this distinction between gross and liquid resources.

The utility of resources and hence the perception of prestige also depends on the target's valuing process. Apart from ingrained values the target should perceive a resource as of greater utility as its scarcity increases. Also, the larger the number of situations for which a given resource is appropriate, the greater the perceived utility of that resource. The more recurrent the *kind* of situation for which a given resource is appropriate, the greater the perceived importance of the resource as a basis of social power (Rosen, Levinger, & Lippitt, 1961).

Source prestige may affect in several different ways the quantity of influence attempted. First, the individual born with a silver spoon in his mouth has many advantages over his ghetto-born counterpart, and it would be surprising if such an edge did not lead the advantaged to more successes than the disadvantaged. Prestige should be directly related to self-confidence, which, in turn, is directly related to SEU calculations.

Second, the law of decreasing returns should apply to the costs of influence. The more resources a person possesses, the less each unit of expenditure is worth to him. Thus if both high and low prestige sources made exactly the same objective expenditure in exercising influence, the subjective worth of the expenditure would be less for the high than for the low prestige source. If the utility of costs is less for the high prestige source, then his SEU for exercising influence is greater, and he should initiate more influence attempts than would a low prestige source.

Finally, a high prestige source must learn that because he possesses the requisite resources his threats and promises are more likely to be believed than if he had few resources available. The possession of great resources should therefore reduce the expectancy of target resistance and should reduce the expectation of incurring target-based costs such as retaliation. Obviously a high prestige source has many interrelated reasons for attempting more influence than would a source of lower prestige.

A high prestige source of influence should prefer those modes of influence that rely directly on the control of resources. Thus the modes of influence preferred by those of high prestige should include threats, promises, and reinforcement control rather than modes that stress information control and persuasion.

Although the amount of fluid resources a source possesses has never been systematically manipulated in experiments on dyadic interactions, the amount of punishment subject sources could administer to others has been. If subjects who are given the ability to impose severe punishments on a target may be conceptualized as high in prestige, and subjects with limited punishment capability are conceptualized as low in prestige, then several experiments can be reviewed in order to evaluate the hypotheses derived from SEU theory.

Fisher (1969) gave both of two subjects high, both low, or one high and the other low punishment capabilities in the context of a bargaining game. The task posed on each trial for each dyad was to divide 90 points between them. On every trial each subject was assigned a minimum necessary settlement (MNS) of between 10 and 60 points. The MNS was subtracted from the subject's bargained-for share of the 90 points to yield his net gain on that trial. Consequently, if a subject accepted less than his MNS on any bargaining trial he lost points. Subjects were given the capability of threatening and fining their opponents but were assigned opportunity costs for exercising their punishment power. Subjects with low punishment capability could fine their opponent three points at an opportunity cost to themselves of two points. Subjects with high punishment capability could fine their opponent 30 points at an opportunity cost of 15 points.

The results clearly confirmed the hypothesis that the greater the capability of the threatener, the more often threats would be used. High capability subjects in the high–high and high–low conditions used more explicit verbal threats than did subjects who possessed only low punishment capability. High capability subjects in the high–low condition actually used the threatened punishments more frequently than subjects in all other conditions of the experiment. Since the costs of potential retaliation (i.e., target-based costs) in the high–high pairs was greater than the comparable costs for the high capability person in the high–low pairs, it is not surprising that subjects in the high–high condition used punishments with more restraint.

An interesting finding emerged with respect to the use of manipulation. Although the high capability individual in the high–low pairs had a clear material power advantage, he won less than did his low capability counterpart both before and after punishments were subtracted from their final scores. One look at the overall data reveals why. In the high–low pairs the low capability member seldom threatened and almost never used fines. It was probably obvious to these subjects that the direct use of power against a well-armed opponent could be disastrous. Instead, these subjects used manipulation as a means of outwitting their strong-armed opponent. The low capability member of the asymmetric dyads started his bidding higher than did the high capability member. Also, he lied about his MNS value more frequently. These differences in the manipulation of information did not emerge when the parties were power equals. In effect, the low power member of the dyad was forced to use deceptive, manipulative tactics in order to compete with and beat a person with greater material power.

In a similar study Smith and Leginski (1970) had subjects participate in a bargaining game against a programmed robot. Subjects were given a table that included three issues to negotiate, each containing 20 possible levels of agreement. Of course, each outcome level carried different point values for subjects and robots. As the points for subjects increased, the point values associated with outcome levels for the robot decreased, and vice versa; hence their interests were directly opposed. Subjects were limited to passing notes that announced offers, agreements to a proposed contract value, threats of a fine, and an announcement of the actual use of a fine.

Subjects were given the capability of fining the robot 20, 50, 90, or 140 points, and could impose the fine in either a precise or an imprecise fashion. Subjects with precise power could fine anywhere from one point up to their maximum punishment capability on any given threat occasion, but subjects with imprecise power were required to use their full capability on threat and punishment occasions. When subjects could exercise their power precisely they sent more threats, threatened greater punishments, and fined more frequently the greater the capability of the source. The exact opposite pattern of behavior was found in the imprecise power conditions.

One interpretation of the differences between the precise and imprecise conditions of the experiment was that a source with precise power could respond more flexibly to his opponent's provocations, making the punishment fit the crime, and could demonstrate his resolve (i.e., intent) by processes of escalation and de-escalation. He therefore was more likely to be successful in coercing his opponent than was a source who was inflexibly tied to large magnitudes of punishments, which was like killing a mosquito with an elephant gun. As long as the source could flexibly use punishments the direct relationship between source prestige and the initiation of coercive influence attempts was supported.

The target's perception of the source's prestige reflects both the capability and the intentions of the source. Intentions are likely to be communicated by commitment strategies, rationalizations of actions, impression management tactics, and other ploys. Some of the most subtle and complex forms of human interactions center around the communication of intentions, and very little is known about the process at present. Apart from alerting the reader to the problem, there is little to offer in terms of testable hypotheses or evidence that would clarify the process.

In summary, the Fisher and Smith and Leginski studies support the hypothesis that source prestige is directly related to the frequency with which threats are used. High prestige sources are also more likely to back up their threats with punishments. These relationships do break down when both parties to an interaction have high prestige, since the danger of retaliation in such cases is quite high (see also Hornstein, 1965). These results, remember, were not obtained from the direct manipulation of slack resources; rather, the amount of punishment subjects could administer was varied, but no expenditure of resources was involved. Again, any conclusions must be adopted tentatively until more direct tests of the hypotheses are performed.

Choice of a Target

Often a source has next to no choice in determining his target. In defensive influence, for example, the source must influence the person who is trying to influence him. But quite often a person can pick his opportunities and choose his targets. Any theory of how power is exercised must specify why one target is chosen over another. The major consideration in determining the choice of a target is the source's expectation that the target possesses or controls significant values—values that the source wants. Given that a population of targets all possess the desired values, the guiding principle in selection of a specific target will be the source's attempt to maximize SEU.

What a source wants or expects to receive from any social interaction is determined primarily by three factors: his preference orderings or value structure, his comparison level, and the current allocations of resources among the members of the groups to which he belongs. The development of values and preferences presumably occurs through learning and the socialization processes. The second factor is definable according to the individual's comparison level (Thibaut & Kelley, 1959) and depends on his previous social experience. How much the individual aspires to acquire depends considerably on his history of past successes and failures. The more successes in goal attainment the person has had in past interactions, the higher are his aspirations in current interactions. The reverse trend would be true for a person with a predominant history of failures.

The third factor in determining the individual's expectations—the distribution of rewards in his membership group—has been brought to our attention by the theory of distributive justice (Homans, 1961) and by equity theory (Allen, 1965). Both theories state that an individual will expect to receive outcomes from the group commensurate with his investments relative to other group members. That is, the individual expects his input–outcome ratio to be proportional to the input–outcome ratios of other group members. Thus if two male graduates of the same college, who have about the same experiences and are about the same age, go to work in the same organization, they would expect to receive about the same starting salary. However, if one had a master's degree while the other had only a baccalaureate degree, the master's holder might expect to start at an initial salary higher than that of his less-educated schoolmate. The master's degree represents greater inputs and deserves better outcomes.

Individuals will go to great lengths to ensure the operation of equity norms (cf. Allen, 1965). For example, if a worker feels that he is receiving less than his just share he might attempt to influence management either to give him a raise in salary or to lower the salaries of other group members. Or he might slow down his own work output to make it proportional to the amount of work he thinks commensurate with the low salary received.

Once a source has determined, on the basis of the above considerations, what he wants, he will choose that target who possesses the desired commodity. If more than one target possesses the commodity sought, that target will be chosen who maximizes the source's SEU for influence. In determining which target the source will choose to influence, two other factors are quite important—interpersonal attraction and relative power.

INTERPERSONAL ATTRACTION

Lott and Lott (1968, p. 68) have stated that "learning to like a particular stimulus person is essentially learning to anticipate reward when that person is present. . . ." It follows that in their social interactions liked persons would be expected to be and actually would be more cooperative than disliked persons, a hypothesis that has received considerable empirical support in mixed-motive games (Kaufmann, 1967; Krauss, 1966; Oskamp & Perlman, 1965; Scodel, 1962; Tornatzky & Geiwitz, 1968; Wallace & Rothaus, 1969).

Knowing that a potential target likes him should lead the source to increase his estimate of the likelihood of success of an influence attempt, thereby increasing SEU for influence. The SEU model leads to the prediction that more influence should be directed toward liked than toward disliked targets. Once again, the modes of influence cannot be ignored in making predictions. Bramel (1969) has stated that one should give those he likes what he thinks they want and those he dislikes what he believes they don't want. If Bramel is correct, then a source should tend to use influence modes that offer advantages to a liked target (e.g., promises, persuasion, and manipulation) and should use influence modes that offer disadvantages to a disliked target (e.g., threats, warnings, and manipulation).

Krauss (1966) has provided some empirical support for these predictions. Positive or negative attraction was induced between players by means of manipulating the perceived similarity or dissimilarity of their attitudes on an opinion questionnaire. Subjects were told that based on past research their judgments of the other person would be either valid or dubious. They then participated in a trucking game. During the game the subjects were provided with gates and could use them to block the opponent's access to the shorter and more profitable of the two available routes to the destination. When subjects believed that their judgments about the other person were valid, they used the threatening and punishing gates more often against the disliked than against the liked person. However, when subjects believed that the other's attitudes could not be validly used to assess liking, the attraction manipulation did not affect the exercise of coercive power.

Schlenker and Tedeschi (1972) used an attitude similarity–dissimilarity manipulation to induce attraction or disattraction in subjects for a simulated player in a modified prisoner's dilemma game. The subjects were given unilateral reward power, unilateral coercive power, or both. That is, subjects could send only a contingent promise of the form "If you make Choice 1 (the cooperative choice) on the next trial, I will add 10 extra points to your score"; could send only a contingent threat of the form "If you don't make Choice 1 on the next trial, I will take 10 points from your score"; or could choose either the contingent threat or the contingent promise. Subjects could, of course, actually reward or punish the simulated player as appropriate.

The results indicated that attraction had little effect on the choice of influence modes, but the manner in which the source used promises was affected by liking for the target. Subjects who liked the target used promises more accommodatively (i.e., cooperated more often on the promise-relevant trials of the PD), while subjects who disliked the target established higher credibility for their promises.

The interpretation of these differences was drawn from Blau's distinction (1964) between economic and social exchange. In economic exchange the terms of the exchange are spelled out in detail by the parties and are known before the transaction. An example of an economic exchange is a contract, wherein one party promises to perform a certain action in exchange for the other party's promise to pay or otherwise reward the first for his services. In a social exchange the terms are vague or only tacitly understood by the parties; it is even considered rude to bring them to light. For example, it would be considered rude to reciprocate a friend's invitation immediately after being a guest in his house. By reciprocating the invitation without delay, an element of distrust is communicated. The hasty reciprocation may indicate that the person did not want to remain in debt to the host for any time at all.

Contingent promises are contractual and appear to be a form of economic exchange, whereas noncontingent promises are unilateral gestures in social exchange that leave implicit the expectation of reciprocity. It could be expected that contingent promises might be used more frequently by strangers or even enemies, while noncontingent promises would most often be used by friends.

Schlenker and Tedeschi (1972) suggested that the subject sources who liked the target used the explicit contingent promises as if they were noncontingent promises: they acted accommodatively on promise-relevant occasions, thus giving the target an opportunity to share in mutually beneficial outcomes, but failed to give the irrelevant side payoff. Conversely, subject sources who disliked the target may have perceived the contingent promises as contractual: the promises had no implication for whether they would exploit that target on message-relevant trials, but the source was obligated to provide the side payoff. An experiment to test this interpretation would manipulate interpersonal attraction and provide the subject a choice of contingent or noncontingent promises to send a robot target in a modified PD. Unfortunately, the study has not been done.

Contrary to Krauss's (1966) study, Schlenker and Tedeschi (1972) found no differences between attraction groups in their use of threats. Also, contrary to several studies previously mentioned, no differences were found in overall cooperation as a result of attraction. The distribution of power in the dyads could account for these conflicting results. In Krauss's study and in those that found effects of attraction on cooperativeness, the source and target were power equals; both either did or did not possess threat capability. In the Schlenker and Tedeschi study the subjects had a unilateral power advantage over their simulated targets.

From these differences in the distribution of power it may be hypothesized that when an individual's power is less than or about the same as his opponent's, he will take interpersonal relationships into account when responding to or exercising influence. However, when the source has a unilateral power advantage and possibly believes that he will never meet the target under reversed power relationships he will tend to disregard personal relationships in determining the frequency, manner, and resolutness with which he exercises his power. Perhaps this hypothesis is a scientific way of restating the observation of Henry Adams (1931, p. 108) that "a friend in power is a friend lost."

RELATIVE POWER

The choice of a target is often characterized by an asymmetry in power between source and target. The principle that states that a source will choose targets who possess the commodities he wants implies that he will attempt to influence persons who are more powerful than he. Powerful persons possess prestige, status, or esteem and are more likely than weak persons to possess those things that a potential source wants. However, powerful persons can also exact more in exchange for their wares. Hence the temptations associated with the potential target's possession of the utilities the source wants are tempered by the probability of higher costs of obtaining them. These considerations lead to the prediction that sources will choose that target who is the weakest person in possession of the desired resources.

Tedeschi, Schlenker, and Lindskold (1972) reviewed evidence that supports the hypothesis that relatively powerful persons are frequent targets of influence attempts, at least of a persuasive and manipulative sort. It is worth noting that this hypothesis suggests that people have a natural tendency to go through the channels of authority within organizational settings.

The relative power of the source and target should greatly affect the mode of influence the source chooses. It would be foolish for a source

to attempt to coerce a target who possessed far greater punishment resources. The chances are that no compliance would be obtained and that
counterthreats or retaliation would impose costs and a net loss to the
source for his trouble. Directly confronting an authority of high status is
also apt to be counterproductive, since other group members are likely to
restrain or punish or by some other means influence the source to leave
the authority alone. Bribing an authority with the use of contingent
promises is considered improper or illegal in many groups and societies.
The source should also hesitate before debating with or in other ways attempting to persuade a person much more expert than himself. Depending on the characteristics of the target, then, the source must choose that
mode of influence that will maximize his SEU.

When individuals of low power interact with persons of high power,
the low power persons tend to use manipulatory modes of influence. Persons of low power cannot offer large rewards or threaten great punishments to others because they don't have sufficient capability to back their
words with deeds. Neither do they have the reputation for being especially competent or wise so that their use of persuasion would have telling effects. Picture the court jester giving advice to the king or, worse yet,
threatening his monarch. When the person is on the wrong end of the
asymmetry of power he must rely on the weapons of the weak. These include the manipulatory forms of information control.

Kipnis and Vanderveer (1971) showed that ingratiation can be an
effective means of influence in gaining favors from a more powerful target. Subjects were asked to be the industrial supervisor of four workers in
a simulation of a factory setting. The subjects were to do their best to ensure that the workers were productive in their tasks. The supervisor subject could communicate to the workers—who, in fact, were simulated—
via an intercom unit, and the experimenter had the workers send back
written notes to the subjects.

Subjects could use a variety of influence tactics to control the workers'
behaviors. They could promise or reward the workers with 10 cent pay
raises; they could threaten or punish the workers with 10 cent fines; they
could threaten to transfer or actually transfer the workers to a more boring job; or they could fire a worker. Two of the workers were average in
productivity, a third was clearly superior, and a fourth was a problem either because he was inept or because he had poor motivation and attitudes. One of the average workers sent ingratiating notes to the subjects,
including such messages as: "Count on me for help—what can I do?" "If
you want me to go faster, let me know." "I was afraid a college kid
would boss me around, but your assistant (a note deliverer working for
the experimenter) is a real nice guy and you seem to be, too."

The results showed that subjects promised as many raises to the ingratiating worker as they did the superior worker; generally the ingratiating worker received more promises and more raises than the other average worker, whose performance was objectively the same as that of the ingratiator. In addition, when subjects evaluated the quality of the workers' performance, the ingratiator was evaluated as favorably as the superior worker and much more favorably than the other average worker. It was quite clear that the ingratiator had succeeded in changing the subjects' attitudes and behaviors toward him and that ingratiation in these conditions did pay off.

Emerson (1962) has pointed out another means by which a relatively weak source can improve his position vis-à-vis a more powerful target. The weak person may attempt to establish power equality or superiority over the target by recruiting additional group members to increase the size of the group and then form coalitions against the powerful person. The study of coalition formation provides insights into alternative ways in which a weak person can increase his outcomes without directly facing a more powerful person. We will pursue this line of inquiry in greater depth in Chapter 6.

The reader may view intentional ingratiation as a form of hypocrisy, the solicitation of group members for the purpose of forming coalitions against the leader as a kind of disloyalty and untrustworthiness, and a liar as morally reprehensible. It is probably not accidental that most of the influence modes available to weak individuals are considered immoral; those who are most powerful in a given society support a moral order that successfully defends their prerogatives against pretenders. It is rather easy to be virtuous when powerful, since to possess power means that one can use moral means, but lack of power forces the source to adopt immoral means. The interesting exception to this generality is the recourse to strategies of nonviolence; however, the effectiveness of this moral alternative for the weak is very much in question.

When the source has relatively greater power than his potential target he obviously will have a much greater latitude in his choice of influence modes. There are constraints on his behavior, however. If the source expects to continue interactions with the potential target over a long period of time he may refrain from incurring the target's enmity. As has been noted, the source's liking for the potential target sometimes restrains him from using threats or contingent promises. Thus a shortsighted person may obtain his immediate objectives by successfully influencing the target in any way he can, but if he considers his longer term policies and interests he will be concerned not only with his objectives but also with his means.

Situational Factors Affecting the Use of Influence

Individuals sometimes find themselves in situations in which they interact with persons they did not expect to meet; the situation determines who interacts with whom. Third parties sometimes contrive situations so that other persons will meet and interact with one another. Artificial seating arrangements imposed by a teacher in a classroom might determine future friendships, as studies of propinquity seem to show. Clearly, situational contexts often have important implications for the exercise of influence. Among the most important situational factors are the intensity of interpersonal conflict, the opportunities for and restrictions on communications, and the physical and social arrangements of the actors. We will consider each of these factors.

CONFLICT INTENSITY

Boulding (1965, p. 172) has facetiously defined conflict in terms of the Duchess's Law, borrowed from *Alice in Wonderland,* which reflects the idea that "the more there is of yours, the less there is of mine." Distributive bargaining in which the interests of the two parties are directly opposed constitutes rather intensive conflict. The number and values of opposed interests will also relate to the intensity of conflict. The conflict can be intensified by the interdependent actions of the two parties involved, by one person's accrual of additional scarce benefits that the other believes vital to his own long-term interests, or by fortuitous or contrived circumstances beyond either person's control.

Intensive levels of conflict imply that important or scarce values are at stake and that decisions cannot long be put off. Some type of conflict resolution ordinarily must be effected, either by one party's complete capitulation or by some form of negotiation and compromise. When actions are perfectly coordinated in an integrative relationship, little communication is needed. In conditions of pure or nearly pure conflict, communications become irrelevant and force becomes necessary. Through the intermediate ranges of conflict intensity, as conflict increases, the requirements for communication and influence also increase. Simulation studies of international conflict as well as analyses of the Cuban missile crisis show that at times of international crisis the flow of communications increases sharply (Hermann, 1970).

When conflict intensity is low, rewards seem to form the basis of man's social interaction patterns. Individuals frequently go out of their way to reward others, implicitly or explicitly recognizing that the favor is likely to be reciprocated later. Rewarding others not only encourages that reciprocity but also mediates positive attraction, itself a resource that is apt to be beneficial for longer term influence effectiveness. Miller and Butler

(Butler & Miller, 1965; Miller & Butler, 1969; Miller, Butler, & Mc-Martin, 1969) have shown experimentally that when conflict intensity is low and the cooperative nature of the situation is salient, subjects will prefer the use of rewards to punishments in their interactions with one another.

When conflict is intense, psychological factors reduce the effectiveness of most modes of influence and devalue source characteristics that ordinarily enhance the source's power. Conflict undermines the perception of the expert's trustworthiness and hence decreases the effectiveness of his persuasive influence attempts. Intense conflict creates distrust for an authority, thereby reducing the perceived legitimacy of his influence attempts and creating suspicion about his attempts to manipulate or persuade a target. Conflict often makes enemies of friends because they cannot rely on those unilateral gestures that have smoothed over their differences in the past. Promises will be viewed with skepticism, and unilateral gestures will be perceived as tricks or as diabolical strategies involving "one step backward in order to take two steps forward." In high conflict, therefore, the opponents can be expected to seek advantage through the use of threats. All in all, during intense conflicts it is much easier to believe that the other person will fulfill his threats rather than his promises. Once threats are used, enmity, misperceptions, and further intensification of conflict leads to a cycle of escalation that often gets out of control (Pruitt, 1965).

Conflict escalation may carry the parties to the point that their potential losses far outweigh any gains that could be obtained through the resolution of their conflict. When this stage of escalation is reached a sudden shift in policies may occur. The parties will be forced to look for their areas of agreement and/or trade off concessions to restore their interaction to an orderly level. An example of this type of change in policy has been demonstrated by the world powers after their recognition of the dangers of brinkmanship. Empirical evidence similarly reflects this process. Several studies have shown that as the conflict between bargainers increases and the bargainers possess relatively equal power, contracts are more frequently formed between them (Murdoch, 1967; Thibaut, 1968; Thibaut & Faucheux, 1965).

AVAILABILITY OF INFLUENCE MODES AND COMMUNICATION OPPORTUNITIES

Naturally, whether a source will use a particular influence mode will depend on his access to communication channels and the availability of the proper resources. Tourists who cannot speak the language of the country they are visiting sometimes find that they must use the tacit communications associated with gestures in order to communicate to the native people. Sometimes a person will limit himself and refuse to use certain influence modes, either for ideological reasons, as in nonviolent resistance campaigns, or because the source does not feel that he possesses sufficient prestige, status, esteem, or attraction to make the particular mode effective. In any case social psychologists have artificially restricted subjects to one or a few influence modes in order to examine carefully the effects of such limitations on the exercise of influence.

The evidence indicates that when a very limited set of communications is provided to a source he still will be able to convey numerous different meanings depending on his concomitant behaviors. In his criticism of the trucking game Kelley (1965) observed that the use of gates to block the direct route to the goal could be interpreted as threats (as Deutsch and Krauss suggest), as punishments, as signals to imply coordination of alternating use of the direct route, and so on. In a communications game that was logically similar to the trucking game, Shure and Meeker (1967) found that subjects used the warning signal to coordinate cooperative alternating rather than as a warning or threat and phenomenologically reported that they thought from its first use that that was what the signal was meant to convey. Anderson and Smith (1970) found that threats of fines actually promoted cooperation when no other channels of communications between bargainers were available.

Finally, Schlenker, Bonoma, Tedeschi, and Pivnick (1970) and Bonoma and Tedeschi (1971) found that explicit threats of punishments could be used as coordinating signals in a modified prisoner's dilemma if they were the only means of communication available and the source's behavior was accommodative on the threat-relevant trials. Our ability to communicate many meanings despite limitations on the modes available to us confirms that in some conditions words can mean whatever we want them to mean.

PHYSICAL AND SOCIAL ARRANGEMENTS

The spatial features of the environment are important in serving the dual function of structuring communication networks to facilitate or hinder interactions. The way in which man regulates the spatial features of his environment and, conversely, the impact of that environment on his subsequent behavior has been labeled *proxemics* (Hall, 1963).

Hall advanced a classification scheme of distances in terms of their meaning for the interactions between people. *Intimate distance,* 0–18 inches, combines visual, olfactory, and thermal sensations to signal unmistakable involvement with another. Tactual contact is the most intimate relationship of all and arouses intense emotions. *Personal distance,* 18 inches to 4 feet, is a distance within which persons can comfortably interact. Patterson (1968) likens it to a protective sphere maintained by the individual. *Social distance,* 4–12 feet, reduces involvement with the other person. Distances greater than 12 feet are referred to as *public distance* and substantially reduce persons' involvement with one another. Theoretically, as the distance between individuals increases, the intimacy of the content of their conversation decreases. These interpersonal distances should produce effects on the types of influence communications a source uses, and, conversely, a source should fix his distance from the target in a manner appropriate to the influence mode being employed. Thus unilateral, noncontingent promises would not be shouted from a distance, nor would a source attempt to persuade a target from a great distance. Distance might favor the use of obscene and threatening gestures.

The orientation of the body within spatial distances also has an impact on interpersonal relationships. Moscovici (1967) found that subjects who faced each other, even when separated by a screen, used typical spoken language, while those seated side by side or back to back used language in a manner more appropriate to written communications. Moscovici interpreted this finding as implying the loss of gestural and postural signaling ability in the nonfacing groups. Argyle and Kendon (1967) found that a more conversational and cooperative atmosphere prevailed in a discussion conducted over the corner of a table than in one carried out across a table. Thus heads of state meet across a table when negotiating the details of a treaty, but they pose side by side when in front of newsmen to suggest progress and good will.

Mehrabian and Williams (1969) found that the sheer frequency of nonverbal activity a source exhibits directly effects the target's perception of the source's persuasiveness. Such cues do not exist in isolation, however, and take on meaning depending on the content of concommitant explicit communications. Ellsworth and Carlsmith (1968) found that a high incidence of eye contact in a pleasant context led to positive feelings, whereas a high incidence of eye contact in an unpleasant context led to negative feelings; the results were reversed when eye contact was minimal. These results imply that a source probably will adjust his nonverbal behaviors to fit in with the type of influence mode being used. Thus the ingratiator would probably look his target straight in the eye while building up his own attractiveness.

Sufficient spatial distance to reduce intimacy may be important in increasing the effectiveness of some influence attempts, depending on which characteristic the source wants to saliently present to the target. Albert and Dabbs (1970) found that social distance (4–5 feet) yielded greater perceived expertise for the source of a persuasive communication than did either personal or public distances. Results that Lott and Sommer (1967) found suggest that a similar intermediate distance enhances perceived status. Presumably, more personal or intimate distances would make the salience of attraction (or disattraction) greater. Sensitivity groups tend to focus on self-disclosure, trust, eye contact, and tactual proximity, and hence might be interpreted as breaking down or reducing the effectiveness of other source characteristics on interpersonal influence. Unfortunately, if this is so then the transfer of effects from sensitivity groups to work groups or other formal settings would be maladaptive.

When printed or electronic (nonpictorial) means of transmitting messages are used there is, of course, a loss of most nonverbal forms of communication. This loss brings about a process of dehumanization or deindividuation (Festinger, Pepitone, & Newcomb, 1952), in which the target takes on the characteristics of a thing rather than a person. The ordinary norms of conduct are abrogated in such deindividuated conditions, as is illustrated in the notion that it is easier to kill an enemy by bomb or rifle than to strangle him. As depersonalization increases it becomes easier for the source to employ otherwise distasteful and negative forms of influence. That is, the SEU for using threats increases relative to other influence modes because the costs to the source in terms of such factors as guilt are decreased.

Milgram (1965) has nicely illustrated the behavioral changes caused by increasing distance. In a set of ingenious studies subjects were instructed to deliver increasingly painful and dangerous shocks to another person (who was actually an experimental confederate) under the rationale that they were teaching the confederate appropriate responses on a task. Although the subjects were all too willing to do the experimenter's bidding, they delivered fewer shocks the less the distance between them and their hapless victim.

In the context of a message-modified prisoner's dilemma game, Gahagan and Tedeschi (1970) found that subjects cooperated much more when they were together in the same room than when they were in separate rooms. The implication, as Nemeth (1970) has suggested, is that physical separation does mitigate social norms as factors determining behavior in mixed-motive games. Such deindividuation effects should be taken into account before findings obtained in the laboratory are too readily generalized to the real world.

A closely related situation is one in which a source expects never again to meet his target, as opposed to the more typical situation in which the same individuals are encountered daily. Continual interaction with the same targets forces one to justify any previous behaviors that have negative connotations. Unless a source has excellent reasons for any potentially distasteful behaviors, he will face the disapproval of not only the target but also anyone who might observe the tête-à-tête or be told about the situation at a later date. Therefore, an individual's behavior should be quite different depending on whether he expects to see his target again.

Marlowe, Gergen, and Doob (1966) found experimental support for these generalizations. They had subjects participate in a prisoner's dilemma game against a simulated opponent who was portrayed as either similar to the subject and quite humble or dissimilar and quite egotistical. Subjects further were told either that they would meet the other person after the experiment and discuss their behavior during the game or that they would not meet with the other person. It was felt that social norms, operative when future interaction was expected, prescribe that one should help other people and cooperate, especially when the other person is a humble, nice person. Conversely, egotists should be cut down to size. However, when no future interaction is anticipated, behavior justification is less necessary; so subjects would gain most by exploiting the humble person but would be careful to placate the egotist by cooperating because the egotist might reciprocate exploitativeness. The results supported these predictions.

Other situational factors affect the influence process. Centrality in a communication network, proximity to resources (e.g., a boy next to a snowbank where someone had prepared a large number of snowballs), cues that indicate that the source of persuasion is being coerced to make certain communications, and many other situations create opportunities for or restrain the use of power and influence. Consideration of these factors would carry us too far astray, and, indeed, evidence from which to draw any firm conclusions is not yet available.

Conclusions

In this chapter we have reviewed a theory that specifies processes and proffers predictions about how social influence is exercised in relatively direct social interactions. Decision theory notions were used to generate predictions about when influence will be exercised, who will be chosen as a target of influence, and what mode of influence the source will choose. The guiding hypotheses were that influence will be exercised more frequently when (1) the utility of the commodities to be gained through influence increases, (2) the probability of successfully exercising influence increases, (3) the utility of the costs of exercising influence decreases, and (4) the probability of incurring costs through influence decreases. The source's personality characteristics, status, esteem, and prestige, the source's liking for the target, and the target's relative power—all were hypothesized to systematically affect the source's estimation of the SEU for initiating an influence attempt and thereby affect the frequency of influence and the choice of a mode and target of influence.

The theory offers the potential for integrating diverse areas of social psychology, such as ingratiation and leadership, under the same general theoretical framework. However, the theory is only in its beginning stages. Empirical evaluation of many of the predictions of the SEU theory of influence is nonexistent. Numerous experiments provide support for other predictions the theory makes; yet much of this evidence was accumulated before the theory was formulated. The evidence that does support some of the basic hypotheses of the theory sheds little light on the processes that are actually serving as the basis for the subjects' behaviors. For example, evidence has been obtained (as per predictions) that indicates that self-confidence is directly related to the frequency of use of influence. However, no available data indicates whether high self-confident subjects frequently used influence because they thought they had a high probability of being successful and a low probability of incurring costs, or whether other causes produced the result. If the ongoing processes as well as the predictions of the theory are supported by empirical data, then the theory will be even more compelling.

5

Bargaining Behavior and
Complex Games

The preceding chapters have considered either of two actors (source or target) who are interdependent for their outcomes and can choose between only a few possible response alternatives. Although such simplification is necessary and important for gaining understanding of the processes operative in conflict and social influence, everyday interactions are much more dynamic than our analysis would indicate, including as they do a multitude of response alternatives, strategies and counterstrategies available to each participant. Each actor is in reality both a source and a target, unrestrained in response choice and in pursuit of complex and multidimensional values or utilities. Many of these rather uncontrolled and free interactions have been conceptualized as *bargaining problems,* conjuring up such images as a flea market in Africa, tobacco auctions in South America, or the contract negotiations of management and labor.

Webster's dictionary defines a bargain as "an agreement between parties settling what each gives or receives in a transaction between them." Deutsch and Krauss (1960) have pointed out that the definition of agreement can be enlarged to include tacit and informal pacts as well as the more explicit outcomes specified in game theoretical analyses of the bargaining problem. Deutsch and Krauss list the following as essential features of dyadic bargaining situations:

(1) Both parties perceive that there is the possibility of reaching an agreement in which each party would be better off, or no worse off, than if no agreement was reached. (2) Both parties perceive that there is more than one such agreement that could be reached. (3) Both parties perceive each other to have conflicting preferences or opposed interests with regard to the different agreements that might be reached [p. 181].

Sawyer and Guetzkow (1965) proposed a similar definition of bargaining: "bargaining is when two or more entities interact in developing potential agreements to provide guidance and regulation of their future behavior [p. 466]." In addition, Deutsch and Krauss stress the importance of social norms to the bargaining process.

Nash (1950) has provided a definition of the bargaining process from the perspective of classical game theory. He defined bargaining as a cooperative game that contains a large number of possible outcomes, any of which the players could jointly agree on. A cooperative game is a non-zero-sum game that allows both players to employ explicit communications and to make binding agreements, much like the message-modified prisoner's dilemma game described in Chapter 2. According to Nash, neither actor (bargainer) comes to the cooperative interaction empty-handed but can be said to possess a *status quo point*, which represents the utility to the actor of *not* reaching an agreement during bargaining. In many instances the status quo solution leaves the bargainers in about the same position they occupied at the start of the bargaining, minus the time, energy, and other costs expended during the cooperative game. Thus a seller and a buyer may each retain the commodities and/or money each brought to the interaction, but both might be somewhat hoarse, frustrated, and tired after an unsuccessful bargaining session.

Nash's determination of a status quo point takes into account the respective threat potentials of the two bargainers. A target's failure to comply to a source's threats will not merely leave the two parties at the point where bargaining began but could leave both individuals worse off, the target because he suffers punishment, and the source because of the costs associated with exercising power. It can be seen that studies employing two-choice, nonzero-sum games ordinarily do not allow for a status quo solution, since each party *must* make strategy choices on each play of these games; in essence, a bargain must be achieved. The game studies considered so far, then, may be thought of as rather simplified bargaining interactions conducted under compulsory regulations requiring that the principals strike a bargain on each trial of the game.

In general game theories of bargaining such as Nash's assume, among other things, that each party has perfect information about his own and the other's utility functions. Two-choice, nonzero-sum games typically display to both parties the possible mutual outcomes that can occur as a function of their strategy choices. However, the most interesting aspects of interpersonal bargaining derive from the situation in which each actor is ignorant of the other's utility function. Efforts to discover or change the other's utility function and disguise one's own constitute some of the most important moves in a bargaining game. Thus, although much of the language of decision theory is retained, social psychologists usually prefer a definition of bargaining more inclusive than game theorists offer. Mc-Grath (1966), for example, suggests that a formal negotiation situation is one in which "representatives of two or more parties interact in an explicit attempt to reach a jointly acceptable position on one or more issues about which they are in disagreement [p. 101]." According to McGrath an informal negotiation is one in which the requirements of representation and explicit awareness of an intent to resolve differences is dropped. Hence the informal situation is the more general one.

The theory of social influence presented in the last two chapters is a limited type of bargaining theory. The payoffs have been unambiguous and have been assumed empirically to involve a single commodity (most often game points); the conflict between source and target was generated by the rules of the interaction as much as by opposed interests; and both players have had full information about their own and their opponent's payoffs. Further, the response choices and communication options of the two parties have been severely limited to one of two game choices—a threat or promise message when the experimenter makes it available and the side payoffs associated with coercive or reward power.

Questions arise about what happens to parties to such conflicts as we move to more free responding situations that might be labeled *free bargaining behavior*. What happens as the actors' response alternatives are expanded? Does the course of conflict change when important as compared to trivial values are at stake? Does ignorance about the opponent's utilities impede or facilitate the coordination of interests? What functions can free communications serve within the context of a bargaining situation? These and other questions will occupy us throughout this chapter.

Expanding and Labeling Response Alternatives

Shubik (1968) has distinguished games that are "environment rich" from those that are "environment poor, free, or rigid." The rich games typically have various elements added to the basic abstract matrix representation of a two-person, nonzero-sum game. When a subject is placed in front of a game board in an isolated and small experimental cubicle, it is unclear just how much of the analog presumed between the laboratory and the real world is preserved. Though the experimenter through the prism of his theoretical vocabulary may view the subject's behaviors in terms of such motives as cooperation, competition, deceit, trust, forgiveness, and repentance, and can visualize applications of his data to crises of international politics, subjects may have quite another conception of what is occurring. The subjects may be confused by the matrix, may not fully appreciate the interdependence of their response choices, and may not perceive the other person's behaviors in terms of the experimenter's

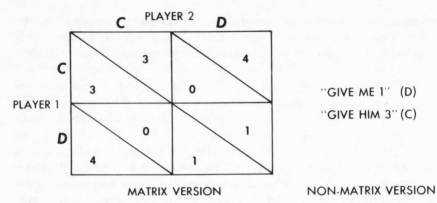

FIGURE 5.1. *Decomposed prisoner's dilemma game (modified from Evans &*
Crumbaugh, 1966).

theory. Schelling (1960) has pointed out that the very labeling of a strategy selection may change its meaning, so that making *Choice 1* in a prisoner's dilemma game might not be perceived in the same way as would
the same response alternative labeled *cooperative choice.*

In an attempt to increase subject understanding of the prisoner's dilemma and to provide subjects with a greater sense of control over outcomes, Evans and Crumbaugh (1966) and Pruitt (1967) have decomposed that game. The nonmatrix version of the game used by Evans and
Crumbaugh, shown in Figure 5.1, is presented to subjects by giving each
two slips of paper printed with either "Give me 1" or "Give him 3." On
any play of the game a subject has the choice of placing down before him
either of the two slips of paper. If both subjects place down the slips
"Give him 3," the cooperative cell of the matrix is entered; if both subjects place down the slips stating "Give me 1," the competitive cell is entered. If one puts down "Give me 1" and the other puts down "Give him
3," the second has cooperated and the first has competed. Hence the matrix and nonmatrix versions of the game are structurally identical, although they do not seem to be psychologically equivalent.

A general result of the comparison of matrix and nonmatrix (decomposed) versions of the prisoner's dilemma is that the nonmatrix version
produces more cooperation between subjects. Several reasons for these
findings have been posited. Subjects may feel that they exert greater control over outcomes, since they can take or give points (Gallo, Funk, &
Levine, 1969). If this perception of increased control over one's own fate
reduces the uncertainty in taking a chance and giving the other person
something, then less perceived risk would be associated with cooperation
in the decomposed game.

A related hypothesis is that norms of reciprocity or social responsibility are activated, since the give-and-take of the decomposed game resem-

bles social exchange situations described by Blau (1964) and Homans (1961). As Nemeth (1970) has observed, it is possible that when the prisoner's dilemma is decomposed "the socially proper behavior for the subject becomes clearer, that is, the subject recognizes that giving 3 points is generous and 'good,' while keeping 1 point for himself is selfish and 'bad' [p. 304]." The decomposed game, though, may obscure the exploitative opportunities for subjects and may lead to more cooperation than does the matrix form of the same game because the matrix form may be psychologically more complex and may more clearly invoke mixed motivations of accommodation *and* exploitation. In addition to cuing the subject to make cooperative responses by obscuring his understanding of exploitative opportunities, the procedure in the decomposed version of the game leads the subject to perceive that choices are made successively and that he always goes first. This perception may persist even though the choices actually are made simultaneously; the usual procedure is that the subject receives or gives his points first and afterward receives the final outcome for that trial. The consequences of failure to give as many points as he can to the other player may be perceived to differ between the person who chooses first and the one who chooses last.

Several experiments have attempted to label response alternatives (or otherwise give them mundane realism in terms of the meaning systems of subjects) and/or increase the number of response alternatives in the context of nonzero-sum games. Expanding the range of alternatives allows subjects to choose intermediate or compromise gestures without having to resort to their strongest or weakest strategies. Sawyer and Friedell (1965) invented an interaction screen, which is a prisoner's dilemma with continuous rather than discrete choice alternatives. Each player can move a pointer incrementally and by turn across a grid; one player moves across the horizontal and the other moves across the vertical plane. The point in geometric space at which both players' markers coincide determines the outcome to each bargainer. Results show that subjects who are allowed to vary the degree of their cooperation or competition are more cooperative than are subjects who must make the usual all-or-none responses in a prisoner's dilemma (cf. Messé & Sawyer, 1967).

As the number of response alternatives is increased arithmetically in a mixed-motive game, the number of cells in the generated matrix increases geometrically. For a two-choice game subjects must comprehend four cells; for a three-choice game, nine cells; for a four-choice game, sixteen cells; and so on. A game with many discrete choices therefore presents formidable comprehension problems, since even in two-choice games a small number of college students must be discarded from the subject pool because they cannot understand the relationships between their choices and the resulting outcomes.

Gallo, Funk, and Levine (1969) investigated the effects of the number of discrete response alternatives on social conflict. In one condition of the experiment each subject was given a single poker chip with "Give him 20 cents" printed on one side and "Give me 10 cents" printed on the other in the usual two-choice game. A six-choice version of the same decomposed game was produced by giving each subject five chips, each one with the printed payoffs "Give him 4 cents" and "Give me 2 cents." Similarly, an 11-choice game was obtained by giving each subject 10 chips with the printed payoffs "Give him 2 cents" and "Give me 1 cent." This last version corresponds to a 121-cell prisoner's dilemma game!

Gallo et al. found that when subjects were playing for real money the six-choice decomposed game produced greater cooperation between subjects than did any other condition. When subjects were playing for imaginary money the six-choice game produced the greatest amount of competition. The conclusion seems warranted that there is some optimal number of alternatives for effective conflict resolution. "Too few may inhibit unilateral gestures of cooperation because of the risk involved in nonreciprocation. Too many may be incomprehensible or may so dilute the gesture that it may not be properly interpreted by the other party in the conflict [Gallo et al., 1969, p. 243]." We will have more to say later about the effects of monetary reward.

Pilisuk, Potter, Rapoport, and Winter (1965) explored the effects of attaching meaningful labels to response alternatives. For some subjects they labeled different sides of poker chips as either *factories,* meant to represent cooperative and productive choices, or *missiles,* meant to represent competitive choices; for other subjects they just called one side of a chip *blue* and the other side *white.* A payoff system was worked out so that depending on the pattern of choices the subjects made they received outcomes in accord with the rules of the PDG; for example, if one person turned over more missiles than the other he would exploit the other and receive greater payoffs. Despite the differences in the semantic meaning of the alternatives, the real-world jargon of an arms race generally produced no more cooperation or competition than did the less colorful abstract version of the game.

While these results indicate that differences in the labeling of alternatives *do not necessarily* produce behavioral differences, labeling may cue a subject as to what the experimenter expects him to do during the game. An experimenter who implies during the instructional phase that he believes a cooperative strategy is the mark of a rational, intelligent, and good person is likely to obtain results quite different from those of one who implies that a cooperative response is the mark of a gullible and socially inexperienced fool.

W. Berkowitz (1969), who used a complex prisoner's dilemma game in a study of escalation, reported similar negative results with regard to realistic instructions and labeling. In the two relevant conditions of the experiment some of the subjects were simply told to maximize the positive point difference between themselves and the other player under conventional (Choice 1–Choice 2) PDG labeling techniques and in a relatively neutral environment. The remainder of the subjects were given the same instructions but in very different circumstances. These subjects entered a "war game room" (the experimental cubicle), were exposed to several minutes of martial music before being instructed, and faced an apparatus with response choices labeled *bullet* and *target*. No behavioral differences were disclosed as a result of these treatments during the 63-trial game.

The effects of rewards and the motivation of subjects in mixed-motive games have been a matter of controversy. One position is that subjects do not really care about the imaginary points they are instructed to amass and that they make up a new idiosyncratic game as a means of relieving the boredom of the repetitive choices presented to them. The typical goal the experimenter gives the subjects is to maximize their own cumulative point totals. Instead, the subjects may invent a game of their own in which the goal is to trick or exploit their opponent, beat their opponent, or minimize the difference in points between themselves and their opponent. The predominance of competitiveness among subjects is accounted for by these conjectures.

A series of studies has investigated the effects of having subjects play for relatively substantial sums of real money, hence making the utilities of the game no longer trivial for subjects. The results have been quite confusing. Oskamp and Perlman (1965) and Radlow, Weidner, and Hurst (1968) using a prisoner's dilemma, McClintock and McNeel (1966, 1967) using a maximizing difference game, Gallo (1966a) using a trucking game, and Kelley et al. (1970) using a bargaining game found that monetary incentives as compared to abstract points created more cooperation. Oskamp and Kleinke (1970) found that money had little effect on the first few trials in a prisoner's dilemma game, but effects became increasingly apparent as the number of trials increased. Several other studies found no differences between large and small incentives (Evans, 1964; Gallo, 1966b; Knox & Douglas, 1968; Wrightsman, 1966), but still other studies found a reverse effect—decreases in cooperation with increases in monetary reward (Gumpert, Deutsch, & Epstein, 1969; Oskamp & Kleinke, 1970). These differences between experiments are perplexing and are probably to be explained by the differences in games, subjects (male versus females, for example), instructions, and demand characteristics.

The important generalization seems to be that even when the absolute levels of cooperation or competition are affected by changes in utilities, the effects of other manipulated independent variables seem to be preserved, and the same basic functions are observed. It is likely, therefore, that the issue, though worthy of pursuit and clarification, is not crucial to the use of experimental games as research tools to investigate hypotheses concerning social conflict.[1]

In summary, we have briefly reviewed some modifications of simpler games to ascertain how subjects' strategy choices are affected by different forms of presentation, expanded response alternatives, different labels or other means to make the conflict more realistic, and variations of utilities. Several tentative conclusions can be offered about these effects in the context of mixed-motive games in which the outcomes are known to both participants, no status quo solution is allowed to the bargaining problem, choices are made simultaneously, and no communications are allowed.

Decomposed versions of the prisoner's dilemma lead to more cooperative responding than do matrix versions, perhaps because in the decomposed versions the exploitative opportunities are obscured and the social exchange, norm-laden character of the relationship is emphasized. An optimum number of alternatives can allow for careful articulation of responses so that more cooperation can be coordinated than if too few or too many alternatives are available. Meaning-laden labels do not always produce effects different from those obtained by more abstract ways of presenting the game to subjects, but if relevant norms are invoked by such meaning labels more cooperation can apparently be obtained in the interaction. Finally, variations in utilities, including points and money, have produced equal and opposite effects, sometimes increasing, sometimes decreasing, and sometimes having no effect on the cooperative choices of subjects. Where utilities do produce effects, the functions of other independent variables with cooperation are generally preserved.

These conclusions specifically apply to situations in which bargaining to a solution is compulsory—a characteristic of the prisoner's dilemma and trucking games. Allowing subjects to accept a status quo solution to a bargaining problem (i.e., allowing them to not bargain) and providing them channels to communicate freely and/or exercise coercive or reward power considerably changes the nature of the interaction. Unfortunately, freeing subjects of experimental constraints also relinquishes control over

1. Although this conclusion is generally valid, several interactions have been found (e.g., Gallo, Funk, & Levine, 1969; Pruitt, 1967) between situational variables and other independent variables, such as between the number of response alternatives and the type of payoff (real versus imaginary money). These findings suggest that in conditions that have not been specified the relationship between dependent variables and levels of independent variables may be altered relatively as well as absolutely. The present authors are somewhat divided in their reactions to this issue; JTT sees less cause for concern than do BRS and TVB.

their behavior, but the richness of the observations obtained may more than compensate (at this stage of our scientific knowledge) for the precision or reliability of our results. No sophisticated formal theory of bargaining exists, and our approach to bargaining processes is based as much on experience, observation, and intuition as it is on systematic scientific knowledge. Nonetheless, the basic bargaining problems can be abstractly analysed in a manner calculated to inform us of the possible strategies and tactics an actor can employ to affect bargaining outcomes.

Factors Relevant to the Bargaining Process

Walton and McKersie (1965) distinguished four possible processes that might be discerned in any bargaining situation: distributive bargaining, integrative bargaining, attitudinal structuring, and intraorganizational bargaining. *Distributive bargaining* describes situations in which the parties are in basic conflict and competition because of a clash of goals. The situation is more precisely described as a constant-sum game in which anything that one party gains, the other loses; for example, a buyer who comes up two dollars in price loses that two dollars to the seller. This is the type of relationship laymen commonly refer to as bargaining. *Integrative bargaining* describes situations that have some areas of mutual concern and complementary interests. The situation is a variable-sum game such that by working together both parties can increase the total product they can divide between them. *Attitudinal structuring* involves interpersonal exchanges designed to alter the nature of the relationship by altering each other's attitudes—for example, the degree of friendship, trust, respect, and accommodativeness in the relationship. *Intraorganizational bargaining* occurs whenever one or a few individuals within an organization represent their fellows at the bargaining table, and it involves the efforts of the chief negotiator to bring the expectations of his own constituents into alignment with his bargaining objectives.

Most of the empirical research to date has been in distributive bargaining. The experimenter usually studies two individuals (no robot) in a distributive bargaining situation without integrative opportunities, with highly restricted opportunities for communications, and with no group for the individual to represent. Limited communication opportunities typically obviate attitudinal structuring, and even when bargainers are acting as representatives of a group (which is not often so), rationalizations and influence processes involved in intraorganizational bargaining are prevented. Our discussion will be limited to the distributive bargaining situation so that research can be used to evaluate existing hypotheses.

The distributive bargaining problem can be best illustrated as follows. Suppose that a used-car salesman had invested $2,000 in obtaining a particular automobile. Given his overhead, other expenses, and a minimal profit, he will not accept less that $2,200 for the car; any price lower would result in a loss. This is the minimum price that the seller would accept rather than maintain the status quo and not sell the car. Various researchers have given this minimum goal several labels: minimum disposition (Iklé & Leites, 1962; Sawyer & Guetzkow, 1965), concession point (Harsanyi, 1962a), equilibrium point (Stevens, 1963), resistance point (Walton & McKersie, 1965), break-off point (Kelley, 1966), fall-back position (Pruitt, 1962), and comparison level for alternatives (Kelley, 1966; Thibaut & Kelley, 1959). There is also some price that the dealer would *like* to receive (say, $3,000). This goal has been alternatively called: forward goal (Pruitt & Drews, 1969), level of aspiration (Siegel & Fouraker, 1960), target point (Walton & McKersie, 1965), and comparison level (Kelley, 1966; Thibaut & Kelley, 1959). The dealer also has an initial asking price (say, $3,400), which is above his level of aspiration and from which he can hope to retreat to a more attainable but still quite desirable price.

A potential buyer for the car has a maximum amount of money that he can either obtain or borrow and that he is willing to invest in an automobile. Suppose that the potential buyer would be reluctantly willing to go as high as $3,000 for the right car. The buyer's minimum disposition thus is $3,000, the amount of money he would spend at the most rather than accept his status quo point and not acquire the car but retain his money. The buyer's level of aspiration might be to obtain the car for $1,800, an outcome that would give him both the car and $1,200 savings. In order to get the ball rolling and give himself an intially favorable bid from which he can progress and still attain a desirable price, the buyer might initially bid only $1,400.

Table 5.1 presents the situation as we have described it. The automobile dealer does not know how much the buyer is willing to pay for the car, and the buyer does not know how little the seller will take; in other words, neither party knows the utility function, minimum disposition, or level of aspiration of the other. Such mutual ignorance provides the basis for the bargaining problem. Many of the tactics used in bargaining are directed toward discovering the utility function and minimum disposition of the other party or toward disguising the utility function, minimum disposition, and level of aspiration of the actor. An omniscient observer would know that the actual *bargaining range* falls between the minimum dispositions of the two parties, in this example between $2,200 and $3,000.

Siegel and Fouraker (1960) developed a research paradigm that rather faithfully captures the buyer–seller situation just illustrated. Subjects are presented with a bargaining chart pertaining to one or more issues and containing a large number of possible levels of settlement. Neither

TABLE 5.1. *The bargaining problem*

Seller Profit	Sales Price of Car	Buyer Savings
1200	3400	−400
800	3000	0
400	2600	400
0	2200	800
−400	1800	1200
−800	1400	1600

(Bargaining Range shown between Seller Profit / Sales Price and between Sales Price / Buyer Savings spanning the 3000–2200 rows.)

Seller's Asking Price = $3400
Sellers's Level of Aspiration = $3000
Seller's Minimum Disposition = $2200

Buyer's Initial Bid = $1400
Buyer's Level of Aspiration = $1800
Buyer's Minimum Disposition = $3000

Status Quo Point = No Agreement, Seller Has Car, Buyer Has $3000.

player knows what outcomes are listed on the other's chart for each possible settlement, but each is aware that the more he gets, the less the other gets. Multiissue bargaining may simulate labor–management problems and include such issues as hourly wages, sick benefits, vacation periods, and working conditions. Issues may be decided one at a time, or logrolling may be allowed so that a subject might make a large concession on one issue in order to gain from his opponent a large concession on another issue.

Communications between bargainers serve four major functions (see Smith, 1968) : (1) a discovery function designed to secure information about preference and utility schedules, the nature of the interpersonal relationship, and procedural details; (2) a coordination function designed to allow the bargainers to locate and increase areas of common agreement and mutual concern; (3) a formal delivery function allowing bargainers to communicate bids, offers, counteroffers, and acceptances; and (4) a manipulative function involving the use of influence tactics to affect the opponent's behavior. Influence tactics may include impression management, face-saving, bluffs, ingratiation, misinformation, threats, promises, warnings, mendations, and introduction of the relevance of norms of justice or fairness. Not only does a bargainer disguise his own preferences from his opponent and probe to discover the opponent's preferences, but he may also use influence tactics to change the opponent's preferences.

We will evaluate the available empirical evidence about bargaining in terms of the bargainers' goals: (1) discovering the opponent's utility function, (2) disguising their own utility functions, (3) manipulating the opponent's utility function, and (4) altering the relationship patterns between the bargainers.

Discovering the Opponent's Utility Function

If the buyer knows how much the seller will minimally take in a bargaining transaction, but the seller does not know how much the buyer might be prepared to give, one would believe that the buyer would have the advantage in the situation. Since the possession of information about the opponent's utility function is believed to give the actor the bargaining advantage, much bargaining behavior is devoted to probing to discover what the opponent's utility function is. Harsanyi (1962a) has reasoned that if two rational bargainers know each other's utility functions and each has complete information about the other's preferences, game theory could predict the bargaining outcome. In other words, there is a rational solution to every bargaining problem; if the bargainers are rational and possess sufficient information, they should recognize and accept this bargaining solution. By examining situations in which players are ignorant about each other's utility functions and by systematically studying the effects of increasing information on bargaining processes and outcomes, evidence should throw some light on these issues.

Studies have indicated that even when bargainers were not provided with information about the other's bargaining schedules or utility functions and could not reveal their own schedules to the other party, they reached agreements that maximized the joint profits to the pair (Fouraker & Siegel, 1963; Siegel & Fouraker, 1960). Schenitzki (1962) suggested that these rational solutions were a consequence of each bargainer's systematic exploration of his opponent's reactions to the value of possible contracts. He assumed that after an individual gained some information about the minimum disposition of his opponent he would make a concession based on the information gained. A bargainer who discovers that his opponent cannot accept less than, say, $2,000 from a contract would not continue to insist on a contract worth only $1,900. Schenitzki's interpretation is quite consistent with game theory, since he really presumes that as a result of probes each bargainer ends up with rather complete information about his opponent's utility function and bargaining schedule. This information allows the bargainers to discover the bargaining range and ultimately the bargaining solution, which as rational players they accept.

When the information available to the bargainers is relatively complete, it could be expected that the bargaining process would take on a character different from that in conditions of incomplete information. No longer do the bargainers have to probe in order to discover each other's minimum disposition or level of aspiration. Tactics meant to deceive the opponent about one's bargaining schedule no longer serve any useful purpose.

Liebert, Smith, Hill, and Kieffer (1968) suggest that most of the time and tactics involved in bargaining are directed toward developing realistic levels of aspiration, which are based to some degree on the minimum disposition of one's bargaining opponent and in the absence of complete information can be inferred from an opponent's initial bid and concession rate. In conditions of incomplete information initial bid and concession rate serve as tactics to convince an opponent that one must settle for a relatively large amount. In conditions of complete information these tactics lose whatever effectiveness they might have. Liebert et al. placed subjects in the role of an automobile seller opposing a programmed robot in the role of another car dealer who wanted to buy the automobile. Each subject was told that he could not accept less than $2,500 for the car; that is, his minimum disposition was $2,500. Half of the subjects knew that the buyer could pay as much as $3,500 for the car; the other half did not know the buyer's minimum disposition. The robot buyer opened the bidding with an initial bid that was either favorable ($3,050) or unfavorable ($2,615) to the subject.

These researchers found that when complete information about the buyer's minimum disposition was available, the buyer's initial bid had no effect on the value of the final contractual outcomes. The subjects knew the bargaining range and could hold out for what they perceived was a fair contract. However, when they had no information about the buyer's minimum disposition they made greater profits when the robot started out with a favorable rather than an unfavorable bid. Apparently when a bargainer does not have complete information about his opponent's minimum disposition he becomes dependent on his opponent's bids and concessions in selecting his own level of aspiration and final outcome.

It might be concluded that bargaining would be more ruthless and power-oriented in conditions of incomplete information. Friedman (1969) reviewed several experiments that investigated the behavior of experimental oligopolies (i.e., a few industries or organizations that control a market). The two conclusions that emerged from these studies were that: (1) very competitive behavior characterizes incomplete information situations; and (2) subjects with complete information display tit-for-tat behavior, becoming more cooperative the greater the cooperation of their rivals.

Schelling (1960) hypothesized that too much information about an opponent's preference schedule may actually be detrimental to a bargain-er's cause. By knowing what an opponent should reasonably receive from the interaction, a bargainer is likely to temper his demands according to what he considers fair. If the opponent is exploitative, does not know what is fair, or perceives the first bargainer's concessions as a sign of weakness or a low minimum disposition, the first bargainer will be at a disadvantage.

Cummings and Harnett (1969) examined the effects of asymmetrical information distribution in a bargaining triad. Two subjects acted as sell-ers and one as a buyer. The bargaining task consisted of reaching a single contract, which was binding on all three parties. Each bargainer had a different bargaining schedule; that is, each earned different amounts de-pending on the contract value reached, and seller A found himself in a conflict of interests with seller B and buyer C. In all conditions of the ex-periment seller A had complete information about B's and C's schedules, so that he knew exactly how much they would make for every possible contract. B and C were given either full or no information about A's schedule. When B and C knew A's payoff schedule they yielded more concessions over the bargaining interaction than when they were ignorant of A's utilities.

In a second experiment using the same bargaining problem for a triad, Harnett and Cummings (1968) allowed triads to bargain to contract agreement in a number of asymmetrical conditions of information and communication opportunities. The results showed that when a bargainer must negotiate a single agreement with two opponents he can conclude a more profitable agreement with a completely informed adversary than with an uninformed one. Uninformed bargainers typically began bargain-ing with high initial bids, took longer to reach agreement, and gained more in their negotiations than did informed bargainers.

The effect of permitting a bargainer to communicate with an opponent was very similar to providing him information. Communications between two informed bargainers included threats, promises, or strong suggestions for a fair solution. An informed bargainer generally did not make such demands of an uninformed opponent but tended to use information to encourage his ignorant adversary to make reasonable offers. Uninformed bargainers, though, did not seek information; they seemed to be aware that knowledge would weaken their bargaining positions. Both informed and uninformed bargainers who lacked the power to communicate in a one-way communication channel had a distinct bargaining disadvantage as compared to the same position without any incoming communication possibility.

The conclusions were reaffirmed in a study of bilateral bargaining by Harnett, Hughes, and Cummings (1968). A completely informed bargainer did experience disadvantage stemming from his knowledge. Apparently an actor should not depend on competitive information as a means of increasing profit. If he possesses such information it might be wise to reveal his own utility schedule to his adversary.

Disguising One's Own Bargaining Schedule

Offers, counteroffers, and concession rates tacitly communicate to an opponent one's minimum disposition or level of aspiration. A not surprising consequence is that subjects typically make high initial bids before scaling down their demands during the interaction (Kelley, 1966; Kelley, Beckman & Fischer, 1967; Pruitt & Drews, 1969; Siegel & Fouraker, 1960). Presumably subjects first attempt to feel out the opponent and then begin to scale down to their actual levels of aspiration. Subjects may shift their levels of aspiration during an interaction (more than once) in the light of new information. Bids and offers may serve to disguise from the opponent the actor's preference schedule and at the same time serve as probes to discover the opponent's schedule. If the opponent gains the impression that the actor has a low minimum disposition, the opponent should rationally attempt to force the bargaining solution down to the actor's minimum disposition—hence the credible notion that a tough bargainer may often reap great benefits.

Toughness has been defined as setting a high level of aspiration, increasing demands, making few concessions, and frequently using bluffs (Pruitt & Drews, 1969). On the basis of a number of experiments Bartos (1970) concluded that "toughness plays a dual role and has contradictory consequences. On the one hand, toughness *decreases* the likelihood of an agreement, while on the other hand, it *increases* the payoffs of those who survive this possibility of a failure [p. 62]."

The empirical manifestations of toughness give rise to the bargainer's dilemma (Kerr, 1954; Podell & Knapp, 1969). When a bargainer appears strong, unlikely to make concessions, committed to the position he defends, and likely to hold on to his initial level of aspiration, then he will be perceived as quite firm and unyielding. A bargainer would need to either make concessions to the tough opponent and thereby appear weak himself or drop out of the bargaining and accept the status quo point. The bargainer's dilemma arises from the difficulty of appearing strong while still making concessions in a reasonable effort to find a bargaining solution. If both bargainers make concessions, agreement may be reached and both may achieve their objectives; if neither makes concessions, no agreement is possible. If one bargainer makes a concession and appears weak while the other remains tough, the result would be a bargaining solution in which the tough opponent gains more than the weak one. Bartos

(1966) found that the fewer concessions made by a bargainer, the less likely it was that a bargaining solution would be reached, but if a solution was reached, the bargainer who made the fewest and/or smallest concessions attained the greatest profits.

Earlier it was pointed out that bargainers infer their opponent's level of aspiration and minimum disposition from, among other things, the opponent's concession rate. As we have just seen, the judicious selection of an appropriate concession rate can be used as an influence tactic designed to conceal one's own utility functions. Pruitt and Drews (1969) found that subjects perceived a bargaining opponent programmed to produce a slow concession rate as tougher and as having a higher minimum disposition than an opponent who made greater concessions. Similarly, Komorita and Brenner (1968) found that tough strategies consisting of slow or no concessions resulted in more subject yielding. A bargaining strategy adopted by a bargainer who sought a fair solution, which included making an initial offer that was considered fair and then firmly holding at that price, was not an effective means of reaching an agreement.

When a bargainer makes regular, noncontingent, and consistent concessions not only does he appear weak but also the opponent comes to expect his concessions. The opponent need only hold firm and wait for the bargainer to sweeten the bargain. Hence, consistent concessions have been found to have no effect on the size or rate of an opponent's concessions (Liebert, Smith, Hill, & Kieffer, 1968; Pruitt & Drews, 1969). However, when a bargainer makes irregular concessions he appears stronger, and the subjects' own concessions roughly follow a similar rate and size (Chertkoff & Conley, 1967; Pruitt & Johnson, 1970).

When time limits exist for reaching a bargaining solution, the actor must decide whether to maintain a tough bargaining posture and risk returning to the status quo point when the time runs out or to make one or more concessions to reach accommodation with his opponent at the cost of possibly appearing weak. Early in the bargaining process, time is available to try out various tactics and early concessions may be perceived as weakness. Later, however, each actor may perceive that this best interests lie in making concessions and reaching a solution, as when the hour for a strike draws near, and management is faced with the possible costs of such a strike and the union the possible loss of wages.

Stevens (1963) suggests that when time pressures are salient a concession by one of the parties may more easily be perceived by his opponent as a sign of good will rather than weakness. Pruitt and Drews (1969) and Pruitt and Johnson (1970) used a task similar to one devised by Siegel and Fouraker (1960) and found that salient time pressures did lower subject bargainers' levels of aspiration, lowered their demands, and reduced the frequency of bluffing for the first few minutes of bargaining.

However, as the actual length of bargaining time increased under such time pressures, subjects reverted to normal bargaining tactics and goals.

A tough bargainer attempts to convince the other party that he cannot change his offer and make further concessions because he is committed to a particular minimum position. The tough bargainer attempts to manage the impressions his opponent has of him in a manner calculated to communicate that a reasonable position has been taken and further concessions would reduce the actor's position below his status quo point. Often the bargainer will, as a commitment strategy, publicly stake his reputation on his stated position. Schelling (1960) has characterized this tough bargaining strategy as follows: "In bargaining, the commitment is a device to leave the last clear chance to decide the outcome with the other party, in a manner that he fully appreciates; it is to relinquish further initiative, having rigged the incentives so that the other party must choose in one's favor [p. 37]." The bargainer should wish to make an irrevocable commitment as close to his opponent's minimum disposition as possible without going below it. However, there is the danger that the bargainer will remain committed to an untenable position, since the commitment usually requires that he follow through with the consequences.

Deutsch and Lewicki (1970) conducted an experiment designed to assess the effects of commitment on the course of bargaining in a version of the adolescent game of chicken. A trucking game was used, and the subjects were told that if their trucks met head on on the one-land road a collision would take place and they would lose money for that trial. None, one, or both of the high-school-age subjects were given a commitment device that allowed the truck owner to lock his truck in forward gear and head down the one-way road. A light on each person's panel informed him when his opponent was using the commitment lock-in device. Unfortunately, the results of the experiment were equivocal, because many subjects were reluctant to use the commitment device. No consistently significant differences were found between conditions on most dependent variables. Indications were, however, that if the commitment device was used *and* a crash did not occur, the person who used the lock-in device increased his profits. More research on this issue seems warranted.

If a chief negotiator is given specific instructions by the group he represents, he may find it easier to maintain a tough bargaining posture. That is, he can no longer afford to make concessions unless they are first approved by his constituents. If his group makes these instructions public, the negotiator's commitment to his bids and offers is unlikely to be perceived by his opponent as bluffing or probing. Also, the bargainer known to be preinstructed by his group may be perceived as more reasonable in his demands, since his actions and goals are not arbitrarily his own but represent the goals of a larger number of people.

The orientation of parties to a bargaining task influences the likely out-comes. Druckman (1967) asked subjects to meet in a prenegotiation ses-sion. When subjects were told to develop their individual bargaining goals and to elaborate justifications for those goals, few agreements with the opposing side were reached; the bargainers apparently became committed to their own positions. However, when the subjects had discussed the is-sues together under instructions to consider both sides, compromises were achieved. In a second study Druckman (1968) again found that concen-tration on one's own position during prenegotiation experiences produced few agreements during formal bargaining. However, when the subjects in-formally discussed their bargaining positions in prenegotiation sessions *with either members of their own group or members of the opposing team,* many compromises were later achieved. As long as the bargainers were free to discuss aspects of the ensuing negotiation without having to formulate a position, conflict amelioration occurred no matter with whom they discussed the problem.

If complex issues of great value are under contention, attempts to dis-guise one's own aspirations are more likely to be counterproductive than when simple issues of small value are at stake. Deutsch (1969) has noted the difficulty of solving a complex bargaining problem when it is per-ceived "as a conflict over a large substantive issue rather than a small one (over 'being treated fairly' or 'being treated unfairly' at a particular occa-sion), as a conflict over principle rather than the application of a princi-ple, as a conflict whose solution establishes large rather than small substantive or procedural precedents [p. 1090]." Roger Fisher (1964, 1969), a professor of international law, has argued that international conflicts also may be more easily negotiated to a compromise settlement by fractionating large issues into smaller ones. The smaller issues then may be traded off as concessions, there is less likelihood that emotions will cloud the perceptions of the decision makers, and there is less danger of uncontrollable conflict escalation.

When conflicts are large or intense and a bargaining solution is thereby difficult to achieve, the bargainers may take great risks, including the use of threats that would otherwise be unproductive. Deutsch, Canavan, and Rubin (1971) explored the ways bargainers use threats in situations varying in conflict intensity. They defined conflict size as "the expected difference in the value of the outcomes that a person will receive if he 'wins' compared with the value he will receive if the other 'wins' [p. 259]." Conflict size was operationalized by varying the proportion of the main road in the trucking game that was one lane. Thus, 20, 50, or 90 percent of the main route was one lane, and the greater the percentage, the greater the conflict size. When the one-lane route was short (low con-flict) it was an easy matter to back up a few spaces, let the other truck pass, and then proceed on one's own way. When the one-lane route was long (high conflict) retracing paths consumed a great deal of time and hence was more costly in terms of getting the trucks to their destinations.

The results of the experiment revealed that as conflict size increased, cooperative or compromising behaviors declined. Consequently, when conflict size was large rather than small fewer trials had positive outcomes, more trials resulted in subjects' receiving the maximum negative outcome possible, more trials occurred on which one or both subjects were forced to use the long alternative pathway rather than the shorter one-lane route, and gates were more frequently used to threaten and block each other.

Fischer (1969) studied the size of conflict and the use of threats in a negotiation game. Subjects were assigned varying minimum dispositions over trials of the game creating either a narrow or a broad bargaining range. The bargainers had less room to maneuver and fewer points to divide when the bargaining range was quite narrow; hence conflict was considered to be inversely related to the size of the bargaining range. The results confirmed that the greater the conflict between bargainers, the more likely they were to send threats to each other.

In conclusion, actors may attempt to conceal or disguise their own bargaining objectives from their opponents as a tactic to gain their own level of aspiration. Tough bargaining strategies may be adopted, including the use of initial high bids, few concessions, and commitment to a bargaining position (even under time pressures). Such tough bargaining moves do increase the actor's outcomes when solutions are reached, but when both bargainers use tough tactics there is much less chance that a bargaining solution will be attained.

Manipulating the Opponent's Utilities

When bargainers are deadlocked and reaching an agreement is important to at least one of them, efforts may be undertaken to induce the opponent to change his bargaining objectives Three major means of accomplishing a change in the outcomes acceptable to the opponent are to threaten him, to seek mediation of the dispute, and to invoke norms applicable to bargaining outcomes.

THE USE OF THREATS IN BARGAINING

A bargainer may seek advantage from the opponent by adopting strategies that will cause the opponent to lower both his minimum disposition and his level of aspiration. Alternatively, the actor may attempt to change the opponent's status quo point by introducing threats into the bargaining process. If a bargainer does not concede under a threat from his oppo-

nent, he stands some chance of being punished. Consequently the bargainer would be worse off than he was before bargaining started and yet
would not have reached any conclusion to the bargaining problem. Of
course, the costs of using coercive power may also lower the threatener's
status quo point, since he, too, would not have gained his bargaining
objectives and would also be worse off than he was when bargaining began (although his subsequent threats would be more believable) .

The use of threats in bargaining may cause the bargainer to become
hostile toward the source of intimidation, especially if they are status or
prestige equals. The target of a threat may raise the ante by issuing a
counterthreat. The original threatener, faced with a counterthreat, must
decide among maintaining his credibility and backing up his original
threat, escalating the magnitude of his threat by issuing a new threat, or
backing down and losing credibility and face. In such circumstances each
side may continually escalate the conflict. The resulting conflict spiral
may become so intense that the contestants lose track of the original issues and concentrate on the new issues (e.g., face maintenance) arising
from the confrontation caused by mutual use of threats. Thus nations
sometimes go to war to settle value conflicts, but the focus then shifts to
other issues (e.g., winning the war) , and the political values that led to
the war may become secondary.

The introduction of coercive power into the bargaining process may be
counterproductive for both parties. In the context of the trucking game
Deutsch and Krauss (1960) gave female subjects no gates, gave one but
not the other a gate, or gave both gates. When no gates were available to
subjects they achieved the highest joint profits of any of the three conditions, indicating that they often were able to coordinate their interests.
Subjects in both conditions of the experiment in which gates could be
used lost money; when both subjects possessed gates they lost more than
subjects in the unilateral gate condition. When gates were not available or
were available to only one of the subjects, profits improved over trials, indicating that subjects did learn to coordinate their interests, even when
one of them possessed an unilateral power advantage. When both subjects possessed gates they did not improve their profits with experience
over plays of the game. The following conclusions were drawn: (1) if either person in the dyad has a threat potential it is best to be the person
who has it; (2) if the other party already possesses threat capability it is
better not to have threat capacity; (3) if neither party possesses threat
capability bargaining outcomes for the dyad are larger than otherwise.

Deutsch and Krauss assumed that two factors caused the pattern of results they obtained: (1) if threats are possessed they will be used; (2)
using threats produces counterthreats, hostility, and competition. Both
of these assumptions have been directly or indirectly supported by subse-

quent empirical results; however, the second assumption must be slightly modified. Several studies (Fischer, 1969; Hornstein, 1965; Smith & Leginski, 1970) have shown that as the magnitude of an available threat increases, so does its use, thereby indirectly supporting the first assumption. The second assumption has been directly supported if it is modified to read "being punished produces counterharm, hostility, and competition."

Anderson and Smith (1970) used an apparatus similar to the trucking game, except that there were no alternate routes, the apparatus was not automated, and the threat mechanism was separated from the harm mechanism by giving subjects a signal light that indicated the intent to deliver a subsequent fine to the other person. They found a high positive correlation (+.80) between the use of fine and counterfine. Willis and Long (1967) also found that harm begets harm in a bargaining interaction. Other studies have indicated that the use of punishment following a threat is directly related to lowered evaluative ratings of the threatener, suggesting that hostility is generated by the use of harm (e.g., Schlenker, Bonoma, Tedeschi, Lindskold, & Horai, 1971).

Whether the use of a verbal threat without subsequent administration of punishment exacerbates conflict is not known conclusively. Studies of threats in prisoner's dilemma games conducted by Tedeschi and his colleagues (cf. Tedeschi, 1970; Tedeschi, Bonoma, Schlenker, & Lindskold, 1970) have obtained results that indicate that the mere use of threats per se may not seriously affect the intensity of the overall conflict between the players, especially when the target could interpret the threats as a nonexploitative gesture.

An actor may make his threats more effective by adopting a commitment strategy, pledging himself in some irrevocable way to backing up the threat even to the point of making punishment for the target's defiance automatic so that the source could not back down on his threat even if he wanted to. For example, it has been suggested that the United States automate its nuclear retaliatory striking capacity so that sensor devices trip off a nuclear strike against predetermined targets as soon as a threshold level of radioactivity is detected in the environment. This threat of nuclear retaliation would involve relinquishment of human control over the threatened action, in effect converting a threat into a warning. Credibility therefore becomes a matter of the probability of electronic failure. The purpose of such a commitment is to affect opponents' minimum dispositions and levels of aspiration by influencing their perceptions of what the actor intends to do. Unfortunately, no research has been conducted to evaluate the many rich intuitive hypotheses about such commitment strategies. For an exposure to some of these hypotheses the reader could find no more rewarding source than Schelling (1966).

As has been seen, the efficiency of threats in bargaining situations depends partly on the target's ability to issue a counterthreat or to retaliate. Both the magnitude and the timing of an opponent's attack have been hypothesized to produce effects on retaliatory behavior. To investigate such effects Teger (1970) devised a game in which subjects could allocate 1,000 units of resources to one of several uses—to secure a fixed income, to make trade agreements with the adversary, or to make arms.

Allocating resources in fixed income produced small but constant earnings irrespective of the behavior of the opponent. A trade agreement could earn greater profits, depending on the amount of resources invested and the amount of the investment the opponent reciprocated. If one bargainer placed into arms more units of investment than the other bargainer, the big investor won a large amount and the small investor lost a large amount. A quick transfer of resources into arms, therefore, was interpreted as a surprise attack. The three allocation alternatives allowed the subjects to withdraw from the game or cooperate or compete in the game.

Robot bargainers initiated surprise attacks against the subjects. The size of the attack (high or low) was operationalized by varying the number of units the robot converted into arms, while the timing of the attack was either at the beginning or in the middle of the interaction sequence. The later attack may have been more surprising because it came later in the interaction and was undertaken only after a sequence of cooperative responses between robot and subject had elapsed. In any case the later attack and the greater magnitude of attack produced more retaliation in the form of subjects' reallocation of resources to armaments, and caused subjects to perceive the robot and themselves as more hostile. Subjects reported feeling "suckered" into defeat in the late attack condition. Because the subjects viewed the robot's earlier cooperation as a sucker ploy, Teger observed that "not only was the attack interpreted in relation to the past cooperation, but the past cooperation was interpreted in relation to the attack [1970, p. 201]."

The perceptions of hostility and entrapment due to the timing of the late attack might be limited to a situation with a competitive context in which an audience is present. If the context were more cooperative the subjects might have forgiven the attack because of the prior history of consistently cooperative gestures; they may have felt that the attack was a result of an accident or a mistake and not really an indication of present and future hostilities. However, when a bargainer is placed in a competitive situation under the watchful eye of an audience (e.g., an experimenter, a group of people, another nation) and then appears to be suckered into defeat, he has a vested interest in restoring his own esteem and maintaining face.

Face-saving behaviors are most likely to occur during aggressive or competitive encounters after an individual's esteem has been publicly punctured. Deutsch (1960) suggests that allowing a threat to go unchallenged would result in a loss of one's own self-esteem and status. In an attempt to restore his own esteem and maintain his social role position, an individual will often take actions that cost him more than they cost his opponent.

Tedeschi, Schlenker, and Bonoma (1971) have suggested that by failing to retaliate against a threat an individual may be perceived as weak and compliant and will thereafter remain a target of threats. They went on to say that even if a person is willing in privacy to accede to a powerful adversary's demands he will resist threats when they are made publicly. The person does not want to encourage others to use coercion against him; his resistance may be motivated not so much by the desire to deter his immediate tormentor as by the desire to deter future possible adversaries. Even if a person knows that his counterthreat will fail, he establishes the precedent that to exert coercive influence against him will result in the threatener's accrual of costs. Hence more reactance should be demonstrated in public than private situations.

Brown (1968) investigated face-saving behavior by having adolescent male subjects participate against a robot adversary in a modified version of the trucking game. The robot player had control over a gate for the first half of the experiment, and the subject had control for the second half. During the first half of the game the aggressive robot exploited the subjects, used the gate quite often, charged the subjects high tolls to pass through the gate, and ended up with a profit much larger than that of the subjects. To make their defeat even more ignominious the subjects were told that a group of fellow adolescents was observing them through a one-way mirror. Midway through the experiment and before the subjects acquired control of the gates, they received evaluations of their behavior from their fictitious peers. They were either told that their peers viewed them as poor bargainers and as weak, a sucker, and pretty bad, or they were told that all things considered they looked good because they tried hard and played fair.

After receiving the bogus evaluations the subjects were given the power to choose from a toll schedule exactly how much they wanted to charge the robot for passing through the gate. The schedule included low or moderate tolls that cost the subjects little or no money to administer and high tolls that cost the subjects a great deal to administer, sometimes even more than the toll itself. Thus, subjects were provided with the opportunity to either maximize their own outcomes by charging moderate tolls at little cost to themselves or save face by hurting the opponent but at a high and otherwise prohibitive cost to self. Half of the subjects believed that their robot opponent knew precisely what their costs were; the other half thought that the robot did not know their cost schedule.

The results indicated that subjects who felt they had looked foolish earlier charged much higher tolls than did the subjects who felt they had looked good. They saved face despite the costs to themselves. Additionally, self-damaging retaliation was more frequent when the robot was said not to know the subjects' costs than when the costs were known. The opponent's knowledge that the subject was harming himself in order to gain revenge suppressed the use of self-damaging tolls.

THE INTERPRETATION OF THREATS

The availability of communication channels and the number of alternative modes of communication available to a source are important in determining how a target will interpret and react to a message. When a source has a rich variety of possible communication channels or influence modes at his disposal he is able to present the target with messages that preserve the nuances of thought he wants to transmit. However, when few modes of communication are available the target may find the meaning of each message more ambiguous than would be so if the source had unlimited opportunities to make his meanings clear. For example, Shomer, Davis, and Kelley (1966) gave subjects who were playing a game board version of the trucking game the ability to illuminate a threat light on their opponent's board and actually fine the opponent. Over half of the subjects used and interpreted the light as a signal to coordinate turn-taking via the shorter one-lane route, since it was the only available communication or coordination signal.

Anderson and Smith (1970) followed up the implications of the restrictive communications on bargaining in a modified version of the trucking game. Half of the subjects were given the ability to illuminate a threat light on their opponent's board and to deliver a fine; the other half were not given threat and fine capability. Additionally, some of the subjects were provided with no communication ability, others were given written intertrial communication ability, and still others were given unrestricted vocal communication ability. When no communication opportunities were available, the lights were more often perceived and used as signals for cooperation rather than as threats; consequently, these subjects were better able to coordinate their behaviors and won more than did the subjects who had no threat light and no communications opportunity. When alternative communication possibilities were available, subjects who used the threats did worse than subjects who did not have threat capability. Given the alternative communications that could have been used, the decision to send a threat more clearly became a hostile action.

Nardin (1968) investigated very much the same problem in the context of a six-choice decomposed prisoner's dilemma game. His conclusions are worth quoting at some length.

Threats do not effect the level of cooperation when communication is minimal, but do lead to heightened conflict when the possibility for exchanging nonthreatening communications is available to the parties. Conversely, although communication results in an improvement in the level of cooperation in the absence of opportunities to threaten, it is not effective in situations in which threat capability exists and is used. Furthermore, individuals are more likely to escalate in response to threats when communication is an available alternative than when it is not [p. 84].

Nardin's subjects most frequently retaliated by escalating the level of conflict when a threat had been sent them, other means of communication were available to their opponent, and the threatener actually administered the threatened punishment. If threats are the only mode of influence available to a source, whether the target will interpret them as coordinating signals or coercive power attempts may depend crucially on the concomitant behaviors of the source—that is, whether the source behaves fairly and accommodatively or unfairly and exploitatively. Similar findings were obtained by Schlenker, Bonoma, Tedeschi, and Pivnick (1970), Bonoma and Tedeschi (1972), and Horai and Tedeschi (1970).

In summary, threats seldom improve and almost always decrease a bargainer's outcomes if his adversary is similarly armed and the values in dispute are important to both parties. Yet when threats are available, bargainers are tempted to use them. If only one of the parties has threat capability he may improve his outcomes by using threats; then a carrot-and-stick approach is likely to be more successful than an exploitative strategy that imposes on the unarmed party a least-of-evils choice. A threatener may increase the effectiveness of his threats by adopting a commitment strategy that communicates the inevitability of threat enforcement. Tacit communications may be interpreted as either threats or signals of intentions to coordinate mutual benefits, depending on the source's subsequent accommodative or exploitative behaviors. The freer the communications opportunities, the more precise and explicit the meanings that can be conveyed between the parties. Within a rich communications environment tacit communications are more likely to be perceived as threats than as coordinating signals. Finally, an accommodative threatener is able to achieve his objectives more easily than is an exploitative threatener.

The Effects of a Mediator on Bargainers' Utility Schedules

When bargainers clearly can gain by reaching a compromise solution but making a concession would be perceived as a sign of weakness to be exploited by the adversary, mediation may be used to facilitate the bargaining process. Mediation involves the intervention of a third party whom both negotiators accept and whose function is to help the contenders reach a fair and peaceful settlement of their dispute. The impact of a mediator is at least fourfold: (1) he modifies perceptions of the meaning of any concessions; (2) he causes both parties to shift their levels of aspiration; (3) he allows one or both parties to save face; (4) he introduces norms of equity, fairness, and justice into the bargaining situation. These four functions are interrelated.

Bargainers and their constituents typically perceive a mediator as an objective third party who has the ability to see both sides and the information necessary to perceive and recommend a fair solution. When a concession is made at the request of the mediator, the likelihood is that all sides will perceive the bargaining move as a function of fairness and good faith (Pruitt & Johnson, 1970). Additionally, a concession made under mediation should not be perceived as a sign of weakness or as an indicator of possible subsequent concessions (Walton & McKersie, 1965). Concessions made under the aegis of the mediator may be perceived as representing a close approximation to the solution of the bargaining problem—a solution not likely to be improved on, since it was suggested by a mediator who should be able to see the fair solution (Pruitt & Johnson, 1970). A mediator's public advice provides the bargainer with a compromise solution that is intraorganizationally salable and saves face with the bargainer's own constituents as well as with his adversary and other third parties (Stevens, 1963).

These ideas have received some empirical attention. Podell and Knapp (1969) found that subjects perceived their programmed robot opponent as being less weak when the robot's concessions came in the presence of a mediator who offered suggestions. Pruitt and Johnson (1970) found that when bargaining occurred without mediation, subjects' perceptions of their own weakness was directly related to the size of their concessions. However, after the intervention of a mediator who offered solutions to the bargaining problem the size of concessions was no longer related to perceptions of weakness. Subjects also made more concessions when a mediator intervened than when he did not.

If the mediator fails to take initiative but merely acts as an observer, his presence could exacerbate the conflict. Face-saving behaviors might increase in front of the mediator, and he may serve as an embodiment of important social norms. Ziller, Zeigler, Gregor, Styskal, and Peak (1969) suggest that each of the principals can take solace in the presumption that his own position is the correct or right one if the mediator does not apply pressure on him to change his bargaining position. Whatever the effects of the presence of a mediator, it could be hypothesized that they would be bolstered by his status, prestige, esteem, and attraction. The place of the mediator in bargaining deserves much more empirical attention than it has received.

The Effects of Norms on the Bargaining Process

The introduction of social norms or rules into a bargaining situation is an effective way of changing the minimum dispositions, levels of aspiration, and status quo points of the bargainers. A social norm is a rule that prevails in a social group and governs acceptable behaviors or prohibits unacceptable behaviors. Violation of the rule may bring about a penalty such as social disapproval or, in instances of legalized norms, a fine or jail sentence. Although such pressures or penalties may bring about conformity to collective rules, often the power of norms to govern behavior arises from the internalized values they serve. Homans (1961) states that "when we say that some people conform to a norm 'for its own sake' we mean that they are rewarded by the result that the norm itself, if obeyed, will bring [p. 116]." If one of the bargainers invokes a norm he is in a very real sense substituting situational rules for more direct personal influence.

To some extent rules and norms govern behavior even in the most intense of conflicts. Shared expectations about the constraints on or the appropriateness of behavior can take several forms. The negative norm of reciprocity, which specifies an eye for an eye and a tooth for a tooth, has already been illustrated by the tendency of parties in conflict to retaliate when attacked. The positive reciprocity norm, which requires that a person give benefit for benefit, may also dictate that the adversary's concession deserves a reciprocal concession of equal value. Equity norms require that persons should be allocated a proportion of the available resources according to the investments they have made. The weaker party to the interaction may attempt to elicit a responsibility norm or principle of noblesse oblige so that the stronger party will provide the benefits the weaker party wants.

Matrix versions of mixed-motive games have not produced results that illuminate the operation of reciprocity norms in conflict situations. Most often it has been found that cooperation in games is not clearly reciprocated, as subjects typically exploit a predominantly cooperative opponent (cf. Gallo & McClintock, 1965; Nemeth, 1970; Vinacke, 1969). Nemeth (1970) has suggested that numerous factors override the operation of reciprocity norms: many subjects are not fully aware of the interdependence of their behaviors and do not completely comprehend the ways in which they can affect their opponent's behavior; instructional sets typically request that the subject concentrate on only his own outcomes; the absence of monetary payoffs often provides no sufficient reason for coop-

eration; and since the subjects do not expect to meet again they have little reason to observe the norms.

Nevertheless, one type of reciprocity has been consistently observed in
simple mixed-motive games. When a robot opponent plays tit-for-tat
strategies higher rates of cooperation are obtained from subjects than
when an opponent is unilaterally cooperative (Solomon, 1960) or follows some other pattern of responding (Gallo, 1967; Komorita, 1965;
Rapoport, 1964). Nemeth has observed that the reciprocity of benefits
often depends on the attribution that an actor intentionally conferred the
benefit. This being so, a tit-for-tat strategy may be effective because it
tacitly but clearly communicates: "I will cooperate with you on a reciprocal basis, but I will compete with you on the same basis if you insist; it's
up to you." If this sort of communication is lacking, as when an opponent
is unconditionally cooperative, reciprocity does not occur, and the subjects simply take advantage of their opponent's apparent stupidity; then
the subjects quite possibly could view the cooperator as failing to understand the game contingencies.

Pruitt (1968) has reported what is perhaps the best single study on the
operation of the reciprocity norm in the context of a bargaining situation.
On each trial of a game, which was structurally an expanded and decomposed PDG, one of the participants was to open an envelope the experimenter gave him, take out the money it contained, and decide how much
of the money to keep and how much to send to the other person. Any
money sent to the other person was multiplied by 1.5 and then turned
over by the experimenter. Since the participants were to take turns receiving the envelope from the experimenter, sending all the money to the
other person would maximize the dyad's total winnings, but sending money to the other person made sense only if it was expected that the other
person would send money back.

On the first trial a simulated player sent the subject: 80 percent of $1
(80 cents), 20 percent of $1 (20 cents), or 20 percent of $4 (80
cents). Subjects were informed that on the third and last trial of the game
the other person would have either $2 or 50 cents to allocate. Subjects
were then given $3 to allocate on the second trial. On the basis of Gould-
ner's (1960) analysis it was hypothesized that: (1) more money would
be sent to the simulated player the more money the subject received from
him on the first trial; (2) more money would be sent the greater the proportion of the other's money received; and (3) more money would be
sent the greater the other's anticipated future resources. The results supported all three predictions.

Equity norms (see Adams, 1965; Homans, 1962) dictate that one
should receive from an interaction an amount proportional to one's inputs to the interaction relative to all other participants. When bargainers

can agree on their inputs, equity norms should operate to provide a clear solution to the bargaining problem. Thus two workers who hold the same job and have the same educational and experiential background should receive the same pay, but a college graduate feels he *should* receive more pay than a high school graduate when they both start work in the same plant. Morgan and Sawyer (1967) and Messé (1969) found that subjects who believed they had equal inputs chose to divide the available resources equally.

Messé (1971) studied a situation in which bargainers' inputs were not equal but were known precisely by both parties. When subjects arrived at the laboratory they participated in a prebargaining task that took 80, 70, 60, 50, or 40 minutes; these times represented their contribution or input. Five bargaining groups were then formed: 80–80, 80–60, 70–50, 80–40, and 80–0. The allocation of money between the parties in the bargaining task closely followed equity predictions; for example, when inputs were 80–80 subjects split the money evenly, when inputs were 80–40 the first subject received twice as much as the second subject. Additionally, solutions to the bargaining problem were reached very rapidly, as if the solution were obvious to both bargainers. Messé concluded that "it could be that agreement on an outcome might be a somewhat trivial problem once agreement on inputs has been reached [p. 290]." In many real-world negotiations the participants spend much of their time trying to convince their adversary of the size and value of their contributional inputs.

Norms may be employed in bargaining to promote a smooth running and efficient bargaining process, thereby preventing a breakoff in the interaction and generally helping the principals to attain their goals. For example, rules of procedure may be developed, like Robert's rules of parliamentary procedure, to facilitate intragroup communication and to ensure the consideration of issues in a committee. Thibaut and Faucheux (1965) investigated some factors that affect the development of norms within the context of a bargaining situation. They suggested that when faced with a large threat to the survival of a potentially profitable interaction the participants will attempt to develop rules that reduce the destructive possibilities.

This hypothesis was tested in a rather ingenious experiment. Subjects played a mixed-motive game under modified conditions that gave one player, *P*, a relative power advantage. When both players made identical choices (e.g., both made Choice 1) they each received an identical small number of points. When the players made nonidentical choices (e.g., one player made Choice 1 and the other made Choice 2) *P* could decide how to allocate most of the points associated with that cell of the matrix. For example, if 98 points were associated with the cell *P* could keep 88 and give *W* 10, or he could keep 50 and give *W* 48, and so on.

P's power was set at either high or low levels by varying the minimum number of points that *P* was forced to give *W* whenever nonidentical choices were made. When *P* had high power he had to give *W* at least 10 of the 98 points, and when *P* had low power he had to give *W* at least 45 of the 98 points. Either player could choose not to play on any iteration of the game and receive a status quo payoff. If only one subject chose not to play he received the status quo payoff and the other subject received nothing on that trial, but if both chose not to play they both received status quo payoffs. The amount of the status quo payoff was relatively high or low with respect to the matrix values. The ability of the weak player *(W)* to leave the relationship gave him an effective measure of counterpower, especially when the status quo was of great value. The research design, therefore, included high and low power for *P* and status quo payoffs of either large or small magnitudes.

The bargainers were allowed to adopt rules governing their conduct and to attach penalties to the violation of any rules adopted. Three types of rules were provided for subjects' consideration: (1) a rule prohibiting the choice of the status quo alternative; (2) a rule specifying that prebargaining agreements about the distribution of points could not be violated; (3) a rule that required that prebargaining agreements about which game responses would be chosen on the next play of the game be honored. The first rule was desirable for *P*, since it would be to his advantage if *W* was required to play the game. The second rule was in *W*'s interest, since he should want to be assured that *P* would equitably allocate the points. The third rule was included as an innocuous alternative.

When the pressures toward dissolution of the dyad were very high— that is, *P* had great power, and a high status quo payoff was available for not bargaining—the dyads formed almost the maximal number of contracts possible and attached higher indemnities for breaking the contracts than in any of the other conditions. Subjects traded concessions and adopted both a rule to prohibit leaving the relationship and a rule to fairly allocate points. Subjects in each of the other conditions formed significantly fewer contracts. When *P* had little power and the status quo payoff was small, there was much less pressure toward dissolution of the relationship and the bargainers consequently adopted few rules or contracts. When *P* had great power and the status quo payoff was small and when *P* had relatively little power and the status quo payoff was large, neither bargainer had much incentive to form a contract. In the first situation *W* had little choice but to play; in the second *W* had insufficient reason to choose to play. Across conditions of the experiment those dyads that did form contracts won more points and distributed the points more equally within the dyads as compared to dyads that did not form contracts.

Additional studies have elaborated on the above results. Thibaut (1968) replicated and extended the original findings. He found that across different populations, whether one or two bargainers represented each side, and despite changes in the inducement of stress on the group, the greater the mutually disruptive forces in the relationship, the greater the amount of rule-forming activity.

Murdoch (1967) found that instability could be introduced into a bargaining situation by manipulating the bargainers' perceptions of each other and that such instability is a condition that encourages the formation of contractual agreements. When bargainers perceived each other as exploitative and likely to choose the no-play option, more contract formation occurred than when the bargainers perceived each other as accommodative and likely to play the game.

Murdoch and Rosen (1970) found that high conflict of interests and the existence of attractive alternative relationships in an informal work task caused subjects to send frequent verbal threats to each other, fostered many informal normative agreements, and produced high levels of accommodation. Fewer threats and agreements and less accommodation were found when conflicts of interests were less severe and attractive alternative relationships did not exist.

It can be concluded from the converging results of all of these studies on contractual agreements that intense conflicts and articulated incentives provide the basis for the formation of norms. Contrary to common sense, norms do not develop more easily when conflict is low than when conflict is high, but intense conflict is not sufficient to generate normative agreements without the presence of articulated and interlocked incentives for the two parties.

Relational Patterns

The motivational orientations, perceptions, and attitudes of the principals clearly affect the bargaining process. Many plausible hypotheses can be intuitively developed from personality theory and considerations of role perception and behaviors. Caution will guide the following discussion, and generalizations will be tailored to the available empirical evidence.

Most bargaining research has emphasized structural and situational factors rather than the impact of idiosyncratic factors on the bargaining process. There appears to be a growing consensus that the situational pressures on individuals in conflict are typically great enough to override the internalized propensities of individuals. However large the proportion of the variance that structural factors account for, few theorists would deny that the vagaries of the persons involved play some role.

Kelley and Stahelski (1970a,b,c) have suggested that all individuals fall somewhere along a continuum that can be labeled at the end points *cooperators* and *competitors*. In interaction people can choose to more or less cooperate (or compete) with one another, or else they can choose to not interact with one another at all. Some people are predisposed to cooperate with others, and some are more apt to compete with others. Competitors expect others to be predominantly competitive and defensively compete against them. Cooperators perceive the world as more complex, perceive the likely behavioral orientations of others rather accurately, and respond accordingly. Although a cooperator prefers to cooperate, he will defensively compete with a competitor. The perceptions and behaviors of the competitors suggest a self-fulfilling prophesy; they perceive others as competitive, behave competitively themselves, and thereby force their opponent to assume a competitive stance irrespective of the opponent's wishes. Hence the competitor's erroneous perceptions are actually quite veridical; everyone with whom he interacts does wind up competing!

Kelley and Stahelski split subjects into cooperators and competitors on the basis of how they intended to respond in a prisoner's dilemma game. The subjects then played the PD in various combinations: cooperator–cooperator, cooperator–competitor, competitor–competitor. Cooperators cooperated often with each other; cooperators competed against competitors; and competitors were quite competitive against other competitors. Kelley and Stahelski (1970a) relate their analysis to other personality characteristics and specifically cite high authoritarians and isolationists as possible competitors, while egalitarians and internationalists are likely to be similar to cooperators.

Authoritarianism was one of the first personality dispositions to receive attention in the context of mixed-motive games. Authoritarianism is characterized by repressed hostilities manifested in extreme submissiveness to authorities, a repulsion of weakness, an intolerance of deviations from socially prescribed behaviors, a concrete outlook, and a tendency toward aggression against those of lower status. Several studies have found that authoritarians, as compared to egalitarians, were less trusting, less trustworthy, and more competitive in mixed-motive situations (Bixenstine & O'Reilly, 1966; Deutsch, 1960; Wrightsman, 1966). However, Gahagan, Horai, Berger, and Tedeschi (1967) found no difference in these personality types over numerous trials of a game. Their results were represented as demonstrating a washout effect of personality over extended mixed-motive interactions.

Personality dispositions similar to authoritarianism have been found to have effects on interpersonal conflict. Intolerance of ambiguity has been considered a characteristic of authoritarians; hence it should not be surprising that intolerance of ambiguity has been related to protracted conflict and refusal to accept compromises (Druckman, 1967; Pilisuk, Potter, Rapoport, & Winter, 1965; Teger, 1970). Isolationism–Internationalism scales purportedly measure a person's nationalistic perspective and are considered logically similar to authoritarianism. Internationalism is reflected by a trust of other countries, a willingness to see the other side's point of view, and a lack of ethnocentrism; isolationists are described by the opposite tendencies. As might be expected, internationalists are more cooperative than are isolationists in mixed-motive games (Lutzker, 1960; McClintock, Gallo, & Harrison, 1965; McClintock, Harrison, Strand, & Gallo, 1963).

Machiavellianism is a personality constellation that contains such interpersonal orientations as a distrusting and unflattering view of others, a cynical view of the world, and a desire to manipulate the behavior of others (Christie & Geis, 1970). Given the opportunity, high Mach personalities can be expected to attempt to manipulate the behavior of others for the purpose of maximizing their own rewards. Remember that a tit-for-tat strategy is the most effective one for controlling another's cooperative behavior in a mixed-motive game; then it is no surprise that Lake (1967) found that high Machs tended to play a tit-for-tat strategy against their opponents. Both Lake (1967) and Teger (1970) have found that high Machs are likely to meet any deviation from cooperation with immediate retaliation and punishment. Despite these and other findings (cf. Terhune, 1968), the relationship between Machiavellianism and game behavior is not perfectly clear. Several studies have failed to find relationships (Daniels, 1967; Wrightsman, 1966), but other studies have obtained a direct relationship between Machiavellianism and competitive game behavior (Uejio & Wrightsman, 1967).

Cohen (1964) suggests that individuals with high self-esteem are realistic and cope well with whatever circumstances arise, while low self-esteem individuals are defensive, avoidant, and unrealistic in their approach to problems. When told to gain as many points for themselves as they could against a predominantly cooperative robot opponent, individuals with high self-esteem solved the problem well by competing often and thereby maximizing winnings, while low self-esteem individuals cooperated more often and thereby failed to win as much as they could (Pepitone, 1964).

When a highly credible promisor or threatener is added to the interaction and it is in the interest of the subjects to comply to the source's requests or demands, high self-esteem persons comply more frequently than do low self-esteem persons (Lindskold & Tedeschi, 1971b). Throughout all phases of social interaction, including both normal and power-relevant occasions, high self-esteem subjects were more realistic and coped with the circumstances better than did low self-esteem individuals.

Risk-taking propensity as discussed by Kogan and Wallach (1964) refers to an individual's willingness to take a chance in a situation where
there is some probability that either a positive or a negative outcome
could occur. Harnett and Cummings (1968) investigated the relationship
between risk-taking propensity and bargaining behavior in varying de-
grees of uncertainty about the outcomes each party was receiving. When
both bargainers had complete information about all outcomes, risk-taking
propensity had no effect on bargaining behavior; the structure of the situation dominated individual differences. However, when information
about the interaction was minimal, individual differences produced some
effect. Those high in risk-taking propensity made lower initial offers and
showed less inclination to yield from their profit attempting stance than
did those low in risk-taking. High risk-takers frequently bluffed by making unfavorable bids and holding out. Nevertheless, their strategy did
them little good because their profits at the end of the game were not different from those low risk-takers achieved.

Most conflict theorists have stressed the importance of interpersonal
trust in achieving accommodative solutions to conflict (e.g., Deutsch,
1958, 1960; Osgood, 1962; Pruitt, 1965). Individual differences in experiences within conflict situations lead some individuals to develop a
trusting orientation, while others develop a cynical and untrusting orientation. Rotter (1967, 1971) has defined trust as the "expectancy that the
word, promise, verbal or written statement of another individual or group
can be relied upon [1971, p. 444]," and he has developed a scale for
placing subjects along a continuum from low to high trust. An individual
with high trust presumably has had experiences in which, for example,
most people fulfill their promises, and he generalizes similar expectations
to new and novel situations; a low trust individual presumably has the
generalized expectancy that he cannot rely on the communications of
strangers.

Schlenker, Helm, and Tedeschi (1973) investigated the effects on
mixed-motive conflicts of the personality variable of trust as well as the
situational variable of promise credibility. They divided subjects into high
and low trust groups, based on scores on Rotter's Interpersonal Trust
Scale, and made them targets of a simulated player's noncontingent
promises ("I intend to make Choice 1") of either 10 or 90 percent credibility. As hypothesized, subjects did react differently to the promises depending on their own trust scores and the credibility of the promises.
High trust subjects cooperated with the promisor on promise-relevant
trials more than did low trust subjects; high credibility gained greater
promise-relevant cooperation than did low credibility.

Two-choice, nonzero-sum games are quite restrictive of behavioral
choice and hence impose strong restraints on individual propensities. It is

more likely that personality factors will display themselves in experiments that employ enriched games. The findings already gathered provide some strong hints about where the greatest empirical and theoretical yield is likely to be obtained.

In summary, it would appear that most personality variables have an effect on interpersonal behaviors when the situation is not highly structured and does not force certain behavior patterns, when the situation is relatively novel, and when the interaction is in its initial stages. In these conditions personality variables are given some leeway in affecting behavior. Just as important as the individual's personality is the interaction between the personality types of the interdependent parties, a point Kelley and Stahelski (1968a) demonstrate. An excellent survey of the literature on personality and behavior in conflict situations can be found in Terhune (1970).

Numerous experiments have examined the effects of the principals's sex in bargaining situations. Differences in behaviors between the sexes show several rather discernable patterns. Sex role as learned in the socialization process, at least in the United States, disposes the two sexes to develop different styles in interacting with others. Females are more influenceable, more dependent on others, less aggressive, and less adept at problem-solving skills than are males (cf. Janis, Mahl, Kagan, & Holt, 1969; McGuire, 1969; Mischel, 1971). In bargaining situations females tend to react in a more extreme fashion to both the demands of the situation and the behavior of the other party. In general, females adopt an either–or approach to bargaining. If the adversary cooperates, females will cooperate more than would male bargainers, but if the adversary competes, uses threats, or aggressively administers punishments, females will react vindictively, outcompeting their male counterparts.

Terhune (1970) has reviewed the sex differences found in bargaining research. He summarizes the findings in five generalizations.

(1) Women are generally less cooperative in games where they are pitted against another, where there is some interpersonal challenge involved, where strategic coping is necessary. In such situations they tend to become involved in mutually punishing conflict deadlocks and are less "repentent" for their conflictive behavior . . .

(2) Women prefer straightforward accommodative solutions in conflict of interest problems. They generally seek to compromise and will avoid competition. They tend to be more generous and make greater concessions than do men . . .

(3) When placed in a vulnerable position, as when they have been exploited, women react with greater retaliation and apparent vindictiveness than do men . . .

(4) Men use a tit-for-tat strategy more, and tend to be more cooperative in response to a tit-for-tat strategy. Women are more cooperative, if presented

with cooperativeness by the other from the beginning, but once crossed, they are less responsive to cooperative gestures. In contrast, when men are presented with a highly cooperative partner from the beginning, they tend to exploit him . . .

(5) Women have difficulty in comprehending strategic situations, often failing to recognize the "optimal" or "rational" strategy. They fail, for example, to see that threats can be used as signals for establishing and coordinating cooperation . . .

Lindskold and Tedeschi (1971a) argued that females are generally more concerned about presentation of self than are males. Females take cues from both the situation and the behavior of other people to draw inferences about what conduct would look best in the eyes of others. To cooperate and seek accommodation is generally perceived as worthy conduct. Given the opportunity, females will behave in a cooperative and accommodative (good) manner. If others seek competitive advantage, females are concerned (more than males) with saving face and hence react in such situations in a volatile and extremely aggressive manner.

In two experiments designed to test the hypothesis that males are motivated to win (a problem-solving approach) in game situations whereas females are motivated by the "interpersonal nature" of the situation, Kahn, Hottes, and Davis (1971) had subjects of both sexes play a prisoner's dilemma game in which false feedback about the other person's choices was provided. In experiment 1 subjects either were faced with a preprogrammed strategy that was nonreactive to their own strategies or were presented with an adversary who played a tit-for-tat contingent strategy. In a tit-for-tat condition subjects would maximize their own winnings by cooperating, since this action would produce mutual rewards and avoid mutual punishments. In the random strategy conditions competitive behavior would maximize winnings, since it avoids the possibility of exploitation when the random strategy calls for a competitive choice and maximizes payoffs when the random strategy calls for a cooperative choice. It was found that males played in a manner that demonstrated both their problem-solving ability and their desire to maximize gains; they cooperated more in the tit-for-tat condition and competed more in the random strategy condition. Females behaved in a similar manner in both conditions, indicating that they either could not discriminate or would not react to the differences in strategies.

Experiment 2 varied both the strategies of the adversaries and their attractiveness. Males reacted to strategies, and females reacted to the attractiveness of their adversary. Reaffirming the males' problem-solving orientation and maximizing rule, the results showed that males were unresponsive to their opponent's attractiveness but cooperated more when it gained them more to do so (tit-for-tat condition) and competed more when they could gain more by so doing (random strategy condition). Females acted in concert with their concern for interpersonal relationships by generally cooperating more when the other person was attractive and competing more when the other person was unattractive; they were unresponsive to the changes in strategy.

Aside from personality predispositions, attitude structures, and sex, other relationship patterns may be important for the bargaining process. There is substantial evidence in social psychology in general and in the context of compulsory bargaining situations (see Chapters 4 and 5) that source and target characteristics may serve as bases of power or weakness. Unfortunately, no attention has been paid to status, esteem, prestige, and attraction within free bargaining encounters.

Conclusions

A bargaining situation was defined as one in which two or more entities who are in disagreement over one or more issues attempt to reach agreement and arrive at a jointly acceptable solution. In investigating bargaining situations experimentally, social scientists have enriched the typical two-choice game matrix situation by increasing the number of response alternatives available to the subjects and by decomposing the matrix. Although increases in mundane realism per se have little effect on the subjects' behaviors, increasing the number of response alternatives and decomposing a 2 × 2 matrix can increase cooperation. Presumably this increase is a function of subjects' greater feeling of control over their own outcomes and the increased salience of such norms as reciprocity and responsibility.

No adequate theories of bargaining have yet been devised. As a consequence we discussed bargaining and the empirical literature that has been amassed in terms of the processes and goals that can be discerned in a bargaining situation. Four major goals were discussed: discovering the opponent's utility function, disguising one's own utility function, manipulating the opponent's utility function, and altering the relationship patterns between the parties. Finally, the effects of the personality characteristics of the bargainers on the bargaining process were discussed, and evidence was presented to show that the interaction between personality types has a major effect on the bargaining process even when the personality of any one of the parties has little effect.

6

Coalition Behavior in
N-Person Groups

A coalition consists of two or more persons, groups, institutions, or nations that band together to achieve their common objectives against the opposition of a competing party or parties. The importance of coalition behavior can be discerned from the perusal of history textbooks, chockfull of stories and legends about foreign intrigues and political machinations that shaped the fate of nations.

Coalitions occur in all aspects of social, economic, and political life. Most people are aware of a northern Republican–southern Democrat coalition in the United States Senate and of conservative and liberal blocs on the Supreme Court. Similar coalitions occur at all levels of social life, whether it be the state legislature, the city council, or the leadership of the local boy scout troop. Management scientists argue that the dynamic operation of huge corporations cannot be understood without reference to the coalitions that form among executives within and across organizations (March, 1962). The sociological analysis of small groups of necessity involves comprehension of the processes that affect who joins with whom and for what reasons (Mills, 1953; Simmel, 1902). Many of the interpersonal tensions within the family unit result in interfamilial coalitions, such as mother and daughter allied against father, and these coalitions serve to further exacerbate the interfamilial conflicts. In fact, the case can be made that the triad and its omnipresent coalitions are the basic units of social organization.

Simmel's (1902) classical analysis of coalitions did not (until recently) stimulate research on the processes, decisions, and behaviors involved in the formation and stability of coalitions. Almost all of the empirical research on coalitions has been amassed during little more than the past decade, during which time numerous theories have cropped up to explain the behavior of individuals in coalition situations. This chapter will be a review of these existing theories and some of the evidence gathered to evaluate them. Near the end of the chapter we propose an SEU theory of coalition formation that includes many of the ideas and principles of previous theories.

Definition of Coalition Behavior

Coalition processes are the most complex phenomena yet discussed in this book. We have considered primarily dyads up until now, but the minimum number of people involved in coalition behavior is three (i.e., a triad), and any larger number might be involved. The complexity of the processes involved is made evident by examination of the many different kinds of questions an investigator can ask: Who coalesces and why? What size will coalitions of a particular type tend to be? What causes a coalition to win? What determines who will be excluded from a coalition? How will the members of a winning coalition allocate among themselves the outcomes the coalition achieves? As this last question indicates, the bargaining process is integrally bound up with the actual formation of a coalition. The share an individual expects to receive from a coalition plays a large role in his decision about which of several alternative coalitions he will join.

Coalition behavior involves the formation of groups whose intention is to use mutual resources to accomplish some common goal in a mixed-motive situation. The resources that can be pooled include not only material ones, such as money, but also personal ones, such as expertise, status, or attraction. For example, if a coalition of small businessmen is forming to obtain a contract from a large manufacturer, the members of the coalition probably would want to have within it individuals with sufficient money and materials to fulfill the contract once it was obtained, an expert proficient at planning such deals, and possibly a trustworthy friend of the powerful manufacturer. Kelley (1970) has pointed out that it is sometimes difficult to distinguish between behaviors that have been explicitly coordinated for the purpose of achieving some common goal and behaviors that are only accidentally articulated. Thus many unorganized congressmen might coincidentally vote for a bill that was pushed by a coalition of only a very few representatives; only the active group can be called a coalition.

In working toward a goal, a coalition makes a decision that is binding on all relevant parties (some in and some not in the coalition). When a successful coalition in the Congress passes legislation it is binding on the losing coalition of congressmen and on the American public as well as on the coalition members themselves. Ordinarily decisions made as a result of a winning coalition can be binding on a larger group only if all accept some decision rule, such as a majority vote, or if they are influenced through coercion or other means to accept the coalition's decision.

Caplow (1959) suggested that coalitions may take place in three different kinds of situations and that such conditions will have a strong impact on coalition processes. When the object of a coalition in a triad is control over the activities of all three group members in order to obtain control over rewards found in a number of situations, the coalition may be considered a *continuous* one. When a coalition is formed for the purpose of controlling some activities of a group periodically over an extended period of time and across a number of different situations, the coalition may be considered *episodic*. When the purpose of a coalition is to dissolve the group or to redistribute power so that further changes are precluded, the resulting permanent coalition is a *terminal* one. The nature of coalition formation will be importantly affected by whether the situation is continuous, episodic, or terminal.

The context for coalition formation is a group that has within it some conflict of interests. Gamson (1964) stated that only in mixed-motive situations are coalition formation conditions present. In a pure coordination situation the interests of group members are perfectly correlated; hence no reason exists for one subgroup to form to oppose other group members. When pure conflict exists within a group, interests are again perfectly but negatively correlated; only one person can win at the expense of all the others. In such conditions no two persons have enough in common to attempt to coordinate their actions. Thus coalitions can form only when some conflict exists within a group and convergent as well as divergent interests are present. Based on these considerations Gamson (1964) defined a coalition as "the joint use of resources to determine the outcome of a decision in a mixed-motive situation involving more than two units [p. 85]." Similarly, Thibaut and Kelley (1959) considered a coalition as "two or more persons who act jointly to affect the outcomes of one or more other persons [p. 205]."

Theories of coalition formation behavior may be classified roughly into two categories—those that make predictions based primarily on the material resources (capability) of the group members and those that include other interpersonal factors and processes along with those based on resources. Theories in the first group make predictions about which of several possible coalitions will form based on the distribution of power in the precoalition group. The distribution of money, power, votes deliverable on election day—that is, the prestige of group members—plays the major role in determining which of the many alternative coalitions will eventually form and how the coalition that forms will allocate the outcomes it receives. While resource theories postulate processes that occur within the group, their major focus is on the structural or material aspects of the coalition relationship. For the sake of brevity we will refer to these theories as *structural theories* of coalition formation.

Theories in the second group take into account factors other than the distribution of resources, such as the degree of attraction between group members, their statuses, and their concern with norms of fair play. These theories to a greater extent than the structural theories stress the dynamic interpersonal processes that occur during coalition formation; they will be referred to as *process theories.* Both structural and process theories of coalition behavior are concerned with the potential expected gains and losses to each group member as a consequence of his selection of one rather than another coalition partner. Important considerations include the probability that each other group member will reciprocate choices, the probability that each possible coalition will achieve its goals, and the utility of the rewards obtainable in each possible coalition. Let's examine in more detail the various structural and process theories of coalition behavior.

Structural Theories

Most structural theories generate predictions about which coalitions will form on the basis of the precoalition distribution of resources in the group. In one of the first systematic analyses of coalition behavior that yielded empirically testable predictions about which coalitions will form, Caplow (1956) argued that coalition formation depended on the "initial distribution of power" among members of a group. Caplow restricted his analysis to the triad. Although he did not define power he seems to have equated the term with resources, particularly material ones, and is therefore dealing with one component of what we have called prestige. If the members of a precoalition set of people have salient power characteristics, then the following postulates would allow the prediction of which coalitions within the triad will form.

I. Members of a triad may differ in strength. A strong member can control a weaker member and will seek to do so.
II. Each member of the triad seeks control over the others. Control over two others is preferred to control over one other. Control over one other is preferred to control over none.
III. The strength of coalitions takes place in an existing triad, so there is a precoalition condition in each triad. Any attempt by a stronger member to coerce a weaker member in the precoalition condition will provoke the formation of a coalition to oppose the coercion [p. 490].

In a subsequent paper Caplow (1959, p. 492) added two further postulates.

Va. The "chooser" in a triad seeks the maximum advantage or minimum disadvantage of strength relative to his coalition partner.

Vb. The "chooser" in a triad seeks to maximize the strength of the coalition in relation to the excluded members.

If Caplow's postulates are correct, predictions can be made about coalition formation based only on the structural factors in the situation. Table 6.1 shows the predictions made by Caplow's theory for various distributions of power in a triad. Persons A, B, and C are assumed to possess relevant resources—money, votes, or power—and the distribution of resources will determine which coalitions will form. We will consider case 5 in Table 6.1 because it has been a critical one for differences in predictions by various theories. In case 5, A is more powerful than B, B is more powerful than C, but the combination of B and C in a coalition is more powerful than A by himself $[(A > B > C, A < (B + C)]$.

During the precoalition phase A is the most powerful person and has control over both other persons as he interacts with them on a head-to-head basis. Caplow reasons that if A feels he must join a coalition to keep B and C from uniting against him and gaining power over him, he should be indifferent to whether he joins with B or C. In either case A will still control two persons; he will have more power than his coalition partner, and the coalition will have more power than the excluded member.

During the precoalition phase B controls one other person, C, and is controlled by one other person, A. If B were to form an AB coalition he would still be controlled by one person, his coalition partner A, and he would control one person through the coalition, the excluded C. If B were to form a coalition with C, though, he would have control over two persons. He would have more power than his coalition partner C, and the coalition itself would control the excluded A. Therefore, a coalition of B and C represents an increase in control for B and should be most preferred by him.

The relatively powerless C has control over no one during the precoalition phase. Should C join a coalition with either A or B he would increase his power. Either coalition represents a gain in power through control over the excluded member of the triad; C should be indifferent to whether he joins with A or B because he would still be controlled by his coalition partner.

In the triadic situation just considered, A should be equally likely to choose B or C as a coalition partner, C is similarly indifferent between A or B, and B clearly prefers a coalition with C. In order for a coalition to form, a person's choice of a coalition partner must be reciprocated. Ac-

TABLE 6.1. *Triad types, predictions from various theories, and representative results*

Triad Type	Coalitions Predicted by Caplow	Coalitions Predicted by Game Theory	Coalitions Predicted by Gamson	Weights Used by Vinacke-Arkoff	Results of Vinacke-Arkoff
1. A = B = C	Any	Any	Any	1–1–1	Any
2. A >B, B = C, A < (B + C)	BC	Any	BC	3–2–1	BC
3. A < B, B = C	AB or AC	Any	AB or AC	1–2–2	AB or AC
4. A > (B + C), B = C	None	None	None	3–1–1	None
5. A > B > C, A < (B + C)	BC or AC	Any	BC	4–3–2	BC
6. A > B > C, A > (B + C)	None	None	None	4–2–1	None

(From "Sociopsychological Theories and Research on Coalition Formation" by Jerome M. Chertkoff, in *The Study of Coalition Behavior: Theoretical Perspectives and Cases from Four Continents* edited by Sven Groennings, E. W. Kelly and Michael Leiserson. Copyright © 1970 by Holt, Rinehart and Winston, Inc. Reprinted by permission.)

cording to Caplow's analysis either coalition AC or BC should form, since in both cases reciprocated choices are predicted. Caplow went on to assume that in instances where reciprocated choices are observed for more than one dyad, all such dyads should occur with equal frequency.

Caplow makes no clear assumptions about nor does he explicitly consider the allocation of winnings within a coalition. It should be noted that in many of the cases Caplow discusses—for example, case 5—any coalition that forms would win irrespective of the absolute amount of resources members of the winning coalition possessed. In order to make specific predictions based on group members' resources, Caplow appears to assume that two separate concerns of the group members are operative simultaneously. First, members of the triad want to belong to a winning coalition so that they can share in the outcomes accruing to the winners. Second, each person wants to maintain or enhance his power relative to other members of the group, but not just in relation to the outcomes that accrue to a winning coalition on any one particular occasion. Caplow does not consider the bargaining process and subsequent allocation of the resources a coalition wins as important factors in predicting which coalition will form.

In many situations a fixed prize or reward is at stake, and any coalition that forms will automatically win this fixed prize. As long as the probability that *any* coalition that forms will win fixed rewards is held constant, the initial resources or weights of the group members are logically irrelevant in determining the allocation of rewards and/or the formation of coalitions. For example, in case 5 of Table 6.1, where A > B > C, A <

$(B + C)$, it does not matter which two of the three individuals form a coalition, since the coalition that forms wins. The excluded member—no matter who he is—wins nothing. A's slight resource advantage is actually illusory; for all practical purposes he is only as powerful as everyone else.

Vinacke and Arkoff (1957) used such reasoning in developing a *game theory* solution to coalition problems. Actually, game theory itself allows for many different types of analyses and solutions, but for purposes of historical continuity we will call the Vinacke and Arkoff analysis the *game theory* interpretation. As presented in Table 6.1, the game theory solution predicts that since all members of most triads are logically equal in power, any of the possible coalitions should form, and they should form with equal frequency. The only exceptions to this prediction occur when A is stronger than the combined forces of B and C (cases 4 and 6 in Table 6.1). In these instances no coalition should form, since the outcome is predetermined.

Shapley (1953) derived predictions about coalition behavior from a theory of bargaining behavior in n-person groups. His theory presents a normative rather than a descriptive analysis; that is, it prescribes how people should behave rather than describing how they do behave. In his *value theory* Shapley concentrated on bargaining processes and thought that a person should receive an amount proportional to the amount of the long-run rewards his presence secures for a coalition. He assumed that all coalitions will form randomly, given an infinite time span and numerous identical coalition situations. He also assumed that people join coalitions in a particular fixed order (e.g., first A, then B, then C) and can leave a coalition only in the same order. A coalition member has pivotal power when his presence turns a formerly losing coalition into a winning one. For example, if a majority of five is needed to win, the fifth person to join the coalition will be pivotal. The vice president of the United States can be pivotal when Senate votes are tied. He is the last person to vote, and his vote determines the outcome.

Shapely proposed that an individual will receive from a coalition a percentage of the total rewards equal to that person's long-run pivotal power. Pivotal power can be formally defined as the number of times that a person is pivotal in deciding the issue divided by the total number of permutations (all the possible orders of entry of group members into the coalition). On any one trial of an experimental game a pivotal person should be able to demand all of the winnings going to the coalition on that trial, since he turned a losing coalition into a winning one and is therefore responsible for the victory. Everyone will occasionally be pivotal to a coalition, but some persons (those with great resources) will be pivotal more often than others (those with lesser resources). The number of times a person has been pivotal to coalitions is a measure of his value (i.e., power), and in the long run powerful persons receive more rewards than do weaker persons. Harsanyi (1963) has extended Shapley's analysis so that predictions can be made about the allocation of rewards within a single bargaining game.

The assumptions Shapley made obviously do not describe the actual processes that occur during coalition games, a point Kelley (1970) stresses. Nothing is wrong with Shapley's logic, and he has a perfect right to prescribe how pivotal persons ought to act, but there is a clear difference between what people ought to do and what they actually do. Of course, Shapley is quite aware of these considerations and does not contend that his value theory explains actual behavior. Certainly individuals do not demand all of the winnings of a coalition on any given trial of a coalition experiment; the identical conditions for coalition formation do not repeat themselves a large number of times; and persons do not enter and leave coalitions in a fixed pattern, with the last player who enters being considered the most powerful by other coalition members. However, a pivotal person might be perceived as crucial or all-powerful when no replacement could possibly be recruited. Among other things, Shapley's theory serves the heuristic purpose of focusing our attention on the bargaining aspects of coalition formation.

Gamson (1964) has suggested that the theories of Shapley and Harsanyi could be made descriptive, predictive theories. Gamson reasoned that individuals might recognize the importance of pivotal power and demand from a coalition an amount proportional to their pivotal power. The coalition should form that has the minimum possible winning size in terms of pivotal power, which allows the coalition members to maximize their own outcomes by not allocating a share of the spoils to superfluous members. Gamson has referred to the modification of the Shapley value solution as *minimum power theory*. Resources are important to the prediction of the coalitions that form and the way the outcomes are divided, but only as they determine when a coalition will win. Resources thus are taken into account in minimum power theory, but is a manner quite different from Caplow's theory.

In the cases in Table 6.1 minimum power theory predicts the same result as the Vinacke-Arkoff game theory solution; that is, all coalitions should form an equal number of times, and the outcomes should be divided equally among the coalition members except when one person can win by himself, which would obviate coalition formation. This situation is so because the weights chosen for most laboratory experiments allow any coalition that forms to win; so all persons are equals in pivotal power even when they differ in the absolute amount of their initial resources.

Gamson (1961a, 1964) has proposed a *minimum resource theory* of coalition formation that considers both the initial distribution of resources of group members and the problem of bargaining over the allocation of winnings. The core of the theory holds that "a coalition will form in which the total resources are as small as possible while still being sufficient" to win (Gamson, 1964, p. 86). The hypothesized preference for the smallest possible winning coalition derives from consideration of a parity norm that determines the allocation of winnings. A parity norm is a shared belief "by the participants that a person ought to get from an agreement an amount proportional to what he brings into it [Gamson, 1964, p. 88]." The parity norm is identical to Homans' (1961) principle of distributive justice and Adams' (1965) equity principle. The coalition member with the greatest amount of resources can claim the greatest amount of the winnings, since he made a proportionately larger contribution to the coalition. Thus, resources serve two functions in Gamson's theory: (1) resources determine which coalition can win, since unless the coalition is more powerful than any single person or any other coalition, it will not win; (2) resources determine how the payoffs should be divided among the members of the winning coalition.

Minimum resource theory does assume that all individuals are motivated to maximize their winnings and minimize their losses (i.e., maximin). If all individuals behave in accord with a parity norm they can maximize their winnings by ensuring that the coalition to which they give allegiance has as few members as possible. Also, assuming that each individual's resources are fixed, the person can maximize his proportional share of winnings by joining the coalition that possesses just enough in resources to win.[1]

The predictions that Gamson's minimum resource theory makes for each of the six triad types Caplow proposed are presented in Table 6.1. With the logic of minimum resource theory to predict to a case of coalition formation, let's once again consider the triad-type where $A > B > C$, $A < (B + C)$.

Assume that any coalition that forms will automatically win and that $A = 4$, $B = 3$, and $C = 2$. A, who is the wealthiest or most powerful person, should want to form a coalition to forestall a potential coalition between B and C, since a BC coalition would cause A to lose (or at least fail to win). Considering the distribution of the winnings after the coalition is formed, and accepting a parity norm (and expecting that other potential coalition members also accept a parity norm), A should prefer to form a coalition with C. C is the weakest member of the triad and only 50 percent as powerful as A. A can split the winnings 4 to 2 with C but would need to divide the winnings 4 to 3 with B. B would also prefer a coalition with C, because an AB coalition would leave B with less than half the winnings, but in a BC coalition B would receive more than half in a 3 to 2 split. It is clear that C cannot receive as much as half the win-

1. Riker (1962) has independently derived a similar version of minimum resource theory that applies specifically to zero-sum situations with side payments.

nings no matter what he does, but he can certainly do better in a BC than in an AC coalition. Hence, C will prefer B.

In sum, both A and B should prefer C, while C should prefer B. Anytime an individual's choice of a coalition partner is reciprocated, the coalition should form. Therefore, a BC coalition should occur. This prediction differs both from Caplow's and from game theoretic viewpoints for a triad of the type case 5 represents. Before going on to examine process theories of coalition behavior, we will evaluate the structural theories described previously in light of the available experimental evidence.

Empirical Evaluation and Some
Other Emerging Theories

In a test of the predictions of some competing structural theories of coalition behavior, Vinacke and Arkoff (1957) conducted an experiment that has become the prototype for many succeeding coalition studies. Triads of male subjects played a modified parcheesi game in which only the outside 67 spaces were used; power differences were established between group members. The goal of the game was to be the first to travel from the start box to the goal box; the person or persons who accomplished this goal were given a total of 100 points.

On each play of the game the experimenter threw a single die, and the players moved their pieces the number of spaces shown on the die multiplied by a weight assigned to each player. The players' weights (the multiplication factors) represented the resource distribution within the triad and were drawn by the subjects before the start of every third game of the 18 games played. Each player played with six different weights during the course of the experiment; each person's resources changed five times. Weights were distributed so that each of the six types of triads, using the specific weights indicated in Table 6.1, occurred three times during an experimental session.

At any point during the game the subjects could form a coalition by coming to an agreement over division of the 100 points that could be won. When a coalition formed, the two players added their weights together, multiplied this total resource number by the value shown on the die on each play of the game, and moved their pieces the appropriate number of spaces. Once a coalition formed it was indivisible for the remainder of a game. *All* players moved *simultaneously* on each throw of the die, and the actual playing of the game was academic once a coalition formed, since this coalition by the nature of the game had to win.

The results of the Vinacke-Arkoff study are shown in Table 6.1. By and large, the results show substantial support for both Caplow's theory and Gamson's minimum resource theory but show little or no encouragement for either game theory or minimum power theory. The gross predictions of minimum resource theory were supported, and the only real failure to support Caplow's theory was in case 5. When A > B > C, A < (B + C), the coalition BC predominated as predicted by Gamson's minimum resource theory. Caplow predicted that coalitions AC and BC should occur equally often, when, in fact, the BC coalition occurred about two-thirds of the time. The finding that subjects actually do exclude the resource-laden A from coalitions gives rise to the paradox that weakness is strength and strength is weakness, or the so-called *power inversion effect* (Gamson, 1964). The presumably powerful A is continually excluded from winning coalitions and so continually loses, while the less powerful B and C form coalitions and share in the winnings.

In an effort to revitalize the predictive power of Caplow's theory, Chertkoff (1967) has offered a revision of the theory that makes the same predictions as Caplow in all cases but the recalcitrant case 5. In order to explain not only why BC has been found empirically to be the pre-

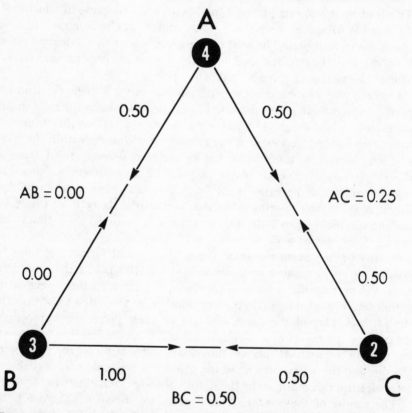

FIGURE 6.1. *Proportions of choices and the resultant proportions of forming coalitions according to Chertkoff (modified from Chertkoff, Jour. Exp. Soc. Psych., 1967, p. 175; copyright © 1967 by Academic Press.)*

ferred coalition but also why a BC coalition does not invariably form, Chertkoff argued that one must look not only at the choices each person makes but also at the proportion of times each choice is made. The proportion of times each individual chooses either of the other two persons as coalition partners must be ascertained; the probability that a coalition would actually form is the product of the probabilities that each pair of people choose each other. Figure 6.1 presents the proportions of individual choices for a case 5 triad, where the weights are distributed as follows: A = 4, B = 3, and C = 2.

According to the logic behind Caplow's formulation, A would be indifferent to choosing B or C and hence should choose each 50 percent of the time. C should similarly be indifferent to choosing A or B and hence should choose each 50 percent of the time. B should always choose C as a coalition partner. When the proportion of times each person chooses each other person is computed, it is found that an AB coalition should never occur (since B would never choose A), an AC coalition should occur one-fourth of the time (since A and B choose each other 50 percent of the time, thereby reciprocating choices only 25 percent of the time), and a BC coalition should occur one-half of the time (since B always chooses C, and C chooses B 50 percent of the time). In the remaining fourth of the cases no choices should be reciprocated and no coalition should form; for example, B chooses C, C chooses A, and A chooses B. Thus, in the long run BC coalitions should be twice as frequent as AC coalitions. Chertkoff (1967) examined data from Vinacke and Arkoff (1957), Kelley and Arrowood (1960), and Chertkoff (1966), and found that the modified predictions quite nicely account for the obtained results.

Thibaut and Kelley (1959) criticized the Vinacke-Arkoff procedures on the grounds that the experiment did not allow a proper test of the logical game theory solution. They felt that by having the subjects periodically change weights during the course of the experiment confusion was generated and the subjects never were able to adequately comprehend that they were actually equals. The changes in weights may have focused the subjects' attention on the resources and consequently caused them to assume that the weights were relevant for the formation of coalitions.

To test the hypothesis that confusion was generated by these extraneous experimental conditions, Kelley and Arrowood (1960) used only one triad type (case 5) and gave subjects the weights A = 4, B = 3, and C = 2. The subjects kept these weights throughout the numerous trials of the experiment. It was found that although subjects predominantly perceived A to be the most powerful at the beginning of the game, excluded him from more coalitions, and allotted him over half the allocated winnings when he was included, there was a clear decrease in such perceptions and behaviors over trials. By the end of the game A was excluded from coalitions no more frequently than would be predicted on the basis of chance alone, which supported their initial hypothesis. However, no differences were found in coalition behavior between the first three trials and the last three trials; therefore, any subject understanding of the specious effects of the resources must have come early, probably during the first or second trial. Nevertheless, even after a considerable number of trials (up to 70 for some triads) there was still a significant tendency to perceive person A as most powerful and to exclude him from coalitions relative to the coalitions that formed between B and C.

Chertkoff (1966) found similar results that more clearly indicated that subjects do come to recognize that they actually are power equals during the course of a coalition game. Although he found that BC was the most preferred coalition initially, the frequency of BC coalitions declined as trials progressed. By the end of the game Chertkoff's subjects were forming each type of coalition equally often.

Apparently the resources do mean something to the subjects, at least initially, and this meaning can change during the game. Minimum power theory, though, has received enough support to remain interesting. In an attempt to assess the impact that an understanding of the rationale behind game theory and Caplow's theory would have on subjects' behavior, Vinacke, Crowell, Dien, and Young (1966) specifically informed subjects about both. During the instructional phase subjects were told that some people viewed the person with the highest resource weight as more powerful than persons with lesser weights, while other people viewed all of the weights as equally powerful, since the weights could in no logical way affect the outcomes for the participants. Even after subjects were given this information, providing reason to disregard the weights, the BC coalition occurred most often. Since the subjects played 24 games it seems unlikely that they were confused or that they were not provided the opportunity to put their information to the test during the course of the experiment. Apparently something more than the mere understanding of the power relationships is necessary to eliminate all vestiges of a power inversion effect.

Minimum resource theory has been rather consistently supported by empirical data. Numerous investigators have obtained overall support for the theory (e.g., Chaney & Vinacke, 1960; Chertkoff, 1966, 1971; Gamson, 1961b; Vinacke, 1962; Vinacke & Arkoff, 1957). Transcripts of subjects' comments during and after coalition games indicate that in line with the rationale behind the theory they perceive the individual with the greatest resources as the person with the greatest power and as the person who is most justified in receiving a larger share of the payoff. As we have seen, this effect does tend to diminish during the course of several games.

Nevertheless, minimum resource theory is far from perfect. In the Vinacke and Arkoff (1957) experiment it was found that although the predicted BC coalition predominated it occurred on only two-thirds of the trials. Minimum resource theory predicts that it should always occur and offers no reason why any other coalition should ever occur. Additionally, Chertkoff (1971) found that although his results generally supported minimum resource theory it did not adequately predict the behavior of the weakest members of the groups. The weak members generally expected and received more in the allocation of winnings than was dictated by parity considerations.

Minimum resource theory presumes that the group member with the greatest resources is rejected by the other group members because they expect him to demand a larger parity share of the winnings. Caldwell (1972) found that when the formation of a coalition per se did not guarantee winning, the member with the greatest resources had little desire to join a coalition, preferring instead to go it alone. Caldwell noted that the high resource player tended to "price himself out of the market rather than being thrown out [p. 279]."

Minimum resource theory was weakened further by Gamson's (1961b) experiment. Subjects participated in five-person groups and were told that each was to assume a role as a delegation chairman at a series of political conventions. Each subject controlled a number of votes and was to use his resources to obtain political patronage or jobs for his constituency. A controlling majority of convention votes constituted a winning coalition, but the task of dividing up the available jobs had to be decided before a coalition could form. In one condition of the experiment Gamson gave five individuals different weights (i.e., votes) of 35, 35, 15, 10, and 6. A coalition of 51 or more votes out of the total of 101 would win. Minimum resource theory predicts that a coalition of 35, 10, and 6 should form, since this combination totals exactly 51, the minimum necessary to win. Yet the 35–35 coalition was the most preferred; it occurred in 6 out of the 24 trials.

Gamson (1961b, 1964) suggested three possible interpretations of the results. First, individuals might prefer to form simpler rather than more complex coalitions. It is simply easier to form a coalition between two persons than among three. While the three persons are attempting to coordinate their actions and get together for a discussion or final agreement, one of them might join another group and walk off with the spoils. As reasonable as this explanation sounds, though, Chertkoff (1971) found that subjects do not necessarily prefer coalitions that involve the fewest formation steps.

Second, Gamson (1964) suggested that people might prefer coalitions between equals if such a state were possible. An equitable division of the rewards between resource equals is immediately obvious; the outcomes are divided equally. The costs of debating over a solution, exacerbating interpersonal conflicts, and determining the equitable solution according to a parity norm are eliminated. If equality does compete against equity, the conditions in which each prediction would hold are yet to be worked out.

Finally, Gamson suggested that the parity assumption may be slightly in error. People might behave according to a parity principle, but in a lesser fashion than he previously supposed. If subjects made a compromise of norms regarding allocation of resources, then departure from the prediction of minimum resource theory in the Vinacke and Arkoff and the Gamson studies can be partially accounted for. However, post hoc interpretations of this sort usually imply that the phenomena under investigation are more complex than the available theory can explain.

Chertkoff (1967) has presented a modified version of Gamson's theory that makes predictions both about which coalitions should form and about how the outcomes should be divided. Chertkoff believes that the existing data can be organized best by assuming that potential coalition partners expect that their share of the winnings from a coalition will be halfway between the parity norm and an equal division of the spoils. Hence Chertkoff's theory combined the virtues of minimum resource theory (parity norms) and minimum power theory (equality). Unfortunately the rationale behind the modification seems less forceful than the rationale behind either theory singly, and the interpretation carries an empirically-oriented flavor. The argument for this equivocation between parity and equity suggests that a strong coalition partner will recognize that he could not have won without the weak member and hence will give the weak member more credit than is justified by considering only his resources. Presumably the weaker party thinks in a parallel way, since Chertkoff assumes that the weaker party will demand more than is justified by his weight.

A person is assumed to choose that coalition partner (or partners) who maximizes his *expected reward*. Expected reward for a person is some share of the total reward to a winning coalition that is halfway between parity and equality. The halfway point is an entirely arbitrary constant included only to allow for predictions to the available data; the constant is revisable in the light of future experimental work. In a recent test of the predictions of most of the structural theories we have discussed, Chertkoff (1971) concluded that although his theory was about as accurate as minimum resource theory in predicting coalition preferences and coalitions that formed, "examination of the data on expected reward and final reward division showed clearly that [his theory's] basic assumption about expected reward is inaccurate [pp. 381–382]." The subjects' expected rewards were closer to the parity norm than to a compromise between the parity norm and equality.

Process Theories: Factors other than Capability

Kelley and Arrowood (1960) suggested that misunderstanding or confusion often focuses the subjects' attention on the resource variable. If confusion were to be further increased subjects might respond in an entirely random fashion, choosing whichever coalition partner is handy. Gamson (1964) expressed his belief that high levels of confusion during coalition games occur more frequently than is often thought. "Pivotal power or resources may not be as relevant to the players as the accidents of propinquity or loudness of voice [p. 102]." Gamson cites evidence from several studies that indicate that subjects may well choose their coalition partners in a random fashion. Interestingly, this *utter confusion theory,* or rather antitheory, predicts the same thing as does game theory or minimum power theory in most triadic experiments; all three predict that the possible coalitions will occur equally often. Gamson suggests that confusion will be generated whenever time pressures are great, numerous potential coalition partners are present, the subjects are unsophisticated (e.g., children), communication difficulties exist, the experimental instructions are complex, and/or the group members are total strangers.

In addition to the possibility of confusion, there is the omnipresent danger that subjects will misunderstand some instructions or misinterpret an experimental situation in terms of their own previous experiences. For example, Chertkoff (1971) reported that in one of his earlier experiments using a political convention paradigm one subject applied his knowledge of real political conventions to considerably alter the meaning of the game. He reports that "one subject in the 20 position in a convention where votes were divided 40–30–20, explained that he chose 40 over 30, because with 30 the margin of victory would be too small. If a few delegates defected from the coalition, the coalition would not have sufficient strength to win [p. 372]." In the experiment no delegate could possibly defect, since the numbers represented indivisible resource blocs.

Vinacke and his associates (e.g., Amidjaja & Vinacke, 1965; Bond & Vinacke, 1961; Uesugi & Vinacke, 1963; Vinacke, 1959; 1962) have found that subjects often do not follow the instructions to maximize their outcomes in coalition games. Rather than play in an exploitative fashion to maximin their outcomes, many subjects behave in an accommodative manner oriented toward maintaining good relations with the other participants and perhaps manage the impressions that the experimenter has toward them. These relational concerns are most pronounced in females. As compared to males, females often formed unnecessary coalitions when one person could have won without a coalition, formed coalitions of the entire triad in order to include all persons in the distribution of rewards, and agreed on equal allocations of the spoils gained by the winning coalition. Vinacke (1959) concluded that males are more concerned with winning, and females are oriented toward accommodative relations.

Similar conclusions about male interest in strategic interactions and female concern with good interpersonal relations have been proposed in other game studies that did not involve coalition formation (e.g., Kahn, Hottes, & Davis, 1971). Gamson (1964) has named these strictly empirical conclusions the *anticompetitive "theory."* According to anticompetitive theory at least some people are more interested in avoiding competition and achieving accommodative solutions than with maximining outcomes associated with money or points in the context of an experimental game.

If anticompetition does occur it should be expected that in some circumstances subjects who are behind in total cumulative payoffs would form coalitions against the person (s) who is ahead in order to achieve some type of overall equality. Several studies have shown that subjects do coalesce against the person who is ahead at the time (Bond & Vinacke, 1961; Emerson, 1964; Hoffman, Festinger, & Lawrence, 1954). Such behavior indicates that in the long run subjects may attempt to equalize not the number of coalitions each enters but the *total cumulative payoff* each person receives.

An overall equalizing process appears at face value to be contradictory to minimum resource theory, since payoff equalization implies that subjects are not attending to the resources arbitrarily distributed by the experimenter (and, we have seen, that behavior is affected by these resources). However, subjects might be performing in accord with minimum resource theory or some other theory on each individual trial as they attempt to equalize the total cumulative payoff to each person. It has been shown that during the course of an experiment all possible coalitions form, and each person receives some payoffs. On any individual trial the winnings may be divided in conformity with a parity norm. According to a parity norm, in either an AB or an AC coalition A would receive the lion's share of the winnings; B and C must form coalitions more frequently together if an equal overall share of the available total winnings are to be distributed across all three parties. Unfortunately, none of the available studies present enough data to fully evaluate this possibility.

If subjects equalize payoffs over the course of an entire experiment, then they might be behaving according to a type of parity norm that most experimenters have not noted. Subjects in a coalition game are faced with two facts: (1) the experimenter gives them unequal resources, and (2) they are peers, usually students at the same school and in the same class, participating in the experiment for about the same reasons, and making about the same investment in time and effort. An equal overall distribution of resources would be consistent with a parity norm, since subjects would be dividing the total outcomes based on the premise that they are status equals. Yet the experimenter has imposed on them an artificial and arbitrary distribution of resources; the joint effect might be that they respond to the experimenter's manipulation (as good subjects) on each trial and they respond fairly to their peers over the course of all trials.

Anderson (1967) presented an argument very similar to the one just elaborated, and he specifically proposed that status differences enter into the formation of coalitions. He defined status rather ambiguously as any evaluative ranking of characteristics that members of groups possess. Anderson's definition thus includes what we have differentiated as attraction, status, prestige, and esteem. Any time that individuals perceive status characteristics among themselves and perceive some goal object (such as a winning outcome) as a payoff that should be distributed according to some status-relevant dimension, the individuals will divide the goal object in proportion to their status inputs. In most coalition situations, the subjects should perceive themselves as equals and divide the total payoffs equally.

This *status theory* has not received sufficient empirical test to warrant firm conclusions. However, Anderson cites as support studies by Emerson (1964) and Hoffman, Festinger, and Lawrence (1954), which show that subjects do try to equalize outcomes by forming coalitions against the person who possesses an advantage in winnings, and Vinacke's (1959) evidence that coalitions of the whole do occur when permitted. The Hoffman, Festinger, and Lawrence (1954) study manipulated status differences prior to a coalition bargaining game. In one group, members were led to believe that one person had an IQ much higher than those of the other group members; in another group all members were led to believe that their IQs were about equal. If we assume that IQ is a relevant status dimension, then status theory would predict that the high IQ person should enter into more coalitions and win more points than the other players. The results supported Anderson's hypothesis.

While subjects might prefer to often change coalition partners to equalize outcomes, switching partners too frequently in high conflict situations can be a rather dangerous practice. Lieberman (1964) proposed the notion of i-trust, or interest trust, by which he means a tendency for subjects to stick with a coalition partner once a stable coalition has formed. In an earlier study, Lieberman (1962) had noticed the development of stable coalitions and felt that subjects come to recognize the importance of a trusted and trusting ally on future plays of the game. A person who frequently changes coalition partners might be viewed as a poor long-term risk and hence be excluded from subsequent coalitions. Consequently, a person might even be willing to sacrifice some small amount of immediate monetary gain that could be obtained by defecting from a coalition in order to develop trust between himself and his coalition partner (s) . If the person can rely on the other person's choosing him (and vice-versa) , the resulting stable coalition may well be in the long-term interests of both parties.

Pressures toward maintaining an established relationship probably occur in laboratory experiments only when a fairly high degree of conflict is present. With lower conflict levels the participants might not mind switching often, since they have less to lose. It might be predicted that the larger the stakes, the more likely the formation of stable coalitions becomes. Also, individuals who are quite high in fear of failure may be more likely to search for stable coalitions than would their low fear of failure counterparts. Many similar interesting hypotheses are generated by the notion of i-trust, but none of them have been systematically studied in the laboratory.

Beginnings of a Decision Theory Analysis

Until now most of the theories and experiments discussed have dealt with situations in which any coalition that forms automatically wins. Yet people seldom can be certain that just because they form a coalition they will win. Rather, a coalition typically has only more or less probability of achieving some goal and winning. Gamson (1964) suggested that decision theory might be used to make predictions in probabilistic situations: "where the probabilities of success of different coalitions vary, the total payoff may be conceived of as the expected value of that coalition [p. 98]." Each player will examine the expected values of each possible coalition and then determine what he can expect to win (according to a parity principle) by multiplying his proportionate weight in the coalition by the expected value of the coalition.

Gamson's suggestion can be readily illustrated. Suppose that when a coalition formed it *might* win a fixed amount of money, say $100. Also assume that the weights assigned the players are: A $= 4$, B $= 3$, and C $= 2$, and that the weight of a coalition is directly related to the probability that the coalition will win. If the probabilities are AB $= .8$, AC $= .6$, and BC $= .4$, then the expected values for these coalitions will be $80, $60, and $40, respectively. What each player can expect within a coalition is based on parity considerations and is a function of his relative weight within the coalition. The expected value of the AC coalition, for example, is $60 (.6 x $100), and the amount won will be split 2–1 in favor of A over C. Thus the expected value of the coalition for A would be $40, and the expected value of the coalition for C would be $20. In our example both B and C should prefer to form a coalition with A, and A should prefer a coalition with B; therefore, the coalition AB should form most frequently.

Chertkoff (1966) examined the situation in which the probability that a coalition would win was dependent on the strength of the individual coalition members rather than the coalition as a whole. Votes at a simulated presidential nominating convention were divided 40–30–20 among the three experimental subjects. Any coalition that formed would have enough votes to nominate one of its members as the presidential candidate. To form a coalition the subjects had to agree which person would be the candidate and then agree how to divide the 100 jobs available should the nominee go on to win the presidency in a general election.

Four groups were created. The first group replicated previous experiments in that any coalition that formed would automatically win the general election. In a second group the subjects were told that each would have a 50 percent probability of winning the election if nominated. In the two remaining conditions both B and C had a 50 percent chance of winning as a nominee, and A had either a 70 percent or 90 percent chance. The outcome of the presidential election (if not automatic) was determined by having the nominee draw a slip of paper from a box containing Win slips and Lose slips. The proportion of Win and Lose slips matched the candidate's probability of winning.

The results provided strong support for the hypothesis that probability of achieving the coalition's goal is directly related to choice of that coalition partner. When the probability of success in the general election was a factor, the greater the probability that A would win the election, the more often B and C chose him. So great was the effect of probability of success that when A had a high (90 percent) probability of winning he was included in most coalitions. That he was included in most coalitions is all the more impressive because it was found that when probability of success was not a factor—when all of the players had an equal (50 percent) chance of success—the weaker players tended to form coalitions against A.

It may be overly ambitious to construct a coalition theory that depends on bargaining processes, as do most of the theories we have discussed, when no sophisticated theory of bargaining is available. Phillips and Nitz (1968) suggest that coalition processes can be divided into an *initial or contact phase* and a *bargaining or decision phase*. The contact phase involves attempts to establish a reciprocal contact with another person; the bargaining phase may involve both the division of rewards and a de-

cision to form a coalition. Chertkoff (1966) found that virtually all reciprocal contacts in the initial phase resulted in coalitions. The complexity
of coalition processes could perhaps be broken down into simpler component processes with the aid of an approach to coalition behavior that
attempts to isolate processes that determine the choices of individuals
during the contact phase, whether or not a coalition forms, and then attempts to predict the development of stable coalitions from the pattern of
individual choices. Ofshe and Ofshe (1969, 1970a, 1970b) take such an
approach.

Ofshe and Ofshe (1970a) argued that "the notable lack of progress in
explaining behavior in the (coalition) game is due to the attempt to treat
both the choice process (selection of a potential coalition partner) and
the bargaining aspects of the game (division of payoffs between coalition
partners) at the same time and without the aid of powerful theories of either of the separate processes [p. 338]." They point out that most theories consider only the factors of resources and rewards but that the experimental data reflect many other variables. Thus the relationship between
the factors of the theory and the behavior of subjects is often obscured.
Ofshe and Ofshe propose that the coalition game be decomposed and
that theories be built to explain the constituent processes (i.e., the choice
process and bargaining).

Ofshe and Ofshe present an expected utility model of coalition behavior that is designed to predict stable states of coalition *choices* in a repetitive choice situation. Tests of this *stable state theory* typically run
subjects through 100 coalition trials (without bargaining) in triads composed of the subject and two robots. The situation is so constructed that
each subject (A) is told that if he forms a coalition with person B he will
receive a fixed amount (say, 5 cents), and if he forms a coalition with
person C he will receive a different fixed amount (say, 10 cents). Each
subject can be given preprogrammed feedback about whether or not either of the two robots (other persons) chose him as a coalition partner
on a particular trial. In this manner the proportion of times a subject is
chosen as a coalition partner can be manipulated. The Ofshes constructed
a model to precisely predict the stable state set of coalition choices that
individual subjects made. The stable state choices were defined as choices
made on the last 20 of the 100 trials.

Basically the Ofshes' model makes three general predictions: (1) the
greater the probability of being chosen by another player, the greater the
likelihood of an individual's choosing that person; (2) as the utility for
choosing a particular person increases, the probability of choosing that
person increases; (3) the more salient equity norms become in any situation (because of decreasing conflict within the triad, stress in experimen-

tal instructions on maintaining equity, and so on), the more a decision maker should distribute his choices among the other persons in order to equalize the amount of rewards each receives. The utility component discussed in prediction 2 above is comprised of the payoffs the subject would receive should a coalition with another person form. Hence this component is analogous to the outcome a subject would receive from the intracoalition bargaining process; rather than actually allowing the subjects to bargain, thus confounding the selection procedure with uncontrolled variables, these rewards are included as a given quantity. The Ofshes have empirically evaluated these three predictions using a rather precise formula for prediction of the proportion of times a subject should choose each of the other members of the triad.

In testing their model Ofshe and Ofshe had subjects arrive at their laboratory in groups of six or nine for participation in a coalition experiment. Each subject was told that he would participate with two peers, but he would not know which of the other people present would be participating with him. In actuality, subjects interacted with a programmed computer through an on-line terminal that simulated the play of the other two members of the triad.

On each trial of the game each person was to choose one of the fictitious others as a coalition partner (players were designated not by names but by numbers). Whenever the computer's program reciprocated a subject's choice, a coalition automatically formed. All coalitions that formed yielded the subject a specified monetary amount without bargaining; thus subjects could always win if they were included within a coalition, though they might win more or less depending on which coalition they were in. If a person's choice was not reciprocated he was not in a coalition and hence won nothing on that trial. Subjects were told how much they could win by forming a coalition with each of the other parties but had no information about the rewards that would be paid to each of the robots. The number of times each of the simulated players chose the subject and each other as coalition partners was systematically varied so that objective probabilities of selection could be controlled.

The results of a series of studies (Ofshe & Ofshe, 1970a, 1970b) provide evidence that closely conforms to the predictions of the expected utility model. In assessing the probability of subjects' choices they found that the greater the objective probability that a person would reciprocate a subject's choice, the more often the subject would choose that person as a coalition partner. For example, when player 1 chose the subject 70 percent of the time and player 2 chose him 30 percent of the time, the subject strongly preferred player 1. In a subsequent study it was found that holding probability of reciprocation constant, the greater the utility that could be achieved through a coalition, the more often the subject would choose that partner. For example, when a coalition with player 1 was worth 10 cents and a coalition with player 2 was worth 5 cents, subjects preferred player 1 as a coalition partner.

Ofshe and Ofshe also tested the third component of their model, which represents the subject's concern for parity in the situation or, literally, how valuable fairness is to the subject in the situation. This concern for equity is considered to be strong enough so that a subject will be willing to take less for himself so that others in the coalition can gain their fair share of the rewards. In a test of this parity assumption subjects received one of three instructional sets and/or expectations. Subjects in different experimental groups were told that they should: (1) maximize their individual gains; (2) carefully note that by excluding any one of the other persons from coalitions they would cause the excluded person to fail to win money; or (3) they would cause the other person to fail to win by excluding him, *and* all three persons would meet after the coalition game to discuss their response choices. This last condition was meant to elicit expectations of future social censure for failure to maintain equitable relationships.

The results for the first half of the game (first 50 trials) supported the model's predictions. Subjects in the third group did display more concern for equity as indicated by the pattern of the coalition choices, and subjects in the first group (told that they should consider only their own gains) showed the least concern for equity. Group 2 fell halfway between the other two groups. During the second half of the experiment group 3 still displayed the greatest concern for equity, but groups 1 and 2 did not differ from each other. Apparently the instructional set that isolated the saliency of the equity principle by itself (group 2) was not strong enough to affect the subjects' behaviors over the course of the entire experiment.

The data do not precisely answer the question of why only group 3 continued to behave equitably. Such behavior could result solely from the effect of the expectation of future meeting with the other two players (and presumably possible social censure for behaving inequitably) or could be a result of the interaction of instructions making the equity norm salient and the expectation of a future meeting. In any event the major conclusion that the utility for equitable behavior is directly related to choices of coalition partners found some support.

Several other studies have indirectly supported the predictions of an expected utility theory of coalition behavior. For example, Vinacke, Lichtman, and Cherulnik (1967) employed the usual parcheesi board game and gave subjects weights adjusted to fit several of Caplow's types of triads. In a deterministic condition of the experiment two dice were thrown, and all players simultaneously moved a number of spaces equal to their weight times the numbers that came up on the dice. Of course, the person or coalition that possessed the greatest weight (s) automatically won. In a stochastic condition of the experiment each subject threw his own dice and moved independently of the throws of the other subjects. When weights were distributed 1–1–1 in the deterministic condition, two subjects could form a coalition, automatically win, and split 50–50; otherwise the game would end in a tie, and the 100 available points would be split three ways (33–33–33). However, in the stochastic condition a person could win all 100 points without forming a coalition; if he was really lucky he could win alone even if a coalition formed against him. Hence the expected utility for *not forming* a coalition would be slightly higher in the stochastic condition than in the deterministic condition. The results showed that fewer coalitions formed in the stochastic than in the deterministic conditions.

In summary, the application of decision theory to coalition behavior looks very promising. Chertkoff analyzed coalition behavior from an expected reward framework that included the probability that a coalition once formed would succeed and the rewards to be received from the coalition. The Ofshes analyzed coalition behavior from an expected utility framework that included the probability that a choice would be reciprocated and the utility of the coalition. These components can be combined in one general theory of coalition behavior that incorporates some of the precision of the Ofshes' approach and some of the richness and complexity of real world situations.

SEU Analysis of Coalition Behavior

A subjective expected utility theory of coalition behavior should include factors that determine whether an individual will elect to try to get into a coalition and, if so, which coalition partner he will choose. Knowing these decisions for each member of a group provides the basis for a prediction of which coalition, if any, will actually form. One way of presenting the necessary factors involved in a decision theory approach is shown in Figure 6.2. Again we presume that an individual will choose the alternative that has the highest SEU; that is, a coalition will be selected whenever the SEU for joining a particular coalition is greater than the SEU for not joining. When several coalition partners are available, and the SEU for not joining any coalition is less than at least one of the coalition choices, the coalition that maximizes SEU will be chosen.

Person A in Figure 6.2 must elect to form a coalition with person B or person C or remain unallied. The SEU of A's choosing B or C will be de-

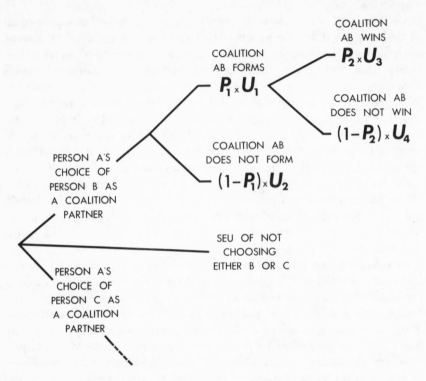

FIGURE 6.2. *Representation of A's choice alternatives in a coalition situation in a triad.*

termined by many factors. First, A must subjectively estimate the probability of reciprocation from B if A chooses B as a coalition partner (P_1);
this is the subjective probability to A that the coalition will form. This
probability is determined by such factors as the objective probability that
in past encounters B chose A and the personal characteristics of B (as
will be seen).

The utility (U_1) of a coalition, irrespective of whether it achieves the
precise goal it set out for (winning), is also comprised of several factors.
For example: affiliation with persons of high status or prestige may be
ego enhancing; satisfaction is derived from not being left out; some material rewards might accrue irrespective of an actual victory; and one's allies provide security. The utility of choosing B, though, might contain
some cost components, such as shunning old friends or forming a coalition with an enemy. Each of these components of the utility of choosing
B must be combined, since they are all associated with the same probability (i.e., that the coalition AB will form).

Once a coalition forms it stands some probability of achieving its goal (e.g., winning). The worth of winning is dependent on A's subjective probability estimation of the AB coalition's winning (P_2) or not winning $(1 - P_2)$ and the utilities associated with each possibility. Factors that contribute to the utility of winning (U_3) might include potential monetary gains, personal satisfaction derived from perceived approval for achieving success, and the accrual of status and/or prestige increments. Of course, winning does not imply that no costs are involved, such as the cost that might accompany defeat of an old friend who was excluded from the coalition. The utility associated with not winning (U_4) may include such factors as loss of monetary gains, loss of status and prestige, dissatisfaction due to disapproval of failure, and possible retaliation from the winning coalition.

If B does not reciprocate A's choice, an event that will occur with a probability of $(1 - P_1)$, an AB coalition will not form. Presumably most of the utilities (U_2) associated with the coalition's not forming after A's selection of B would be negative and might include such factors as loss of face, loss of time, and loss of monetary incentives.

A's SEU for choosing B as a coalition partner is determined by computing the probabilities and utilities of each of the possible consequences of that action; the coalition forms (and then there is some chance it will win), or the coalition does not form. The consequences of the coalition's forming are computed as the probability that the coalition will form times the utility $(P_1 U_1)$.

Should the coalition form, it will either win or not win, and these consequences must be taken into account. They are figured as $(P_2 U_3)$, or the probability that the coalition will win times the utility of winning, and $[(1 - P_2) U_4]$, or the probability of the coalition's not winning times that utility. These two components are added together and then multiplied by $(P_1 U_1)$, since they are contingent on the occurrence of the coalition's forming. The resultant value is the component of SEU associated with the consequences of the AB coalition's forming.

Certain consequences also are associated with the AB coalition's not forming, and they are computed as $[(1 - P_1) U_2]$, or the probability of the coalition's not forming and the utility of the coalition's not forming. The values obtained by computing the consequences of the AB coalition's forming and its not forming must be added together, and this final value represents the SEU for choosing person B as a coalition partner. The entire formula for calculating the SEU for choosing B can be represented mathematically as:

$$SEU_{AB} = \{ (P_1 U_1) \times [(P_2 U_3) + (1 - P_2) U_4] \} + (1 - P_1) U_2.$$

The SEU for the choice of person C as a coalition partner is determined in a similar fashion. Finally, the SEU for remaining unallied and electing not to join a coalition must be determined. A should select the choice alternative that has the highest SEU.

Some basic predictions can be derived from the preceding analysis. First, the greater the subjective probability that a coalition will either form or win, the more likely that it will be chosen. Second, the greater the utility for forming a particular coalition or the greater the utility of winning, the more likely it will be to be chosen. Third, the greater the probability or utility of going it alone, the more likely it will be that a coalition will not be selected. All of these predictions have received support in the literature previously reviewed.

In preceding chapters we have continually noted that source and target characteristics are typically implicated in the influence relations between persons. Except for the possession of resources (i.e., prestige) very little attention has been paid to such personal characteristics in coalition formation. Yet we could expect that source and target characteristics will produce important effects on both the probability and the utility components of SEU and hence the subsequent choices of coalition partners. With little but insecure intuition as a guide we will offer a few very tentative hypotheses.

PRESTIGE

Another person's prestige, it will be recalled, is a multiplicative function of the amount of disposable resources he possesses and the perception that he intends to use them (here for the purpose of forming a winning coalition). Since most laboratory studies that have manipulated resources (i.e., weights) have created conditions in which any coalition could win and a person had to join a coalition if he wanted to share in the spoils, the intention to join a coalition must have been quite high. Thus any person who chooses to join a coalition must automatically use all of his resources to help the coalition, and the prestige component therefore depends primarily on an individual's capability.

Even though almost all coalition experiments are concerned with resources, the effects of prestige on the coalition process is not unambiguously interpretable. The problem is that the experiments have confounded the contact and bargaining phases of coalition formation and have used the number of coalitions formed as a dependent variable rather than subjects' individual choices of coalition partners. Nevertheless, it is possible to discern two competing effects of prestige on coalition behaviors. First, an individual with high prestige normally increases the probability that a coalition in which he is a member will achieve its goal. In most real-world situations resources and probability of winning are positively correlated: the more resources a person possesses, the greater is the probability of a coalition's winning if it includes that person. The SEU for choosing a high prestige person thus will be raised for a member of a precoalition group who must choose between coalition partners. However, when one has an ally with high prestige that ally should demand a greater proportion of the outcomes accruing to the coalition because of the operation of parity norms. Hence the utility that can be gained by joining a coalition with a high prestige person is lowered.

The prestige of potential coalition partners, then, acts to increase the SEU for choosing them because of the increase in the probability that the coalition will achieve its aims, but it decreases SEU because of the decrement in utility to be derived from intracoalition bargaining. Therefore, in situations in which the probability of success component is more salient than the bargaining phase a person's prestige would be directly related to the frequency of choosing him as a coalition partner; in situations in which the bargaining phase is salient a person's prestige should be a detriment to him, and a power inversion effect should occur. Chertkoff (1966) has provided indirect support for these predictions.

ATTRACTION

All else constant, differential liking for members of a precoalition group should bias choices of coalition partners. The more a person is liked and is perceived as reciprocating that liking, the higher will be the perceived probability that choice reciprocation should occur. Also, the utility of being in a coalition with a liked person should be greater than the utility of coalescing with a disliked or neutral person, since liked people are more enjoyable to work with, should cause least conflict and tension in bargaining over the distribution of rewards, and should give the chooser an equal share of the outcomes. Therefore, the SEU for forming a coalition with a liked person should be higher than the SEU associated with coalitions with disliked people. In support of the hypothesis that attraction is directly related to choice of a coalition partner, Trost (1965) found that persons who are attitudinally similar (and therefore presumably are attracted to one another) tended to form coalitions more often than those who were dissimilar. Helm, Nacci, and Tedeschi (1973) obtained similar results in a role-playing study of coalition processes.

A complicating factor may be introduced when both prestige and attraction are differentially distributed in a precoalition group. Attraction probably encourages an equal distribution of rewards in the bargaining phase of coalition behavior, and prestige encourages use of a parity principle during bargaining. It might be predicted that a person who possesses superior resources might avoid forming coalitions with friends, since by so doing he may forfeit the extra share he could claim through a parity principle from a coalition partner where attraction was not a factor in determining coalition choices. Attraction thus can reduce the utility of a coalition when the chooser must shift from a parity to an equality norm during bargaining. No evidence is available to evaluate this hypothesis.

ESTEEM

A coalition partner may be preferred because he possesses special expertise in planning goal-oriented activities or attracting other members to the coalition or can otherwise apply his special competence to increasing the probability that a coalition that includes him will have a higher probability of achieving its objectives. Such special expertise also may imply that a highly esteemed person may gain advantages in bargaining. Thus it might be predicted that esteem will produce exactly the same kinds of contradictory forces on coalition choices that occur as a function of prestige. When winning is stressed, esteem should enhance the probability that a person will be selected as a coalition partner, a hypothesis supported by Helm et al. (1972), but when bargaining is stressed, esteem should decrease the probability that a person will be selected as a coalition partner.

STATUS

Status, defined as the prerogatives associated with a person's role position, should have important effects on coalition formation. High status should contribute to the probability that a coalition would win, since deference to the high status member might be expected from other group members. The high status person's authority may deter opposing coalitions from forming, thereby enhancing the prospects of any coalition that includes him. Also, excluding the high status person from a coalition could portend future retaliation, thereby decreasing the utility of all coalitions that did not contain him. However, the high status person is likely to seek a larger share of the rewards, thus decreasing the other members' utility of a coalition with him. A high status person has a *right* to receive more from a group, and excluding him from a coalition should produce guilt and anxiety, thus increasing the costs for choosing other coalition partners. The net result of all of these considerations is that the loss in material rewards associated with choosing a high status person may cost less than the psychological costs associated with not choosing him.

Michener and Lyons (1970) studied the formation of "revolutionary coalitions"—that is, coalitions that exclude a high status member. They found that a low status person's tendency to form revolutionary coalitions depended on the perception that other low status members were supporting or not supporting the legitimacy of the high status person. When group dissatisfaction with the leader was high, revolutionary coalitions did form frequently. A high degree of support for the high status person from other group members deterred members from forming revolutionary coalitions. Michener and Suchner (1972) suggest that these findings occurred "not only because a high level of perceived support diminishes a person's subjective probability of successfully forming a coalition, but because it palliates his dissatisfaction with the existing status arrangements [p. 259]."

Conclusion

The empirical literature on coalition behaviors is only beginning to grow, and exploration of the area promises an exciting new scientific endeavor. Structural theories of coalition behavior have tended to ignore the social aspects of interpersonal behavior as they center on the power or resources of group members and use these factors to predict coalition behavior. While several well-formulated structural theories exist, they all seem inadequate on empirical grounds. Process theories have attempted to incorporate social factors but, except for some decision theory attempts, have not been adequately formulated.

The SEU theory of coalition behavior stated here attempted to delineate significant factors in an individual's determination of the choice of coalition partners. These factors include the probability of having one's choice of a coalition partner reciprocated, the utility of forming a coalition, the probability that the formed coalition will achieve its goal, and the utility of the goal. Prestige, attraction, esteem, and status were assumed to systematically effect one or more of the above factors and hence play a crucial role in the selection of a coalition partner.

The study of coalition behavior has focused on continuous and has ignored episodic and terminal coalitions. Many real-world coalitions are formed as defensive alliances to protect the status quo rather than to offensively seek additional gains; yet only accrual situations have received research attention. Certainly much more work must be done before the principles underlying coalition behaviors can be clearly discerned.

7

Games as Research Tools

In recent years much heat and controversy has been generated about the purposes and usefulness of experimental games. Games have been considered as theories, models, simulations, and experimental paradigms; some have viewed games as analogues of real-world conflicts on an international scale; others criticize research with games as too trivial to tell us anything of merit about human behavior. We will examine the various viewpoints and will conclude that games are experimental paradigms and as such need to be examined in terms of validity questions relevant to any experiment. Questions of the relevance or merit of game research usually are questions about theories, not experiments. Game experiments, it will be argued, are valuable if they provide evidence for or against theories of social conflict and power.

Some General Viewpoints on Games

The rationale for advocating the central nature of games in understanding broad laws of human interaction probably came first from George Herbert Mead (1934). He argued that each individual comes to define his very self-concept as a distinct entity by engaging in play and games with peers. In games, Mead noted, the individual participates in organized social activity and hence learns to distinguish himself from the other players and to distinguish both self and others from the generalized (societal) rules or norms governing the interaction. Huizinga (1950) has taken a somewhat similar view of play and games in the development of both individuals and societies, and has even suggested relabeling the human species *Homo Ludens* (Man the Player) to reflect this basic game-playing propensity in human behavior.

Coleman (1969) has propounded a generalized view of the socialization processes and life as a supergame, complete with rounds and time-outs. Coleman suggests that gaming techniques used by the social sciences capture the essence of much social behavior. The argument of gaming advocates is simply that the processes of securing one's identity, learning cultural roles, and just plain living can be represented as game-playing behaviors. According to gaming advocates, then, it follows that the use of games in the laboratory has the potential for unraveling many of the dilemmas that have confronted social scientists for so long.

Those who hold detracting opinions about the usefulness of games view gaming advocates as especially inclined toward Kaplan's (1964) law of the instrument: "Give a small boy a hammer, and he will find that everything in sight needs pounding [p. 28]." The critics of gaming techniques argue that (1) indiscriminate application of gamelike analyses to policy planning has led to unfortunate consequences because the focus tends to be on conflict and coercion to the exclusion of ethical and political alternatives (Rapoport, 1964; Wilson, 1968); (2) research evidence has been erratic, unreliable, chaotic, and immune from theoretical integration; and (3) the arbitrary rules and trivial outcomes experimenters provide do not tap the rich behavioral repertoires of subjects and do not elicit powerful motives. Hence the results from experiments that use games are judged to be trivial and uninteresting.

Before a middle ground between the two extreme viewpoints can be offered, some conceptual ambiguities must be clarified, the criteria of good experiments must be examined, and the question of the application of scientific knowledge to problems of everyday life must be considered. Some confusion exists in distinguishing between computer models, man–machine simulations, and experimental games. Games often are evaluated on the basis of criteria applicable to computer models or criticized because of deficiencies noted for man–machine simulations instead of strictly on the merits of research design and experimental controls. Analogies to real life can be drawn easily from game situations and seduce some into generalizing from a single experiment to make prescriptions for problems of everyday life. Yet, that hasty generalizations occur does not reflect so much on the research tool as it does on the lack of practitioner judgment. We will examine each of these problems in turn.

Machines, Models, Simulations, and Games

Metatheoretical discussion often bogs down because of the difficulty of gaining consensus about the basic assumptions and definitions offered in behalf of a presented thesis. Of course, definitions are arbitrary. The value of any definition is in where it leads us in dialectic or theory. With this in mind, we will offer our definitions and attempt to follow the path they establish.

We will define a *model* as a closed mathematical, verbal, or pictorial system based on an analogy and proposed as a simple but inclusive representation of some aspect of the real world. A model is an attempt to simplify an aspect of the real world that is of concern to the model builder, and it contains all those variables in the real world that the model builder deems necessary for accurate representation of the phenomenon under consideration. The history of science is replete with examples of prominent models. The wave theory of light was based on an analogy with sound waves, and the emission theory of light was built on the image of projectiles moving along a straight line. Insights into the structure of the DNA molecule were gleaned from a model built of tinker-toy components. An example of a practical use of model building is the work of technologists who attempted to provide formal and efficient decision-making techniques for the design of air defense operations during the World War II air battle over Great Britain. Symbolic models and mathematico-deductive processes were devised to predict the effects of various solutions to the defense problem and to determine the optimal solution for defending against German aircraft and rockets. These quantitative techniques constituted what came to be known as operations research.

Formalized analogies or models have sometimes led to important theoretical advances in science; then the model is incorporated into the language of more general theories. That is, a successful model is one that is superseded by a more general scientific theory.

When the electronic computer was invented it was only natural for operations researchers to take advantage of the machine's enormous capabilities for processing quantitative and logical symbols. The result was the development of computer simulations of real-world problems. An *all-computer simulation* is a model of some structure or process written to be examined and evaluated on a computer. It may have as its purpose a careful examination of what happens when one or more values or relationships in the model are slightly modified—that is, an examination of changes in some dependent variables that accompany changes in the parameters of the model. An all-computer simulation provides a rapid mechanism by which a mathematical model can be manipulated systematically to test its assumptions or to closely approximate some criterion for model outputs.

Because in principle almost anything can be simulated, a plethora of simulations have been produced, including simulations of the workings of investment trust offices, department store operations, human thought processes, human personalities, research and development strategies, and agricultural soil testing. Models are not empirically evaluated in the same way as scientific theories, but rather are examined with respect to assumptions, logical consistency, and good fit to the system being modeled.

A recent invention has been an attempt to weld together a partial model with actual human decision makers. In a *man–machine simulation* the model represents the structural features of a situation, which has its own laws and operates in ways to facilitate or constrain the behaviors and/or decisions of the human actors. The outputs of the man–machine simulations depend on both the logical and human components of the system. A simple man–machine system, such as a cadet learning to fly a dummy plane on the ground, may lead to changes in control systems, techniques of teaching, or personnel selection, and hence may be useful for many purposes. However, the more people involved and the less control that the researchers have over the factors that determine behavior, the more ambiguous the interpretation of results is likely to be.

Much of the skepticism directed at experimental games derives from a confusion between games and partial simulations of internation behaviors, where parameters and functions are programmed on a computer, and individuals are asked to act as national decision makers. The human actors (possibly as many as 30 or more in one man–machine simulation) can make decisions on domestic policies, trade and aid agreements, alliances, war and peace, and so on, within the context of a complete model of the world political scene. Such man–machine simulations represent the worst of two possible worlds. As models, no system output is clearly traceable to specific changes in parameters or functions. As experiments a lack of control over the factors that determine human decisions produces irreconcilable difficulties in identifying empirical regularities.

Two basic virtues of man–machine simulations have been claimed. First, Raser (1969) believes that heuristic benefits are likely to be gained because of the ability to observe confrontation, communication, involvement, and role-playing in complex situations. In a sense, one has the world in front of him and is therefore likely to gain insights that would not accompany a view from a greater distance. Second, Coleman (1969) has argued that man–machine interactions can be used successfully as teaching and training aids; for example, students of international relations might develop a better feel for the problems of national decision makers by participating in internation simulations.

However, skepticism about these two claims also exists. Stoll (1970) has reacted to the heuristic argument by saying that intuitive insight can be gained from any source—empirical research, formal logic, mathematical modeling, and so forth. There is no necessary reason why a man–machine simulation should lead to insights that are any more fruit-

ful than reading the Sunday *Times,* and the newspaper is much less expensive and time-consuming than the simulation. In a recent review
Cherryholmes (1966) concluded that student interest is apparently stim-
ulated by man–machine experience, but no evidence exists that there is
any effect on learning or problem-solving efficiency. In any case no virtue of complex man–machine simulations has been so outstanding as to
quiet criticism. The case for man–machine simulations is yet to be proven.

Games have historically been differentiated from simulations in that
games as tools are: less inclusive than simulations (Dawson, 1962) ; employ human participants (Guetzkow, 1968; Raser, 1969) under typically
less stringent and unspecified conditions (Barton, 1970; Dawson, 1962;
Guetzkow, 1968; Raser, 1969) ; severely restrict the number and type of
responses available to the participants to conflict (Abelson, 1968; Zinnes,
1970) or explicitly instruct them on the criterion of task success (Abelson,
1968) ; and are more oriented toward gaining information about human
beings than about the research tool (Raser, 1969) . A reasonable argument
can be made for each proposed distinguishing factor in some specific
cases, but few cases would discriminate all of these distinctions. The one
consistent difference between games and simulations is that while games
concentrate on the structural aspects of, say, a conflict situation and leave
the functional relationships between relevant process variables to empirical
determination through human decisions, simulations attempt to form a
coherent theoretical model of the situation beforehand and then observe
what happens when system parameters are manipulated.

Not only does the prime focus of games differ from that of simulations, but also, as we have seen, the functions that each technique serves
in the strategy of scientific inquiry also sharply differ. Simulations attempt to serve at least a partial explanatory function; the purpose of experimental games is clearly that of empirically testing scientific theories
and aiding in the discovery phase of science by providing new data relevant to conflict interactions. Simulations hold the status of theoretical
models; games are clearly experiments.

Experimental Games

Because the focus of this book is on games rather than on computer or
man–machine simulations, and because there are so many misconcep-
tions about the research use of games, it will be necessary to examine in
some detail a rather formidable array of issues. Many pseudoissues have
been generated by social psychologists who have misused games as research tools or have claimed far too much in the way of generalizing results to value-laden contemporary domestic and international policy formation.

Many social scientists who use games as research tools are action-oriented and use their research results as propaganda in support of their value commitments. Analogues of disarmament, inspection procedures, unilateral initiatives to reduce conflict, and many others have been used as the basis of designing research. The investigator intuitively abstracts from a real-world problem those ingredients he believes to be critical and attempts to build a *logical* analogue of those elements into his laboratory. On the basis of one-shot hypotheses and by moving back and forth between the real-world problems and his laboratory, the action-oriented technologist attempts to arrive at prescriptions for solving problems. Hence, the results of two-person game studies often are interpreted in terms of international relations or racial or domestic conflicts, and prescriptions are offered unblushingly to the appropriate decision makers. These decision makers more often than not will see *relevance* in the technologist's work and will provide funds to further it. To understand why the technologist's approach in using games as analogues of real-world problem situations is misdirected will require an excursion into the nature of scientific theory, the logic of experimentation, the history of research paradigms in psychology, and the applicability of scientific knowledge for practical affairs.

THE NATURE OF SCIENTIFIC THEORY

Science itself may be viewed as a game whose goal is to develop true theories. Each player must abide by a set of rules on the logical and empirical evaluation of theories. In a sense the grand strategy of science is to develop theories, and the tactics involve the use of empirical methods, the most important of which is experimentation. The purpose of a theory is explanation, and the purpose of an experiment is to isolate cause–effect (functional) relationships, which are predicted by a theory.

Observation of events in the world produces images in the minds of men. These images are often explicated in the form of linguistic, logical, or mathematical symbols. Images in any form are highly manipulable. An elephant, for example, may be pictorially represented as small, huge, pink, possessing five legs, or whatever. Relating symbols together in a logically consistent manner represents one requisite in the construction of scientific theories, but the system of formalized images (concepts) must then be articulated with primitive images gained from observations of events under highly controlled conditions. A theory contains (1) a set of concepts that define those aspects of phenomena one wants to understand and (2) a set of postulates about the relationships presumed to hold among the concepts.

Few would be interested in an experimental result that was unique and probably would never occur again. Scientists want to develop such generalizations as "water freezes at 32° F.," but this particular generalization is of a rather low grade nature called an *experimental law*. What has been specified is the relationship between temperature on the one hand and the density of water on the other hand. Although the functional relationship of the concepts of temperature and density has been specified, the observation predicted is very specific and does not allow articulation with as many events as scientists would like. If each scientific theory were limited to the statement of a single experimental law, there would, of necessity, be as many scientific theories as there are recurrent and connected primitive images. In addition, our curiosity is not satiated by the knowledge that water freezes at a particular temperature. The question why remains to be answered.

"Why?" is answered by deduction from theories and constitutes the explanatory function of science. Formal theories are constructed in science just as in mathematics, where definitions are explicated, axioms assumed, and theorems deduced from a set of axioms. A theorem in a scientific theory usually consists of a testable hypothesis. Unlike mathematics, where logical proof is sufficient for the test of the truth of a system of symbols, scientific theories must stand the tests provided through controlled observations. The scientist is faced with three classes of problems: construction of theories, determination of significant fact, and the matching of facts with theories. Schlick (quoted in Frank, 1961) has indicated one criterion for the truth of a theory: "Every theory is composed of a network of conceptions and judgments and is *correct* or *true* if the system of judgments indicates the world of facts uniquely [p. 39]." Of course, if two or more theories can equally well deduce the facts, by this criterion each must be judged to be equally true. It is the inevitable imperfection of the theory–data fit that defines many of the problems scientists pursue.

Experimental laws, which are generalized statements from observed relations, may be said to explain phenomena in that they depict the relationships between antecedent conditions and consequent events. Experimental laws can be developed by systematic research and do not depend on broader theories. By their very nature, however, experimental laws are typically restricted to readily identifiable and qualitatively similar events. Theories, though, can explain (deduce) what appear to the naïve observer to be strikingly dissimilar qualitative events. Newton's laws of motion explain planetary motion, freely falling bodies, tidal action, shapes of rotating masses, and much else. But not even Newton's genius could produce a theory that could explain all the facts with which it could be confronted. And so the search goes on.

In the history of the natural sciences it has been quite unusual for a new law to be discovered or suggested simply through experimentation, observation, examination of the data, and subsequent generalization. Campbell (in Kaplan, 1964, p. 303) asserts that almost all advances in the formulation of new laws follow the construction of new theories to explain the old laws. Conant (1952) agrees and says flatly that "the history of science demonstrated beyond a doubt that the really revolutionary and significant advances come not from empiricism but from new theories [p. 53]." In the context of this book, then, we should not expect that we will discover very many new laws from the use of experimental games as research tools. Rather, we should ask whether this new tool is useful for testing existing scientific theories. The experimental method is inseparable from the development and evaluation of theories.

Theories are systematic organizations of knowledge. The organization is tidier the fewer the assumptions (postulates or axioms) the theory makes. In a sense the scientist has the same goal as the poet, who attempts to use linguistic symbols as economically as possible to express his view of some aspect of the universe and so produce an aesthetic effect. The scientist serves a poetic function, but has the additional burden of testing out his views. The goal of the scientist is not aesthetic appreciation but, rather, a true explanation for some aspect of the universe. As Homans (1967) expressed it in the language of games, "The winner is the man who can deduce the largest variety of empirical findings from the smallest number of general propositions. . . [p. 27]."

The words the poet uses may be quite ambiguous, and a free use of metaphor or simile allows the reader to decipher many different meanings from the same poem. Much of the profoundness discovered from literature is a function of symbolism and ambiguity of interpretation. The scientist's language does not permit ambiguity, since precise deduction of theorems would become impossible, and then no empirical test of the theory could be made. Empirical tests of theorems or hypotheses require the careful explication of the relevant concepts used in the theory. Empirical operations represent partial definitions of theoretical concepts and are often called *operational definitions.*

Operational definitions assign meaning to a concept by specifying the activities or operations necessary to measure the concept in question (Kerlinger, 1964). For example, the concept of *anxiety* may carry complex theoretical meaning, and many partial empirical operations may be performed to measure it. A paper-and-pencil scale may provide one measurement approach; measurement of heart rate, respiration rate, or physiological arousal may constitute other approaches. Although the operational definitions of anxiety may differ, they are hopefully measuring various aspects of the same theoretical construct.

These two facets of scientific inquiry—the collection of data as dictated by the scientific method and the incorporation of a large number of particulars under a small number of precise general statements or laws —operate in a cyclical fashion to promote discovery and explanation in science (Kemeny, 1959; Marx & Hillix, 1963). First, data about some phenomenon is collected in a systematized and controlled fashion; second, these observations are generalized and subsumed by way of explanation under more general laws or in theories; third, the law or theory is reapplied to new situations in the form of specific predictions of hypotheses. Thus, as more formally stated by Marx & Hillix (1963), science may be said to be concerned primarily with the movement from empirical systems (facts and data) to theoretical systems (general explanatory principles) and back again to the empirical domain in the form of theoretically derived hypotheses by way of operational definitions.

All three steps are essential to the tactics of scientific inquiry: without the continuing collection of new facts and data we would speak not of science but rather of technology, which is just the application of existing theoretical principles to new situations. Similarly, without the theoretical "middle space" promoting generalization and systematization of data, one could only speak of compendiums of facts such as are found in cookbooks, seed catalogs, and encyclopedias. Finally, if data were only collected once and then generalized as firm and immutable truth, one would be in the position of the theologian poring over books of doubtful relevance as the sine qua non of dogmatic interpretation. Thus it is not just some of the components but the entire data–theory–hypothesis–data cycle that promotes the advance of scientific knowledge and explanation.

THE LOGIC OF EXPERIMENTATION

The scientific method refers to the means by which evaluation of theoretical propositions is carried out. The method must be rigorous and the results publicly communicable, and the experiment should ordinarily be replicable. More formally, we may define an *experiment* as a test of a cause–effect relationship in which two or more contrasting conditions are observed and all the factors except those of interest are controlled. When experiments are used to test hypotheses (which usually are derived from more general theories) they are called *hypothetico-deductive experiments* (Jones & Gerard, 1967) or *nomological experiments* (Kaplan, 1964). What to control, what to vary, what to measure, and so on, are experimental questions that rely on theoretical considerations; thus theory and experiment are inextricably bound together. Once the theoretical considerations are satisfied, the observed facts can either confirm or disconfirm the hypotheses. As Homans (1967) has put it: "Nature, however stretched out on the rack, still has a chance to say 'No!' [to theories] [p. 4]."

Although hypothesis-testing experiments probably are the most important in science, research often does have other functions. Kaplan (1964) and Jones and Gerard (1967) suggest four purposes besides testing theories. In practice, of course, any single experiment may actually serve more than one of these purposes. *Illustrative experiments* usually are performed for the purpose of demonstration. Every student is familiar with the illustrative experiments in physics, chemistry, and psychology classes. *Methodological experiments* consist of attempts to standardize tests or apparatus, which then can be used for hypothesis-testing purposes. *Exploratory experiments* are based on hunches or just sheer curiosity that elicits questions like "I wonder what would happen if . . ." These experiments usually are heuristic in nature and are more likely to be of benefit in the earlier rather than later stages of a research program.

Finally, *simulation experiments* are experiments on models—that is, examinations of a particular model to see what would happen in the real world in the conditions that are being simulated. For example, one can construct a model of an airplane and put it through its paces in a miniaturized wind tunnel. If the simulation has captured the essence of the real situation one will be able to tell how the actual airplane will fare in actual flight conditions. Similarly, many social scientists build simulations of international conflict and conclude from their simulation experiment that such-and-such should or will happen in the real world. Naturally, the validity of their claims depends on the adequacy of the model, and, as we have seen, man–machine simulations have difficulty in illuminating either the adequacy of the model or the relationships of the model to the participants. Unfortunately, many critics of games confuse the simulation experiment with the hypothesis-testing experiment and believe that games are instances of the first rather than the second.

The purpose of a hypothesis-testing experiment, as has already been pointed out, is to assess the plausibility of a hypothesis about a cause–effect relationship. The experiment is done in controlled circumstances so that the precise process of interest to the researchers can be isolated and examined. The critical question is not "Is there a high degree of fidelity or resemblance to the real world?" but, rather, "Can the results obtained be attributed to the single factor of interest?" This last question is concerned with the *internal validity* of the experiment.

The history of psychology is rife with examples of experimental paradigms that have been extremely important in the development of knowledge. An experimental paradigm is a situation structured to ensure the operation of a particular process so that the process can be systematically studied. In a manner of speaking, the experimenter deliberately introduces constraints so that other contaminating (uncontrolled) factors do not obscure the process of interest. Each experimental paradigm devised builds certain constraints into what can take place and what can be observed or measured.

The internal validity of an experiment is established as much for what it does not allow to happen as by what it does allow to happen. Obviously, then, different techniques probably will be concerned with different processes and events. Pavlov placed his dogs in a harness, soundproofed the chamber, eliminated the presence of strangers and even the experimenter by automating the measurement of the salivary response, and standardized preexperimental handling procedures. He found that when these controls were introduced, making the situation very artificial and unlike the everyday world his animals encountered, the conditioned reflex could be *reliably* elicited. Without these controls the conditioned reflex was a very unstable and difficult phenomenon to produce in a lawful manner. Within the framework of Pavlov's conceptual interests the constraints imposed on the dogs were successful because they enabled him to select from nature and scrutinize those data that would test the hypotheses he was interested in testing.

A similar development of fruitful theory and a body of systematic evidence has accrued from Small's invention of the maze in 1898. He replicated the Hampton Court maze and provided rats with two routes to a goal box that contained food. He found that the animals soon learned to take the shorter of the two routes. That the white rat could master a complex maze and do so rather quickly opened up an avenue for exploration of numerous theoretical problems that are still of interest today. Many methodological studies have been done with mazes. Psychologists have varied and simplified the maze pattern, constructing linear, roundabout, checkerboard, open-alley, and U-mazes. Handling procedures, elimination of cues by painting the maze or building walls and/or ceilings, and variations in procedures, including allowing the rat to backtrack through the maze, dropping a door behind him as he passes each choice point, and not allowing him to choose the wrong arm more than once—all have been systematically studied.

The methodological studies of mazes have been quite useful. Similarly, methodological studies using the operant box have proved quite valuable in the experimental analysis of behavior (Skinner, 1956). Yet the many methodological studies undertaken with experimental games have been severely criticized as one more variation of little interest. Scientists have manipulated payoff matrices, feedback about scores, strategies of robot players, introduction of communications, and so on. These are clearly methodological studies and are quite necessary in gaining clarity about the effects of game parameters on player behavior. Of course, if no reliable effects could be discovered by means of such manipulations one might conclude either that some important factors were not under the experimenter's control or that the research paradigm was of little value because it was insensitive.

The reader should observe that the classical conditioning paradigm,

Thorndike's problem box, Small's maze, and Skinner's operant box are artificial situations; each places numerous constraints on what the organism can do so that the experimenter can isolate and study particular processes of interest to him. The theorist's actual choice of procedure is significant, and quite possibly he has not chosen the best method for testing the hypotheses of his theory. Kaplan (1964, p. 59) has also noted this relationship between theory and experiment: "Consciously or not, the decision to employ a particular piece of apparatus and to use it in a particular way carries an assumption that only certain sorts of circumstances will arise. There are instrumental as well as theoretical expectations, and they have often played a decisive role in scientific development."

Yet an experiment is part of real life, though perhaps not of everyday life. The laboratory may be an unusual place, but it is a real one. When animal subjects are used for experiments their biological needs can be controlled through deprivation and satiation procedures or by recourse to physiological techniques. The most serious problem facing social science is that the motivations brought into play for human subjects in the laboratory may be both very weak and very limited in number as compared with those we would like to investigate. One of the problems is that subjects are knowledgeable that they are serving in the role of experimental subjects. Presumably, if the subjects could be provided with a task that was sufficiently engrossing or intrinsically interesting they might be more strongly motivated and to some degree forget their role of subject.

Goffman (1961) argues that gaming encounters provide us with fine examples of an utterly engrossing task for the participants in spite of the ultimate triviality of the game. That other persons also are involved with a subject in a face-to-face interaction ensures that the engrossment will be steadily sustained despite the flickering of actual interest. If the subject observes that the other person is not spontaneously involved in the game or if the other's identity is suspect in some way, involvement will be weakened. The reality of a game is not so important as its as-if character. It is true that the game cannot be too fantastic, but neither can it be too real to life or it will lose its fun character. This possibility, however, also implies that the strong similarity of games to a real competitive situation will elicit strong everyday motivations. It is this last factor that experiments with games attempt to elicit.

Whether experimental games do elicit these strong motivations and many of the other psychological processes (e.g., anger, trust) that operate in real-world conflicts is a question for theory and data to answer together. Conceptions of the real world will lead us to theoretical concepts, which, in turn, generate experiments. Theory-testing experiments will, in turn, evaluate the theoretical conceptions. Since the preliminary theory-building stage in studying interpersonal conflict has just begun, the question of success cannot yet be judged. However, if the theory suggests that cause–effect relations of a particular form occur in conflict situations and these theoretical propositions are confirmed within the context of experimental games, we must conclude that internal validity has been demonstrated. The application of theory to the real world, though, is another question altogether.

To satisfy one criterion for internal validity an experiment must be controlled tightly enough to truly test the hypothesized cause–effect relationship in question. A second criterion for internal validity is *experimental reliability*. In essence, reliability asks whether measurement of the same set of objects many times with the same or comparable measuring instruments will produce the same results (Kerlinger, 1964). Thus the question of reliability is answered by whether or not the results of conflict experiments are repeatedly obtainable (replicable) when a careful effort to reconstruct similar experimental situations is made. The criterion of reliability, while a good indicator of internal validity, is not sufficient to conclude such validity; that is, it is possible to *reliably* produce an invalid finding, as when a schizophrenic reliably has telephone conversations with God. In sum, to conclude that a particular conflict investigation possesses internal validity it is primarily necessary that the results of the study test the hypothesis and that the obtained data can reliably support this hypothesis.

The internal validity of many game experiments does not appear impressive when the reliability criterion is applied as the basis of evaluation. Disagreement of results across experiments may occur because researchers use different modes of presentation, instructions, apparatuses, subject populations, rewards, and so on. Yet, since many of these studies are methodological it is difficult to say that they tested the same hypothesis and failed to produce the same findings. This book testifies to the reliability of findings derived from the use of experimental games when such games were employed as hypothesis-testing situations. In the authors' views, *games are merely experimental situations, nothing more, and hence should be judged in the same manner as any other experimental paradigm.* To be opposed to a research paradigm would not be good sense; to believe the paradigm does not produce results that can be found in the real world is another matter altogether.

Experimental games probably allow as much control over the behavior of human subjects in social interaction as any other tool in social psychology. This claim is not true, however, when two or more subjects actually are allowed to interact. When two persons play a game the inference problems in isolating the cause–effect relationships are quite difficult. As Hogatt (1969) suggests, with live dyads "the problem becomes one of estimating parameters in a simultaneous system of equations which is not identified. When the robot is specified the model becomes very simple. The robots standardize the situation faced by the subject so we may measure the performance of many individuals against identical situations [p. 420]."

Another advantage of using robots is that subjects may be paired with many types of rival players, and instead of having the problem of esti- mating a different set of parameters for each subject, the experimenter knows the parameters of the robot players. Yet, as Friedman (1969) la- ments, "like most good things, the robots come at a price. If their behav- ior is very singular and unlike the behavior of people, it is possible the subjects play against them in ways they would never play with other subjects. . . . Clearly the ideal is to have robots which behave like peo- ple [p. 412]." If experimenters do use live dyads in game experiments they should probably view the two persons as a single system. Unfortu- nately, the elements of the system continually change, introducing great amounts of variance in data and decreasing the chance that an experi- ment will have high internal validity.

The possibility always exists that a situation produced in the laboratory will be artificial in the sense that it controls *out* something another theor- ist believes is critical for the explanation of human conflict behavior. For example, Alexander and Weil (1969) argue that the ambiguous goal structure of the prisoner's dilemma, which subjects could interpret in such ways as cooperate and win with the other person, compete and beat the other person, stay just a few points ahead of the other person, or make the other person lose as many points as possible, destroys the possi- bility that subjects can make a firm decision to behave normatively or even to maximize outcomes.

Nemeth (1970) has also argued that the two-person, mixed-motive game presented to subjects in matrix form is normless. If one views an experi- ment using the prisoner's dilemma game as a simulation experiment in which all of the essential elements of the real world are included in the structure of the situation (i.e., the PDG represents a model of the world) , then this criticism is quite warranted. The criticism, simply put, is that the PDG is not an adequate model of the real world because the situ- ation is essentially normless. However, the PDG and other games should not be construed as models but as research situations that allow tests of hypotheses; they are hypothesis-testing situations. As long as they meet the criteria for hypothesis-testing experiments they are valid. Thus, these arguments are not really against the prisoner's dilemma as a research tool but against the theorist who claims wider generalization for his results than these critics think warranted.

Like other experimental paradigms, games constrain what the subjects can do. Rules limit the actions that players may carry out and also provide their motivation by defining their goals. Rapoport (1960) has argued that games offer a good experimental situation within which to observe the behavior of people where: (1) conflicts of interest exist; (2) several alternatives are open at each phase of the interaction; and (3) people are in a position to estimate consequences of their choices, taking into consideration the outcomes determined not only by their own choices but also by the choices of others. Arguments about the validity of games should consider whether they do what Rapoport (and many others) alleges that they do. What hypotheses can or cannot be tested within the situation (so defined) is not a critique of the paradigm when it is used to test hypotheses that it can test.

Just as a maze may be used to study learning, discrimination processes, exploratory behavior, or instincts in rats, so can experimental games be used to study differences in motives, levels of aspiration, face-saving behaviors or emotional relationships between people. Consequently, it is an anomaly to call someone a maze theorist or even a game researcher just because he uses games as research tools. Such terminology makes about as much sense as calling Thorndike a problem-box scientist, John Watson a maze theorist, or B. F. Skinner an operant box researcher. You cannot know what a scientist is studying merely by knowing what tool he uses.

Experimental games clearly are not theories or models, and their value cannot be assessed on logical grounds alone. However, the misconception of laboratory experiments as simulations has encouraged some to evaluate research in terms of real-world applicability. We have already mentioned that some game research is motivated by practical concern with pressing social problems. The question raised about the fit between data obtained from an experiment and the real world is one of *ecological validity*.[1]

Chapanis (1961) has expressed the view that experiments are simulations: ". . . there can be no doubt about one thing; our experimental situation is a model of the real world [p. 117]." Yet experiments may be highly artificial situations unlike anything else in the real world. The attempt to isolate subtle processes may require a high degree of control in the research environment. If the concern is for theoretical understanding, the scientist will be completely unconcerned about the correspondence between the laboratory and real-world environments. As Swingle (1970, p. 235–236) has aptly pointed out:

> The findings of experimental gaming situations are not directly applicable to, nor do they directly reflect real life conflict situations, such as the international balance of terror or labor management disputes. The results do, however, provide us with some insight into the existence of structural dimensions in

1. Our use of the term *ecological validity* follows Bjorkman (1969), and should not be confused with Brunswick's use of the same term (Hammond, 1966).

bargaining situations and provide us with an opportunity to develop terms for intellectually manipulating these dimensions toward the development of theory which should, in turn, provide intellectual levers for attempting to explore and understand interpersonal conflict in society at large.

To ask about the ecological validity or technological relevance of social psychological experiments is to ask the wrong question. Whatever degree of generalizability may be attainable from science for the practical world of affairs must be purchased from the available theories, not from single experiments. Theories are more general statements of the relationships between events, and they state the conditions in which various phenomena should be displayed. Festinger concludes (in Kaplan, 1964, p. 169–170) : "It matters not whether such a situation would ever be encountered in real life . . . the possibility of application to a real-life situation arises when one knows enough about these relationships to be able to make predictions concerning a real life situation after measurement and diagnosis of the state of affairs there."

A sound observation is that generalizations should not be made from the results of laboratory experiments without further tests in the natural social environment. Very seldom should an experiment be modified because it was thought to have a low degree of fidelity with an applied setting. Experiments may have little or great resemblance to the real world, but this is not the critical criterion for judging the value of the experiment. The critical question is: Does it contribute to systematic knowledge? Bjorkman (1969) points out that the flow of influence from science to technology can be depicted as shown in Figure 7.1.

The observer develops some conceptions about the real world through

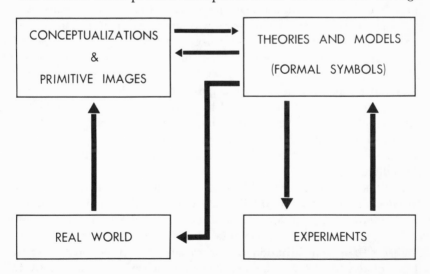

FIGURE 7.1. *Relations between science and the practical world of affairs.*

direct interaction with it. These observations form the basis of intuition, which leads to the development of theories and models, which, in turn, change what seems to be commonsense intuitions. Experiments are derived from theories and models. Experimental results lead to revisions of theory and suggest further theoretical propositions, but the influence of models on experiments is one way. No flow between the real world or its conceptions plays much of a part in carrying out experiments, nor do experiments have much utility for telling us about the real world. However, both theories and models may be useful in applied settings; hence theories and models do directly have impact on real-world problems.

The authors side with the skeptics when the skeptics argue that illegitimate generalizations often are made from experiments utilizing experimental games. The urgency and magnitude of contemporary problems coupled with the lack of social science theory that can be applied to the crises of our world are frustrating impediments to a social scientist who has an action orientation. But such frustrations should not lead one to violate the logic of scientific inquiry. The only likely outcome is to exacerbate the very problem for which a solution is deemed necessary. The cries of relevance from undergraduate students and congressmen urge that scientists spend more of their time in considering social problems. What they want is a good scientific theory. But concentration on the social problem is not likely to attain the desired results. In any case, because of their associated terminology (cooperation, conflict, threats) experimental games suggest to the naïve layman that only a criterion of relevance is a suitable basis for evaluations.

The argument that experimental games are too artificial and consequently useless in telling us how people act in the course of their normal daily lives derives from the above view of an experiment as a model. The real world has many disadvantages from a scientist's point of view. Certain phenomena of great interest occur only rarely; other phenomena of only little interest occur with great and tiresome regularity. Critical processes and events may never be recognizable through naïve and unaided observation. They may be obscured by a profusion of other variables and extraneous events or even be invisible to the eye, as are electrons, and genes. No one would think of criticizing a biologist because he examined chromosomes on slides and under a microscope rather than observing them directly.

The question of generalizability of experimental findings is one of *external validity*. Although specific research paradigms may be extraordinarily useful in the development and testing of a theory, no theory applicable only to a specific experimental situation would be considered very powerful. The generalization of the cause–effect (functional) relationship isolated by a particular experiment to a variety of situations and contexts increases the external validity of that experiment. Campbell (1969) suggests that only additional research will answer the external validity question, and in order to increase the generality of a finding, replications utilizing different research paradigms, subject populations, and conditions must be undertaken. Hence the same function may be discovered in a trucking game, prisoner's dilemma game, and chicken game, whether males or females, children or adults, whites or blacks, nationals or foreigners are used as subjects. External validity thus is the task of assessing our experimental findings over a wide variety of persons, situations, and measures in order to determine the boundary conditions of our knowledge.

PERSPECTIVE ON GAMES

Although there is a theory of games it is more formal and/or normative than descriptive or empirical. One value of game theory is that it has suggested a set of research paradigms and some concepts to describe the parameters of the paradigms. Those engaged in research with games have provided additional descriptions and parameters not derived from game theory; but one can be a game theorist and never do a game experiment, and a person can carry out game experiments without understanding or wanting to understand game theory.

Games are not models except in the sense that any contrived and controlled experimental setting may be called a model. Clearly, however, this use of the term *model* is different from that ascribed to all-computer or man–machine simulations, which not only provide structure but also specify many of the processes and functions that will operate in the model. Of course, it could be argued that the prisoner's dilemma is a model in the sense that a certain structure of rules, payoffs, and responses operate to effect the outcomes as prespecified in the game, but such an interpretation strays a good way from the theoretical model that deals with extreme complexities in an attempt to more concretely specify theoretical possibilities.

Games are almost never used as training devices and have almost no value as applied tools. One problem is that most games really are very simple and can be mastered within a short period of time; otherwise, game research would require specially trained subjects. As concerns their use as heuristic devices, it can be argued that some interesting hypotheses and concepts have been developed from research with games, and the capability of introducing reiterated threats and promises into the situation with verisimilitude has helped to produce the theory of influence stated previously in this book.

Experimental games, like all experimental settings, are used to study specific functions and processes. Subjects can be studied in the laboratory while they are engaged in a partial conflict of interests with another (robot) person. The interdependence of responses requires that subjects pay attention to what the other person does. A prisoner's dilemma in which a subject plays a robot is a situation controlled almost as tightly as a Skinner box. The potential for studying person perception, the effect of the specific social relationship of the two parties on the course of conflict, and the experimental study of reward and coercive power is quite impressive just in terms of what has already been done.

Whether a particular experiment that uses some game as the environmental setting is internally or externally valid depends on careful scrutiny of the particular case. Broad statements about games make little more sense than any such statement that could be made about experiments. Games are simply experiments. Games vary in terms of the processes they attempt to study and the constraints, rules, and procedures that will be employed. When assessing the internal validity of conflict studies using experimental games as the research tool, one should pay as much attention to the derivation and operationalization of hypotheses, the data analyses, and the supportive or disconfirmatory nature of the results as to the structure or characteristics of the particular game used.

The external validity of results obtained with games is directly and empirically ascertainable. By way of illustration, Tedeschi, Bonoma, and Brown (1971) have provided evidence that a modified prisoner's dilemma (to include threats) produces consistent and coherent data about subjects' reactions to threats in interpersonal conflicts. A major finding was that the effectiveness of deterrence increases with the magnitude of the punishment threatened and the probability that punishment will follow noncompliance. The face validity of these findings is obvious. The same function was found when using as subjects college students of both sexes, elementary school children, and ROTC cadets. Further, results from other research settings are consistent with the generalization; national surveys on the effectiveness of legal punishment (including capital punishment) and a study of parking violations on a college campus revealed the same relationships. Thus the external validity of a set of findings generated from an experimental game setting was assessed by confirming the relevant theoretical hypotheses in as many different conditions, situations, and subject populations as were practically possible.

Criteria for the assessment of ecological validity are nonexistent for experimental games. Consider the nature of games: they serve as tools of discovery to be used for hypothesis-testing, methodological, or exploratory purposes. The knowledge discovered through their use serves the inductive phase of science—the development and assessment of theories. Games represent highly artificial part-replicas of conflict situations and sometimes make what would be patently absurd assumptions if the real-world analogue were used as the criterion of judgment. To argue that the results of investigations made with such games could be generalized to the real world runs counter to our entire examination of the strategy of science. No generalizations about social phenomena based exclusively on laboratory experiments could be safely assumed to be applicable in natural social environments without further inquiry. Those who attempt to deal with the real world directly and without sufficient theory will design poor experiments and make inappropriate generalizations. Poor experiments may result from trying to find out too much rather than too little. As Kaplan (1964) warned: "You get what you pay for, and bargains are as much to be distrusted in research as anywhere else [p. 158]."

The most relevant thing a scientist can do is build a good theory. Kurt Lewin is said to have remarked that the most practical thing in the world is a good scientific theory. If the real world faces problems and must make life and death decisions before the scientist can construct a good theory, then policy must be formed without benefit of science. The history of science shows that scientists have sought knowledge of the interrelationships between events, often without concern for its bearing on human values.

The fact is that the insulation of the scientific community from society permits the scientist to focus on problems he feels he can solve. Kuhn (1962) commented that "the contrast between natural scientists and many social scientists proves instructive. The latter often tend, as the former almost never do, to defend their choice of a research problem—e.g., the effects of racial discrimination—chiefly in terms of the social importance of achieving a solution. Which group would one then expect to solve problems at a more rapid rate [p. 163]?"

Conclusions

Inquiry into the usefulness of experimental games began with the claims and counterclaims of adherents and skeptics. To reduce some of the confusion that has caused inappropriate criteria to be applied to the research uses of experimental games, it was necessary to clearly differentiate them from models and their variants, all-computer simulations and man–machine simulations. While these three approaches constitute at least partial attempts at theory construction, experimental games serve the function of theory evaluation. Confusion of the terms *simulation* and *game* is unfortunate. It is too late to do anything about it, but we can register our dismay that emotions have been aroused over what should be a clear distinction between models and experiments.

Whatever else we may require of them, games are essentially tools of experimentation to be used in controlled interaction settings in which certain conflict variables are systematically manipulated. Games are tools of scientific discovery, and results from studies that employ them must eventually be used for the purpose of theory construction or theory evaluation.

Three basic validity questions can be posed for any experimental paradigm. Internal validity asks about the confirmation value of the data for the hypothesis tested in a particular conflict study. External validity is concerned with the generalizability of internally valid findings to other research paradigms. Ecological validity asks whether scientific findings have valid technological application to the real world. The reader can assess whether the theory and research presented in Chapters 2–6 gives an answer to the internal validity question. Chapter 8 will examine the external validity question and will also attempt to explore the ecological validity question. Obviously a social psychology that fits only laboratory settings would be quite disappointing.

Our review of epistemological questions may have been at times somewhat tedious for the reader, but it does support the claim that experimental games are indeed useful scientific tools. Because many social scientists have tuned out game research, we have perceived the need to defend this as *one* approach to the study of conflict. Experimental games are somewhat like the United Nations. Nations may misuse it, but if we did not have it someone would invent it.

8

Generalizations and Applications
of the Theory of Conflict

Several psychologists have raised the very legitimate question of whether a theory that has been generated from and evaluated by laboratory games is generalizable beyond such simple situations (e.g., Alexander & Weil, 1969; Gallo, 1968; Knox & Douglas, 1968; Marwell & Schmitt, 1967; Messé & Sawyer, 1967). Do experimental games really tell us anything about social conflicts, power, and influence, or are the propositions and evidence relevant only for understanding behavior in rather trivial parlor games? As we saw in Chapter 7, this question really must be given at least two answers. The first requires that the external validity of a theory's propositions be assessed, and the second requires some consideration of the applicability of the theory to real-world problems. The external validity question is a scientific one; the applicability question is a technological one.

The External Validity Question

Thomas Kuhn (1962) has distinguished two identifiable historical phases in the development of science—the preparadigm and paradigm phases. The reader should be careful to discern the difference between two types of paradigms. A *research paradigm* refers to specifiable sets of operations and procedures meant to isolate and study particular behaviors or processes—for example, such research tools as a Skinner box or a message-modified PDG. A *metatheoretical paradigm* refers to a specific collection of assumptions, concepts, laws, research findings and tools, and a theoretical superstructure that numerous practitioners of science accept as a relatively integrated whole. Examples of such paradigms include Newtonian dynamics or wave optics, which are sufficiently different from their predecessors (e.g., Aristotelian dynamics or corpuscular optics) to attract new adherents and yet leave unanswered enough questions to give the adherents a common vocabulary, set of working assumptions, and problem areas in their scientific attack.

Kuhn has contended that psychology (and social science in general) is in the preparadigm stage of development and has not yet reached the point where it has developed a well-formulated metatheoretical paradigm. Although this is a rather harsh appraisal of the current status of the science of psychology and related social sciences, it is largely accurate. However, some fields, such as learning theory, have reached the point where they might be called paradigms, and other fields are fast approaching that point.

In the preparadigm stage of a science all facts seem equally relevant to the practitioners. As a result, early fact-gathering is an activity much more random than later theoretically guided research. Theory once developed tells the scientist what is relevant, important, and interesting. Thus when Newton's theory of mechanics was developed, much of the astronomical data that Brahé and Kepler collected was discarded as irrelevant and uninteresting. Theories (scientific laws, generalizations, hypotheses) developed during the preparadigm phase of a science are likely to be rigidly circumscribed. There is a tendency to fractionate the science into small, encapsulated and semiindependent subfields. Theoretical principles and scientific laws are therefore *low grade;* that is, they have little external validity. The emphasis tends to be descriptive rather than inferential, and the scientist typically stays close to his data.

When a metatheoretical paradigm has been developed a coherent tradition is shared and includes theoretical assumptions and principles, research procedures and instrumentation, and applicability of the theory. Thus a paradigm (according to Kuhn) guides both the investigatory and the interpretive functions that are integral to scientific inquiry. The new paradigm not only stimulates new discovery but also must allow for a coherent reinterpretation of established low-level laws. *Normal science* is that stage of science that is firmly based on a metatheoretical paradigm.

The SEU theory used throughout this book does not constitute a metatheoretical paradigm. Rather, it is based on certain assumptions drawn from an economic interpretation of behavior, a philosophical motivational principle (hedonism), and psychological research. As such it is an eclectic theory still searching for an increased precision in the formulation of its concepts, a more thorough exposition of its basic assumptions, a solid foundation of low-level laws, and consensually accepted instruments and research paradigms to generate low-level laws. The eclectic basis for the SEU theory has suggested assumptions, concepts, and procedures that could have been worked into a number of specific theories of conflict of which it is only one.

It was pointed out in Chapter 7 that one of the primary indicators of the truth value, or acceptance, of an empirical or theoretical proposition is the degree to which it is generalizable across other research areas within social psychology. Clearly, although the SEU theory has received convincing experimental support, the data we have primarily reported have been gathered from a restricted number of research paradigms (i.e., varieties of experimental games). Critics would certainly be justified in taking a show-me attitude toward a theory that has been restricted to behavior in simple two- or three-person games, especially when the response alternatives allowed to subjects are so severely restricted. Rapoport (1968) has argued that laboratory games and simulations represent no more than incubators for a science of conflict. Whatever is hatched must be tested in a more complex world as it develops into maturity, and this task will occupy us for much of this chapter.

The areas of research chosen for reinterpretation in terms of the SEU theory are voluminous and central to the discipline of social psychology. To exhaustively review these areas would take several books, each larger than the present one. However, examples of research that represent established principles in particular areas should be sufficient to demonstrate that the SEU theory can find considerable external validity outside the bounds of experimental gaming. Further, such reinterpretations suggest additional research in traditional areas that perhaps would not be intuitively obvious to scientists who are working in those areas. The coherence and plausibility of the reinterpretations should give some indication of how seriously the SEU theory should be taken as the basis of future research.

The growth of research in social psychology has seldom stemmed from other than practical and applied interests. A characteristic assumption has been that if a person's attitude could be changed, subsequent and corresponding behavioral change could be expected. Behavioral engineers, especially during and after World War II, were vitally interested in developing principles and delineating antecedent conditions of attitude change. Any theory of social influence would need to assimilate much of the attitude change literature in order to be seriously entertained by social psychologists. Less obvious applications of the SEU theory can be made to the research on social conformity, verbal reinforcements, modeling and imitation, and aggression and altruism. Naturally, as we attempt to reinterpret these important social-psychological problem areas in terms of the concepts and principles of SEU theory only representative experiments can be reviewed.

ATTITUDE CHANGE

In typical experiments of attitude change, persuasive communications are directed toward an individual subject, and measurements are taken of changes in attitude and/or behavior toward the object or commodity that is the subject of the appeal. Most persuasive communications have consisted of warnings or mendations or some combination of both. As was indicated in Chapter 3, the target of persuasive communications is expected to make his decision among behavioral (or attitudinal) alternatives in terms of maximizing SEU. If a warning is communicated to a target person, he must decide whether to change his behavior and possibly avoid the alleged punishment or to ignore the warning and accept the potential consequences associated with what he is already doing. It could be predicted that, holding constant the probabilities and utilities associated with the outcomes of alternative responses, attitude change would be a direct function of the negative subjective expected utility of warnings. Higbee (1969) concluded from his review of the warning literature that the bulk of recent studies report a positive relationship between the magnitude of punishment contained in warnings and subsequent target attitude change.

Almost all social psychological theories of interpersonal attraction predict that a liked source will be more persuasive than a disliked source (Cartwright & Harary, 1956; Heider, 1958; Newcomb, 1953; Osgood & Tannenbaum, 1955). The contribution of SEU theory in this area is that it defines persuasion in terms of warnings and mendations and provides a mechanism—that is, the systematic biasing of probabilities—by which the effects of attraction are mediated. Substantial evidence confirms the expected relationship between the attractiveness of a persuasive source and the target's attitude change (e.g., Abelson & Miller, 1967; Dabbs, 1964; Wright, 1966). For example, Weiss (1957) probably induced perceptions of similarity and dissimilarity by having a confederate first agree or disagree with the subject on a prior question. (Byrne, 1969, has shown similarity–dissimilarity of attitudes to induce liking–disliking between pairs of strangers.) Targets were then presented with a warning about the dangers of fluoridation of public reservoirs. Subjects were more strongly influenced by the source who was perceived as similar to themselves.

One of the most consistent findings in all of social psychology is that an expert source will produce more attitude change in a target of persuasive communications than will an inexpert source, a conclusion entirely consistent with SEU theory. In a representative study Johnson & Izzett (1969) investigated the effects of source esteem on attitude change toward the position advocated in a warning of the danger of X-rays. The source in one condition was described as a medical authority and an expert in the use of X-rays; in another condition the source was described as a quack who had spent time in prison for medical fraud. The high esteem doctor produced more attitude change than did the low esteem quack. SEU theory presumes that the source's esteem biased target subjects' probability estimations, with consequent impact on the decisions they made.

Aronson and Golden (1962) reported a parallel finding when the source's persuasive communication was a mendation, delivered to sixth grade children, extolling the value of a knowledge of arithmetic. The source was allegedly either an engineer or a dishwasher. The children's posttreatment attitudes toward arithmetic were more favorable when they received the message from the high esteem source than when it came from the low esteem source.

Weiss and his colleagues have taken the interesting research position that in the absence of more direct criteria to permit some numerical scaling of a source's expertise, the *number* of experts endorsing an issue may offer an indirect method for measuring the quantitative relation of source esteem to attitude change. Weiss, Buchanan, and Pasamanick (1964) exposed subjects to speeches that advocated a particular position. These persuasive messages were said to be supported by all of the experts or by somewhat less than half of the experts. As predicted, subjects in the high communicator consensus groups showed more attitude change than did subjects in the low consensus conditions.

In a refinement of the basic paradigm, Weiss, Weiss, and Chalupa (1967) presented targets with persuasive arguments advocated by a group of experts at one of five levels of consensus (0, 25, 50, 75, or 100 percent of the experts). After hearing the communication subjects rated the probability that the communication was true. As predicted, the targets' probability estimates bore a direct and linear relationship to the consensus manipulation.

Surprisingly enough very few studies link status (as defined in Chapter 2) or prestige to the efficacy of persuasive communications. The clearest confirmation of the direct relationship of source status to target influenceability was in an experiment done to investigate ingratiation. Jones, Gergen, and Jones (1963) had pairs of ROTC cadets, status unequals, exchange opinions. In one condition they were asked to stress the accuracy of their opinions; in a second they were told that the purpose of the experiment was to identify compatible commander–subordinate pairs. The low status subjects agreed more often with the opinions of the high status subjects than vice versa, and this effect was accentuated in the compatibility condition in which the need to give deference presumably was tacitly communicated to the person of inferior rank.

In the SEU theory of influence high prestige not only makes a source more successful in his influence attempts but also causes him to seek more influence. Bass (1963) confirmed both of these hypotheses in a single study. ROTC cadets were assigned to five-man groups. They were told that each would be given a weighted value that reflected their power to evaluate the other subjects in the group in reference to their candidacy for advanced ROTC. Three distributions of capability were created: (1) all members of the group possessed equal capability; (2) weights were 3-2-1-1-1; or (3) weights were 4-1-1-1-1. The group's task was to judge the frequency with which five adjectives are used in the English language. Subjects gave their opinions, held a group discussion, and again gave individual judgments. The greater the subject's capability, the more influence he attempted and the more influence he successfully exerted over the others. Several other experiments can be reinterpreted in terms of prestige and reveal the same relationships (cf. Tedeschi, Bonoma, & Schlenker, 1972).

When a persuasive communication is very different from the position a target already holds, the appeal may seem implausible and lower the credence the target places in the new information. Targets may therefore shift even further away from a very discrepant opinion. These assimilation and contrast effects are at the heart of the Sherif and Hovland (1961) social judgment theory and are consistent with the propositions of SEU theory. A contrasting position to which the target gives little credence may imply to him that an opinion opposite to the one the source expresses is more plausible than ever, causing the target to move further away from the source's judgment. Other factors that may affect the plausibility of a communication are whether it is one-sided or two-sided, whether it is given first or second when contradictory appeals are made, and its logical structure.

Of course, many other important phenomena associated with attitude change have not but could have been reinterpreted here. Yet the consistency of the attitude change literature with the propositions and findings of the SEU theory are encouraging and suggest that evidence gathered from experimental games may have its counterparts in numerous other settings.

Verbal Reinforcement Studies

The verbal conditioning literature can be reinterpreted in terms of tacit promises. In a typical verbal reinforcement study the subject is asked to form a sentence using one of several pronouns and a verb presented to him on cards. Over trials the same pronouns but different verbs are displayed for sentence construction. Whenever the subject uses a particular pronoun, the experimenter emits a verbal response, such as good, uh-huh, or fine. The repetition of a verbal reinforcement directly following a particular response provides a basis for the target to abstract a rule that governs the relationship between the responses he emits and the reinforcements received from the experimenter. Our interpretation is that the subject decodes the source's invariant (contingent) response as a tacit communication of the form "If you use the pronoun I, I will give you my approval by saying good." Generally the experimenter establishes 100 percent probability of reward for compliance to his tacit promises.

Our version of SEU theory suggests that the utility of the reward offered and the characteristics of the source should affect the rate of reinforced responses in verbal reinforcement studies. Matthews and Dixon (1968) scaled voices by their preferability and then used tape recordings of the voices to reinforce subjects in a verbal conditioning task. If we assume that voice preferability is related to the utility of the source's approval to the target, then the results can be reinterpreted as confirming our prediction. The number of reinforced responses was directly related to voice preferability and therefore to the SEU of the promises. Similarly, Hemphill (1961) showed that the greater the value of reinforcement given to subjects for voicing opinions and demonstrating leadership, the more frequently they attempted leadership in groups.

The only source characteristics that have been investigated within the context of a verbal conditioning setting are attraction and esteem. Both of these source characteristics should have similar effects on the target subjects' behaviors. Low esteem or low attraction for the source should cause the subjects to deauthenticate the probability of receiving the rewards. High esteem or high attraction for the source should cause the subjects to authenticate the probability of receiving rewards. The authenticating subjects should emit more reinforced responses than those deauthenticating.

Sapolsky (1960) and Brown, Helm, and Tedeschi (1972) have shown that a highly attractive experimenter elicits more reinforced responses from subjects than does a disattractive experimenter, and Helm, Brown, and Tedeschi (1972) have shown the same effects for source esteem. In the Helm et al. study the experimenter either dressed in a suit and tie and introduced himself to subjects as a Ph.D. candidate undertaking his dissertation, or wore casual clothing and told subjects that he was an undergraduate fulfilling an experimental psychology course requirement. Posttest judgments indicated that the manipulation did lead to the appropriate differences in esteem for the experimenter. Supporting the predictions, the high esteem experimenter tended to elicit more reinforced responses from the subjects than did the low esteem experimenter.

The SEU theory provides a mechanism by which verbal reinforcement takes place and suggests new hypotheses to test. No thorough and systematic investigations that manipulate the probability of verbal reinforcements have been done, and the source characteristics of status and prestige have yet to be studied in the context of a verbal reinforcement research paradigm.

SOCIAL CONFORMITY

Conformity is a change in behavior or attitude that can be shown to be caused by real or imagined group pressures. In the typical laboratory paradigm (cf. Asch, 1951), a naïve subject is placed in a situation in which several confederates of the experimenter all give rather consistent and public incorrect responses during the relatively simple and unambiguous task of judging the length of lines. All confederates verbally and successively give each of their judgments before the critical subject responds. When all the confederates make incorrect judgments, the subject is faced with making his deviant but correct independent judgment or conforming to the group by making an incorrect judgment. In Asch's original study fully 75 percent of the subjects made incorrect judgments and conformed on some of the critical trials; subjects without group pressures turned in virtually errorless performances on the same task.

Conformity may be conceptualized as compliance to the social influence attempts of an n-person group. The Asch paradigm may be interpreted in terms of tacit communications. In any group situation each individual anticipates disapproval for failure to conform to the group's dictates and approval for conformity. The critical subject in the Asch-type study probably views the situation in terms of tacit threats of punishment (such as disapproval) if he fails to conform and tacit promises of reward (such as approval) if he conforms.

Subjects, of course, are quite aware that they are participating in an experiment and are usually concerned about how the experimenter views them. If all the other people in the situation make unanimous judgments and have not been disapproved or corrected by the experimenter, then perhaps the critical subject can best gain the experimenter's approval by doing as the others have done. If this interpretation is reasonable, then the group members tacitly communicate warnings or mendations by making unanimous judgments, indicating to the critical subject the wrong, or correct, responses in terms of the probable evaluative reactions of the experimenter. Despite the confounding of these influence modes in a conformity situation, the results that have been amassed are consistent with the expectations of an SEU theory.

Manipulation of the utility for conforming behavior and the probability that conforming behavior will lead to a desirable outcome have been shown to produce results consistent with the maximizing rule of decision theory. Several investigators have confirmed that public conformity behavior is a direct function of the amount of reinforcement proffered for target conformity (Deutsch & Gerard, 1955; Endler, 1966; Jones, Wells, & Torrey, 1958). Endler and Hoy (1967) varied the percentage of both reinforcement and punishment for conforming or nonconforming behavior. The conformity means across groups were perfectly ordered by their expected utilities. The subjective probability of being punished for non-conforming behaviors is decreased when behaviors are private and not under the surveillance of the rest of the group. Raven (1959), Argyle (1957), and Deutsch and Gerard (1955) have found that less conformity occurs in private than in public. Similarly, when another member of the group supports the subject's deviant opinions, the subject should feel that there is less likelihood of punishment. The presence of another deviant in the group may decrease the target's estimate of the cohesiveness of the group and the strength with which the other group members hold their views. Thus it should not be surprising that the presence of an ally in a group decreases the amount of conformity given to the group's judgments.

By now the reader must be asking about the effects of the attractiveness, esteem, status, and prestige of the group on the target individual's conformity. The results are consistent with the hypotheses of SEU theory. After reviewing the literature that shows the direct function between group attractiveness and target conformity Kiesler and Kiesler (1969) conclude that this is "as solid a generalization as one can arrive at in social psychology [p. 66]." In one of a very large number of supporting studies, Sampson and Insko (1964) had a confederate interact with a subject before both made distance judgments about the apparent movement of light (autokinetic effect). The confederate either praised the subject and agreed with many of his opinions or was obnoxious and insulting. Subjects agreed more closely with the judgments of the liked than of the disliked confederate.

Similar facilitative effects of esteem on conformity have been found. Mausner (1953, 1954) has found that students conformed more to the judgments of experts than to those of nonexperts in making artistic or geometric judgments. When confederates were reported to be intelligent (French & Snyder, 1959), high in arithmetic ability (Gelfand, 1962), or skillful in estimating the area of irregular figures (Croner & Willis, 1961), subjects conformed more often than when the confederates were presented as inexpert in these tasks.

Crano (1970) provided a clear demonstration of the power of an expert confederate's opinion judgments on an ambiguous task. Subjects and confederates were recruited in pairs to make estimations about the number of dots projected on a screen. When the confederate arrived after the subject, the experimenter greeted the confederate, noted that he looked familiar, and asked him if he had participated in a similar experiment in a previous term. The confederate acknowledged that he had had some experience at the task, and the experimenter noted that the reason he remembered this particular individual was because the confederate had either done so well (high esteem) or so poorly (low esteem) the last time they met. Given this induction in the presence of the experimental subjects, both subject and confederate made dot estimations for 100 trials. During the first 50 trials the confederate was present; during the last 50 trials the confederate was removed. Not only did subjects demonstrate more conformity to the highly esteemed confederate's opinions when the confederate was present, but the effect also persisted even when the confederate was not around to directly influence the subjects' behaviors.

Torrance (1954) has provided confirmation that status also has a direct role in producing conformity. He asked air force bomber crews, consisting of a pilot, navigator, and gunner, to reach unanimous decisions on four ambiguous problem tasks. Crews generally accepted the high status pilot's suggestions about problem solutions even when his answers to the problems were incorrect. The hierarchical nature of the effects of status was indicated in that navigators, who held intermediate status in the crew, gained more conformity to their suggestions than did the low status gunners.

As far as can be determined, no study of the effects of prestige on conformity has been done. The available evidence does look encouragingly compatible with the results obtained from research with experimental games.

MODELING AND IMITATION

Bandura and Walters (1963) presented convincing evidence that individuals can learn environmental means–ends relationships simply by observing the responses of others. This phenomenon of vicarious learning, or social imitation, has come to be one of the more prominent topics of psychology. The typical experiment may be illustrated by recounting Bandura's (1965) procedures.

Children watched a film of a person who exhibited a series of verbal and aggressive responses. In one condition the model was punished for his behavior; in the second the model was rewarded; in the third group no consequences of the model's behaviors were shown. Subjects were then placed in an environment that was obviously the same as the one in which the model had performed in the film. Children who had seen the model either receive rewards or receive no consequences imitated more of the model's behaviors than did children who saw the model punished. Following the performance test all children were offered a highly valued incentive if they would reproduce the model's responses. When these incentives were offered all of the children showed that they could imitate the model's behaviors; the results cannot be attributed simply to differential attentiveness or memory.

Krebs (1970) suggested that a model's function is to draw the observer's attention to particular courses of action, to supply information about what is appropriate behavior in particular settings by providing an example, and to supply the observer with information about his latitude of available decision alternatives. The model's behavior–outcome contingencies with respect to identifiable stimuli provide the observer with information about the causal structure of the environment. These environmental contingencies include the conditions under which a third party (e.g., the Experimenter) will bestow rewards. Accordingly, from the perspective of SEU theory the model's behaviors serve to communicate to the observer tacit warnings or mendations about environmental contingencies.

In a laboratory subjects are usually in an ambiguous situation and are quite aware that their own responses are under observation. In such circumstances it is completely reasonable that from a model's response–outcome sequences they should develop expectancies about which responses are appropriate or inappropriate and about which the experimenter will reward or punish (cf. Orne, 1962). Thus when a model receives rewards after certain behaviors, these behaviors serve to communicate to the observer a mendation such as "If you make response X, you will receive reward Y from the experimenter." Conversely, when a model is punished after certain behaviors, these behaviors serve to communicate a warning such as, "If you make response X, you will receive punishment Y from the experimenter."

Often a problem arises for the observer because it is not clear that the tacit communication is applicable to him. Watching another person is much like overhearing his conversation. Anyone could tune in to the model's communications, explicit or tacit, but the problem is one of determining the *relevance* of the nondirected communication. The relevance of a nondirected communication may be defined as the target's perception that the communication is useful to him. For example, the greater the difference in the problem and/or environment facing the model and the observer, the less relevant the model's behavior should be. The propositions of SEU theory should hold for all modeling studies in which the tacit communications transmitted are relevant to the target, but not when they are irrelevant to him.

The credibility of the model's tacit warnings or mendations is determined by the proportion of times his behavior leads to punishments or reinforcements. The more success the model has in solving problems, avoiding harm, or acquiring benefits, the greater the credibility of his tacit communications. Lanzetta and Kanareff (1959) manipulated the credibility of the model's tacit mendations. Subjects were asked to identify which of two tones had the higher pitch (actually, the tones were identical 80 percent of the time). Feedback indicated to subjects that a model's judgments had been correct either 84, 60 or 36 percent of the time. The two instructional sets used asked subjects either to keep their judgments as independent of the model's as possible or to remember that they were participating with another person and were part of a group. The group instructions implied that the experimenter would approve of imitative behavior. When the experimenter tacitly approved of imitative behavior (group instructions) subjects imitated the model as a direct function of the probability that the model's judgments were correct. The credibility of the model's mendations was not related to the frequency of imitation when the experimenter had tacitly communicated that the subject was not to use the model's judgments (individualistic instructions).

Aronfreed and Paskel (1968) directly varied the perceived utility of a model's outcomes. Following the emission of self-sacrificial behaviors a model emitted expressions of joy, hugged others in the room, or did both. In the last condition the model apparently received a great deal of satisfaction from her self-sacrificial behaviors, more so than when she was just joyful or when she only hugged some other people. The greater perceived personal utility of self-sacrificial behaviors in the third condition leads to the prediction that more imitation of the model should occur in this condition than in the other two. This prediction was supported and these results were replicated in a very similar study (Midlarsky & Bryan, 1967).

Since the model is considered the source of social influence his or her characteristics should play an important part in studies of imitation. If the model is perceived as similar and hence probably liked by the target, then the model's behavior is clearly relevant to the observer. But when the model is perceived as dissimilar (and hence probably not liked), the observer should not view as relevant to himself the behaviors or outcomes the model receives. If these interpretations are correct, the credibility of the model's communications should affect the observer's imitation when the observer likes the model, but not when the relationship is one of dislike.

Baron (1970) carried out an experiment that can be interpreted as supporting the above reasoning. An attitude similarity–dissimilarity procedure was used to induce positive or negative liking between a confederate (model) and a subject. The model was either successful and won 75 percent of the time or only moderately successful and winning 25 percent of the time in a horse race game. The observer was reinforced 60 percent of the time when he imitated the model's responses. The probability that the model's response gained him rewards (i.e., credibility of mendations) was directly related to the frequency with which subjects imitated the model, but only in the positive attraction condition.

A person's manner of dress gives an observer cues about his status (cf. Goffman, 1967), and Lefkowitz, Blake, and Mouton (1955) have demonstrated that subjects imitate a well-dressed model who violates a clearly marked pedestrian traffic signal more often than they do the transgressions of a shabbily dressed model. These results are consistent with an SEU hypothesis that high status authenticates the SEU of a model's warnings and mendations and thereby increases an observer's influenceability.

Similarly, several studies have confirmed the SEU prediction that a model's prestige is positively related to an observer's imitation. Grusec and Mischel (1966) and Mischel and Grusec (1966) had children interact with a female model who was introduced either as the new nursery school teacher or as a visiting teacher who would be leaving shortly. The permanent teacher can be viewed as possessing greater future control over resources than does the temporary teacher, thus giving more prestige to the permanent than to the temporary teacher. As predicted, high prestige models gained greater compliance (i.e., imitation) than did low prestige models. In another study Bandura, Ross, and Ross (1963) placed a child in a situation with two adult models. In one experimental condition one adult mediated reinforcements for the second adult, and both essentially ignored the child. In a second condition the adult who controlled the resources rewarded the child and ignored the second adult. The child imitated the adult with the greatest capability (i.e., the model who controlled and mediated the reinforcements) in both conditions.

Although no evidence could be found to relate an observer's imitative responses to the model's competence or expertise, it can be claimed that the empirical evidence is consistent with an SEU reinterpretation of the modeling literature and extends the external validity of the SEU theory of influence.

AGGRESSION AND ALTRUISM

The SEU theory of social conflict and influence offers a basis for reappraising the social psychological literature on aggression. Although several social scientists have noted that the concept of aggression cannot be defined without invoking value judgments on the part of the observer who attaches the label *aggression* to a set of behaviors, each has proceeded as if such criticism were not fundamental and crucial for the direction of theory and research on aggression.

Tedeschi, Smith, and Brown (1972) have argued that the behaviors that various experimenters have labeled aggressive are so diverse that theories of aggression have undertaken the impossible task of explaining *all* negative forms of behavior. For example, hitting a doll (Bandura, Ross, & Ross, 1961), asking the experimenter to pop balloons with a needle (Mussen & Rutherford, 1961), tardiness to school and physical coercion (Eron, Walden, & Lefkowitz, 1971) are only some of the responses that have served as dependent variables in aggression research. The central point has been stated best by Walters (1966): "Value judgments are involved in the categorizations of an act as aggressive. The concept of aggression is consequently not purely descriptive and thus has limited usefulness in guiding social-psychological research [p. 61]." Although the criticism is well founded, Walters' conclusion need not be accepted.

If aggression refers to coercive social actions (verbal or behavioral), then the categories in Figure 2.1 may be offered as a more discriminating, analytic, and value-free alternative to the concept of aggression. Instead of merely renaming an action or behavior as aggressive, we can refer to the actions as various forms of coercive power. The actor may use various types of threats and attendant punishments, or he may apply some punishment to a target without giving the target any cues for anticipating the punitive action (e.g., such as walking up to a person and punching him in the face for no apparent reason).

This reconceptualization of aggression may be important for several reasons. First, the actor is now viewed as a source of influence who is using coercion. This perspective may be important because the actual application of punishments will then be interpreted in the context of establishing credibility for threats or as reciprocity or vengeance-like behaviors. Second, attention is directed toward the conditions that lead observers to label certain behaviors as aggressive. Tedeschi, Smith, and Brown (1972) have proposed a number of factors that will determine such evaluation of behavior on the part of a neutral and objective third-party observer. They suggest that *observers must perceive* a behavior as intentional, offensive (rather than defensive), and antinormative in order to label it as extremely aggressive. Whether the actor's behaviors are *actually* intentional, offensive, and antinormative is of secondary concern.

A third reason that the present formulation may be important is that it raises the question, "Is there a difference in the way a target or third party responds to a source of coercive influence as a function of whether the source's behavior is or is not labeled aggressive?" It might be presumed that on the basis of the effort all people (and nations) make to rationalize their coercive influence attempts as completely defensive gestures there would be a large difference in consequences as a function of observer labeling.

The very fact that so little of the available aggression research is relevant to any of these three questions indicates that a reconceptualization of aggression would radically affect the scientist who adopted it. In Chapter 4 we discussed a theory of the conditions in which a source will choose to use coercive influence, and the claim may be made that it is an alternative to existing theories of aggression.

A quite similar reanalysis of altruistic behaviors can be made. Entire classes of positive social behaviors, such as generosity in giving money to charity (Isen, 1970), helping another in physical distress (cf. Latané & Darley, 1969), helping another in need of medical attention (Darley & Latané, 1968; Latané & Rodin, 1969), and accepting pain so that another will not be penalized (Epstein & Hornstein, 1969), can be placed under the rubric altruistic behaviors (cf. Macaulay & Berkowitz, 1970). These classes of behaviors have received increasing research attention and theoretical scrutiny.

Helping or prosocial actions may be categorized in terms of various types of promises and/or rewarding behaviors (see Figure 2.1). A neutral and objective third-party observer would probably view an actor as more altruistic the more the actor's behavior costs him, the less self-interest the observer can discover or attribute, and the more anonymous the relationship between benefactor and recipient. If the scientist's eye is on the actor he will do well to avoid the value-laden concept of altruism (unless to create such an impression is part of the actor's motivation) because the concept implies that an action is good. Unfortunately, what one man considers good may not be so evaluated by another.

Whether the actor who provides help should be considered a target or a source of influence depends on the social situation. If a victim shouts for help he may be considered the source of influence, and the potential benefactor who hears the appeal may be considered the target. Help is or is not provided at the victim's request; so the help may be interpreted as compliance to the victim's influence attempt. The nature of the communication and the relationship between source and target, victim and benefactor, should be important determinants of benefactor compliance. For example, the implausibility of the communication or the ambiguity about which response from the potential benefactor is being requested may reduce the amount of compliance the victim obtains.

Another type of situation is one in which the benefactor initiates the interaction with the person who is to be helped. The benefactor might be viewed as the source of influence who chooses to use positive inducements. If the benefactor is a source of positive influence, then the assumption of SEU theory must be that the actor always *believes* he has something to gain by his actions. Hence the evaluation of an actor's behavior as altruistic depends on the observer's ignorance of the benefactor's goals. Because human behavior is often so complex it is not easy for naïve observers (or even sophisticated psychologists) to discern the reasons for the behavior. Sometimes actors' goals are very subtle. For example, in some cultures a person may offer a complete stranger a gift. We tend to call similar behaviors hospitality, courtesy, chivalry, or just plain manners. The function of such actions may well be to establish a basis for positive attraction, both for purposes of increasing the probability that future (as yet unplanned) influence attempts will succeed with the stranger and because it presumably reduces the probability that the stranger will use coercive influence against the person.

The entire area of altruistic behavior is rather poorly conceptualized, and most of the evidence gathered has been on the basis of one-shot hypotheses. Consequently, no clear theory either explains or guides research. The scattering of evidence provides a small amount of data that is directly applicable to an SEU interpretation of helping behavior. Miller (1971) gave subjects a number of scenarios relevant to possible emergency or helping situations and asked them for their subjective estimates of the probability that their help was needed, how much the help would be worth to them if they provided it (utility), and how likely it was that the subject would actually provide help. Subjects indicated that they were more likely to provide help as their estimates of probability and utility increased. This paper-and-pencil study may be interpreted as also telling us something about how subjects define the social situation. If it is assumed that the subjects' utilities are positively related to the value of the help to the victim, then systematic studies of dimensions of situations that lead to changes in probability and utility estimations should help to identify critical factors that affect interpretations of emergency situations.

From SEU theory it could be expected that interpersonal attraction between a victim and a potential benefactor should affect the likelihood that helping behavior will be emitted. Both Darley and Latané (1968) and Clark and Word (1971) have found that friends as compared to strangers intervened more quickly in emergency situations.

The difficulty of deciding whether a nondirected, overheard communication is meant for him requires that the target develop criteria of relevance. A quite obvious example would be that a person has suffered some physical injury and calls for help, and one of the bystanders is a physician or nurse. The appeal should appear to be more relevant to the medically trained than to the medically nontrained bystanders. Kazdin and Bryan (1971) have found that the probability of target compliance (i.e., intervention) was increased when the target of the appeal for help possessed special skills or expertise relevant to the kind of help needed. Perhaps the strongest argument that can be made for a reinterpretation of helping behavior in terms of SEU theory is not in the existing evidence but rather in the kinds of future experiments that are suggested. A theory should not only explain existing data but also should heuristically lead to new research.

CONCLUSIONS

The theory that proved useful in generating and interpreting results accumulated from experimental gaming paradigms also proved to be quite powerful in coherently organizing data obtained in numerous other research paradigms. It was shown time and time again that results obtained in experimental games generalize to other research paradigms. Nevertheless, the theory has numerous shortcomings. First, the theory considers only a single type of influence message at any one time; yet most social situations, as we saw with conformity, involve complex combinations of influence modes. Second, no propositions have been offered to tell how *combinations* of source characteristics affect the influence process. Almost all of the research has varied everything at once or varied only one source characteristic while holding all others constant. Third, most of the theory applies only to one-way interactions; thus predictions have been made with regard to influence, but very little has been said about counterinfluence. The theory is relatively static.

It is true that the more dynamic processes of bargaining and coalition behavior have been considered, but the level of theory is quite unsophisticated. For example, no attempt was made to integrate into free bargaining situations such message factors as the credibility of promises or threats. In other words, the less controllable the situation is from a scientific point of view, the less relevant the present theory is for understanding or predicting behavior.

Whatever its limitations, the SEU theory of social influence does not appear to suffer more than any alternative theory in social psychology. The external validity of the theory is apparently quite good, and encouragement has been given for making further generalizations and for provoking further reinterpretations of traditional areas of research in social psychology. Yet the limitations of the theory do imply that one should be quite cautious in applying its principles in the real world. In other words, we can be much more confident about the external than about the ecological validity of the SEU theory. While the external validity can be judged by consistency of results across problem areas, research procedures, and populations of subjects, the ecological validity can be judged primarily on the basis: "Does it represent real-world processes?"

Ecological Validity

Shubik (1968) has posed some very serious problems for those who want to make technical applications from the kind of theory presented in this book, although his criticisms were directed at game theory proper. He notes that in complex social situations it is sometimes difficult to identify what game is being played and by whom. As Shubik notes, "It is easy to write down a general formal statement saying, 'Let us consider the United States and the Soviet Union as two players . . .'; it is not so easy to defend the proposition that it was worthwhile to do so [p. 84]." In such a game is the United States one entity, or should we study its diplomatic representatives, or its armed forces, or its political leaders, or its political factions, or its minority groups, or some combination of the above, ad infinitum? The situations are often too complex, even when played by one person, to represent in either matrix or game tree form. This problem would hold even if we could know all the moves available to a player and the utilities that he assigns to the consequences of each.

The problem of measuring utilities is an unsolved one in decision theory, and the best we can often do is to guess or estimate what they are. What's more, it is almost impossible, as Shubik points out, to assign utilities to groups. Whose utility do we apply to the outcome? The consequence of an action is certainly not worth the same amount to the leaders of a nation as it is to its population, its diplomats, or its military leaders. One cannot combine utilities across people in any logical or coherent manner.

With all of these problems (and others besides), it should be clear that whatever applications of SEU theory are suggested, they are offered tentatively and even reluctantly. Yet it has become fashionable to believe that a social scientist shirks his moral responsibility if he does not provide some link between his work and the solution of burning social issues. To avoid being tagged shirkers and also to derive some intellectual enjoyment from playing around with theoretical extensions, we will climb, theory in hand, far out on several social limbs.

It is not altogether unreasonable to expect that our theoretical formulations will shed some light on the complex and utterly confounded sorts of conflict interactions that occur in the nonlaboratory world. We will indicate by analogy and suggestion how a more mature version of the SEU theory might be applicable to clinical psychology, organizational psychology, the effects of portrayals of violence in the mass media, and international problems of war and peace.

CLINICAL PSYCHOLOGY

Although not the first to interpret mental illness in terms of social power, Haley (1963) has stated that various symptoms are really tactics that have succeeded in solving for the patient some problem of social power. For example, he described the relationship between a European-born authoritarian (chauvinist) husband and a wife who very much resented the oppressive domination under which she lived. Like Lady MacBeth, the wife developed the compulsion to wash her hands over and over again. She could not get dirty, nor could she expose herself to bacteria. Now when her husband demanded that she clean the house, wash dishes, or go out for the evening she could not do as he wanted because she could not control her own behavior. She was "mentally ill." Through this device of believing that she could not control her own actions, the wife gained control over the husband.

To vastly overstate the case, abnormal behavior may be defined as behavior that is unexpected and upsetting to some person powerful enough to initiate medical help or institutionalization. If the psychologist is conceptualized as a source of influence (or power) and the client is conceptualized as the target of influence, clear parallels can be drawn from evidence obtained from clinics and the experimental laboratory.

Research has shown that females are more conforming, suggestible, persuasible, cooperative, and honest than are males. Not surprisingly, psychiatrists, clinical psychologists, and other social workers prefer to work with females, since they are the kinds of patients who make the therapist feel efficient and effective in his therapy. Similarly, psychologists do not like to work with sociopaths, who are characterized as seemingly impervious to influence attempts directed toward them. They do not condition to verbal reinforcements, and they fail to learn in a variety of experimental situations. As Tedeschi and O'Donovan (1971) indicated, "what establishes power over other persons does not usually establish power over sociopaths [p. 60]." Clinical psychologists, who are accustomed to wielding a certain amount of power over patients, are threatened by a vague awareness that they are powerless with respect to sociopaths; hence sociopaths are viewed as suffering from a probably incurable disease.

Two problems face the psychologist: (1) the patient is likely to be involved in power struggles in the family and other primary or secondary groups; (2) the therapist and patient are involved in an influence relationship. In the first instance the therapist may take the role of mediator in a bargaining situation. In this role he might want to interview not only the patient but also important other people with whom the patient is in conflict. Additionally, the patient may never have developed skills of interpersonal influence, such as how to gain compliance while remaining liked. The psychologist might attempt to teach these skills either by modeling or by explicating the influence strategies that he uses in his own interpersonal relationships. The patient may learn the value of source characteristics (such as friendship) and impression management strategies. Influence strategies that might be effective in coalition formation in n-person groups would also be worthy of a patient's attention.

Various therapies concentrate on different forms of social influence. Behavior therapies rely primarily on the explicit use of both coercive and reward power; psychoanalysis relies more on information control (persuasion) . The psychoanalyst attempts to influence the patient to view the world and himself through the meaning categories of psychoanalytic theory. Advice (mendations) , consultation (both warnings and mendations plus some matters of fact and value) , and interpretation (decoding tacit communications) constitute descriptive instruction about the nature of reality. Once the therapist's basic assumptions are accepted he has gained control over the patient by virtue of the extremely high credibility and plausibility of his communications. Nondirective therapy uses love-oriented power as the means to treat (i.e., influence) the patient. Whiting and Child (1953) have found that love-oriented punishment, which involves the manipulation of nurturance by withdrawing love, is positively related to the child's tendency to identify with the parent. This finding suggests that positive transference in therapy should increase the probability that the patient will accept the therapist's definitions of reality, including the explicit and implicit communication of values.

Although the therapist's source characteristics have not been the subject of systematic research, there is good reason to believe that they might be connected with the prognosis for therapy. Both the expertise and the status of the psychologist or psychiatrist are made salient in the situation. The patient ordinarily is required to visit the therapist's office and is ushered into the therapist's presence by a receptionist or nurse. The cues make it clear that the patient will provide money and that the therapist will provide help, that the therapist is the expert (the doctor) and the patient is sick. It might be said parenthetically that clinical psychologists usually perceive themselves as somewhat altruistic, but patients may view the situation differently, particularly when the bill arrives each month. The therapist informs the patient about the limits of what each can do, where each will sit in the office, and the rules that will govern their interaction.

In no way can the clinical psychologist avoid the implications of his relationship with his clients. He must make his goals for therapy as explicit as he can; acknowledge that he is in the business of manipulating the attitudes, values, and behaviors of others, however subtly he applies influence; and wield his power in the service of the values he holds. Psychotherapy thus interpreted certainly should be receptive to a theory of social conflict and influence.

ORGANIZATIONAL PSYCHOLOGY

The propositions of SEU theory clearly have application to organizational settings, though they have seldom been applied. For example, we have seen that interpersonal trust is based on honesty and openness of communications. If one backs up his words with corresponding deeds he will be trusted. Manipulatory modes of influence must be avoided by the source who wants to maintain a high level of trust; there is too much danger of discovery in deception. Persuasive communications must be based on facts, and threats and promises must be backed up. For management to meet these conditions secret salary schedules must be eliminated, clear goals must be specified in the promises of rewards offered as incentives to employees, and so on. Townsend (1970) captured these ideas in his best-selling *Up the Organization*.

> Secrecy implies either:
> 1. What I'm doing is so horrible I don't dare tell you,
>
> or
>
> 2. I don't trust you (anymore) [p. 151].

The legitimacy of an authority, the basis of status, rests on the constituency's trust that decisions, allocations of rewards, and assignment of responsibilities will be carried out equitably and in the interests of the group. Persons of status must reveal the decisions that are made and must rationalize those decisions to their constituents. Every decision made without such reasoned elaborations will undermine the trust that the constituents have for the authority and will increase the amount of noncompliance with the organization's rules and objectives. The typical organization in the United States is a political system in that management can gain compliant behaviors from employees without threats or force, and the employees perceive their interests as coincident with those of the organization.

Persons are more or less attractive, competent, or prestigious, and they possess lesser or greater status in the organization. These source characteristics should be related to the degree of success a person has within the organization. If a foreman or manager treats others with respect and dignity, knows his own job thoroughly, speaks with high and consistent credibility, clarifies and rationalizes objectives, and generally sets an example as a model, even if just by reporting to work early and by working hard, then the employees under him should believe that they have a good boss, and they should often imitate his behavior and comply eagerly to his requests.

Viewing the organization as a set of conflicts between various individuals and groups causes one to look for coalitions being formed, bargaining situations, and direct power confrontations. Much contemporary stress is placed on humanistic goals, but the hard-boiled and Machiavellian approach suggested here is not necessarily void of humanistic values. Openness, trust, and concern for the feelings and interests of others are of central concern to an influence-oriented approach; yet many humanists may ignore and, in fact, abhor the use of influence. It may well be that only by concentrating on the power and influence aspects of behavior can some of the humanistic goals be achieved within the context of the constraints posed by the organization's major goals. The future of organizational psychology may be inextricably bound up with the study of power and influence.

MASS MEDIA VIOLENCE

Considerable controversy has been raging about the effects mass media violence has on the behavior of viewers, particularly with regard to the movies and television. The works of Berkowitz and Geen (1966) and Bandura and Walters (1963) suggest that when a person views aggressive behavior on film he is likely to be more aggressive in his own actions. Yet a large-scale study of televised violence (Feshbach and Singer, 1971) leads to exactly the opposite conclusion: boys who watched violent programs subsequently were rated as less aggressive than boys who watched nonviolent fare. The reappraisal of aggression that we have presented suggests inadequacies in the studies done and in the conclusions drawn from the results.

The usual definition of aggression stresses behaviors that have as their intent the doing of harm to other humans. Berkowitz and Geen (1966) investigated aggression by placing subjects in a situation where they were to be a teacher and deliver punishment in the form of electric shock to help a learner confederate improve at his task. What may appear on the surface to be a harmful action (the delivery of shock) has a benevolent intention rationalized for it by the experimenter (it is a teaching technique to aid the learner). From our perspective the interpretation of such an action as aggressive is certainly moot.

In another investigation of aggression Bandura and Walters (1963) gave subjects the opportunity to imitate a model by hitting a big plastic doll that had the words HIT ME painted on it in large block letters. That the doll was not damaged when the adult hit it should lead a child to believe that no harm would occur when he hit it himself. Also it might be conjectured that the child saw the action he undertook as fantasy and play activity. If this analysis is correct there is no reason to expect the child to act aggressively when he interacts with another human being.

The previously mentioned Feshbach and Singer study opens up an interesting possibility. The boys' ratings on aggressiveness were made out each week by a housemother or dorm leader who also watched the programs selected for the boys to view. The ratings may have indicated not that boys who watched violent programs were less aggressive but that raters who watched such programs evaluated the boys' behaviors as less aggressive as compared to the television behaviors they had been watching. Thus the effects of mass media violence may not be that children or adults imitate such behaviors but that the standards of conduct are lowered as a result of using behaviors observed on mass media as anchors or frames of reference to judge and evaluate real behaviors of interacting persons.

This is not the place to pursue this argument (see Tedeschi, Smith, & Brown, 1972), but it should be clear that the concepts of SEU theory have implications for analysing the effects of mass media violence and that an entirely new perspective on the problem can be generated by doing so. If we adopt the position that models tacitly communicate warnings and mendations by their behavior–outcome sequences, questions arise about the type, credibility, and utilities associated with these communications; their relevancy to the viewer; and the source and target characteristics involved. These questions have seldom been explicitly stated, much less researched.

WAR AND PEACE

Kaiser Wilhelm of Germany and Emperor Hirohito of Japan have been quoted as pessimistic about the outcomes of the wars that each chose to enter. The Kaiser has been quoted as saying that at least Germany would make India bleed; Hirohito succinctly expressed his position by pointing out that sometimes there is no alternative to leaping off a tower (Frank, 1967). If, as can be ascertained by their writings, each of these leaders entered a war in which they assessed themselves as having a low subjective expected probability of winning, why did they do so? Historians (Tuchman, 1962) and strategic analysts (Kahn, 1960) suggest that each leader perceived that he had no alternative but to enter such a conflict, and that the alternative to war was perceived as worse than war itself, involving degradation, ignominy, and possible occupation by expanding enemy forces.

These historical events have their analogues in the game laboratory. Tedeschi, Horai, Lindskold, and Gahagan (1968), for example, found that when the differences in the SEU for compliance and noncompliance to threats was zero—that is, the gains and costs were equal for whichever response the target subjects chose—subjects consistently refused to comply to the threats. This result would imply that some psychological costs were not indicated by actual numerical payoffs and that these payoffs were associated with the ignominy of yielding to coercion in the presence of an experimenter. Brown (1968; 1970) and Modigliani (1971) have demonstrated that individuals will go to great lengths to avoid embarrassing situations and will attempt to save face when they can. It would appear that face-saving behaviors are very important both in the laboratory and in international affairs.

The SEU theory provides a basis for understanding the rational criteria decision makers use in conflict-of-interests situations. If the theory is at all applicable to international behaviors, then the arms race, the nuclear balance of terror, and the occurrence of armed conflicts in the world can be viewed as based on the rational and effective assessment of what it takes to retain power and influence among nations. While the SEU theory puts some of the wind back into the sails of the rather gruesome scenarios of nuclear holocaust proposed by strategic thinkers (cf. Kahn, 1960, 1965), it is clear that means of conflict resolution other than the use of threats and force are available. But between nations that are suspicious of one another (attributions of exploitative intentions are made), promises, warnings, and mendations are likely to fall on deaf ears. Bargaining is likely to be unsuccessful without the presence of important mediators, and coalitions are likely to form, causing the intensity of conflict to escalate or grow deeper.

Osgood (1962) has proposed a policy for the mitigation of international conflicts that does not rely on an escalation of penalties, threats, or intensity of the conflict. Graduated reciprocation in tension reduction (GRIT) requires that the nation that adopts the strategy make over time a series of announcements that the source will unilaterally undertake some specific low risk but costly actions; the actions should be designed to benefit the target. Although the promises made should be noncontingent and 100 percent credible, some nonspecified reciprocity could be requested. GRIT is a strategy for developing trust between initially hostile and suspicious nations so that forms of influence other than coercion can be effective in resolving their conflicts. Osgood's strategy has received research support (Bonoma & Monteverde, 1972; Tedeschi, Bonoma, & Lindskold, 1970) and is entirely consistent with SEU theory. However, there is also evidence that GRIT works only when the parties to interaction are of equal prestige (Tedeschi, Horai, Lindskold, & Gahagan, 1968), a finding that would suggest that President Nixon's detente policy would work better with the Soviet Union than with the Peoples' Republic of China.

The SEU theory contains nothing for use as a basis for suggesting foreign policy, and it is likely that decision makers have a source of experience richer than the present theory. Nevertheless, both diplomats and military analysts may draw some suggestive hints from the theory.

CONCLUSIONS

Our foray into the world of clinical psychology, organizational psychology, mass media violence, and war and peace may indicate the long-term possibilities for a general theory of power and influence. The embryonic character of SEU theory at present requires that such forays be modestly interpreted and that they act more as teasers about possibilities than as statements about confirmed realities. However, unless we begin to try out principles developed in the laboratory we may never know how to improve practically on what we are doing. Practical failures may also lead to new insights and theoretical and research questions.

Some Final Thoughts

The worth of a scientific theory must be judged in part by the coherence it brings to the interpretations of existing research and by its power to generate entirely new research possibilities. In the face of apparent anarchy in the research on experimental games, this book has tried to demonstrate that an impressive amount of consistency of results and generalizations is possible when a particular set of concepts is applied for purposes of interpretation.

Incorporated in the theory are structural concepts of conflict, competition, and cooperation, the exploitative and accommodative intentions of the interacting parties, the attraction, status, prestige, and esteem of the involved parties, and the types of messages transmitted and their properties. The action of norms is important in some situations to mitigate intense power conflicts. Application of the concepts of the SEU theory to traditional areas of social psychology, such as attitude change, verbal reinforcement, social conformity, modeling and imitation, and aggression and altruism, indicates that the theory is not bound to the methodology that has spawned it. Suggested applications of the theory indicate that it may have great potential in a wide variety of nonlaboratory settings.

The authors' attitude toward the SEU theory is that it is a useful conceptual apparatus for asking old questions in new ways and for putting together a great deal of data. Where before no apparent connection existed between this area and that, the theory provides some continuity and coherence for social psychology. Yet theories are devised as a means to develop superceding theories. In the process of following the lines of inquiry suggested by the present theory it can only be hoped that it is fertile enough to bear the seeds of its own destruction. The theory must be developed into maturity, a process that will require many changes in concepts, assumptions, and relationships. That task has hardly begun.

Glossary

All-Computer Simulation. A model specifically designed to be examined and evaluated with digital or analog computer technology.

Asymmetrical Contingency. According to Jones and Gerard (1967), a mixed version of the pseudocontingency and reactive contingency interaction patterns in which person A behaves according to the internal or preestablished rules of pseudocontingency, and person B's acts are almost solely reactive to the first's responses.

Attitudinal Structuring. Interpersonal exchanges designed to alter the nature of the relationship by changing each other's attitudes—for example, the degree of friendship, trust, respect, and accommodativeness extant in a relationship.

Attraction. A generic construct usually viewed as an interpersonal attitude, possessing cognitive, affective, and behavioral components. Attraction implies the tendency to approach rather than avoid the attracted individual and is based on such antecedents as reward mediation and attitudinal similarities.

Authentication. An upward biasing of the subjective probability the target assigns to an influence message because of the personal attributes or characteristics of the source of influence.

Bargaining. A situation in which two or more entities are in disagreement over one or more issues and attempt to reach agreement in order to arrive at a jointly acceptable solution.

Bargaining Range. The range of outcomes that fall between the minimum dispositions of each of the parties to negotiation.

Behavior Control. According to Thibaut and Kelley (1959), a type of power in which one party can by varying his own behavior make it desirable for the other party to also vary his behavior. One of two types of interpersonal control. See also *fate control*.

Coalition.   The formation of groups whose intention is to employ mutual resources for the accomplishment of some common goal in a mixed-motive situation.

Comparison Level.   According to Thibaut and Kelley (1959), chronic or average level of reward a person expects from a situation. It is the standard used to determine the attractiveness or acceptability of outcomes and relationships.

Comparison Level For Alternatives (CL_{alt}).   According to Thibaut and Kelley (1959), the lowest level of outcomes a person will accept given his perceived alternatives. It is the standard used to determine an individual's dependence on a relationship.

Competition.   A conflict state in which the incompatibility that exists between the actors extends beyond their immediate activities to include their desired goals or end states for the interaction.

Conflict.   An interactive state in which the behaviors or goals of one actor are to some degree incompatible with the behaviors or goals of some other actor or actors.

Conflict Size.   According to Deutsch, Canavan, and Rubin (1971), the expected difference in the value of the outcomes a person will receive if he wins compared with the value he will receive if the other wins.

Costs.   Outcomes that have negative utility for the individual.

Cue Control.   According to Jones and Gerard (1967), a type of information control in which the source provides stimuli to the target as a means of eliciting preestablished habit patterns.

Deauthentication.   A downward biasing of the subjective probability the target assigns to an influence message because of the personal attributes or characteristics of the source of influence.

Decision Theory.   A system of primarily economic assumptions and postulates designed to explain and/or predict human choice behavior. Variants include classical economics, expected value, subjective expected value, and subjective expected utility theories.

Descriptive Theory.   Any theory that attempts to describe the way individuals actually do behave.

Distributive Bargaining.   Bargaining situation in which the parties are in basic conflict because of a clash of goals.

Ecological Validity.   The degree to which the data integrated into a coherent theory allows theoretical propositions to explain naturally occurring phenomena in the real world.

Esteem.   The perception of another person's degree of expertise and/or ability in a relevant area.

Expected Value. A decision criterion determined as the sum of the products of the objective probabilities of occurrence of events and the associated objective values of the events related to the choice of a particular behavioral alternative.

Experiment. A controlled observational setting in which an investigator systematically manipulates one or more independent events in order to determine their effects on one or more dependent events, and in which the elements sampled from a universe are randomly assigned to the various conditions of the experiment.

Experimental Law. A generalized and reliable empirical relationship between one or a set of independent events and a dependent event.

Experimental Realism. According to Aronson and Carlsmith (1968), the degree to which a subject is forced to take an experiment seriously; that is, the degree to which the situation is realistic to him and has an impact on him. The situation need not be similar to a real-world experience; it need only involve the subject. See also *mundane realism.*

Exploratory Experiment. An experiment based on a hunch or sheer curiosity about the phenomenon in question.

External Validity. Reflects whether the results from a particular experiment generalize to other paradigms, subject populations, and measuring instruments. It represents the problem of interpreting a difference between conditions and generalizing it to new situations.

Fate Control. According to Thibaut and Kelley (1959), a type of power in which one party has unilateral control over the other's outcomes. One of two types of interpersonal control. See also *behavior control.*

Force. According to Bachrach and Baratz (1963), the actual imposition of negative sanctions to a target after the target's noncompliance to the source's threats.

Formal Theory. An abstract level of analysis concerned strictly with definitions, theorems, and the relationships between terms. A formal theory is devoid of any empirical meaning.

Gains. Outcomes that have positive utility for the individual.

Game. A situation in which the outcomes of two or more persons in interaction are conjoint, and the persons are uncertain about which of several outcomes will occur. Some writers add that a game must involve a contest conducted under prescribed rules or that there must be a conflict of interests between the participants.

Game Theory. An elaborate mathematical theory with applications to behavior in conflict situations.

Hypothetico-Deductive Experiment. An experiment specifically designed to test hypotheses deduced from an existing theoretical framework. Also called a hypothesis-testing experiment or a nomological experiment.

Illustrative Experiment. An experiment whose outcome is previously known to the investigator and is performed for the purposes of demonstration.

Influence, Social. Most broadly, any causal connection that exists between the actor's behaviors, attitudes, or actions and another actor or actors' behaviors, attitudes, or actions.

Information Control. A manipulatory influence mode in which the source attempts to control the information the target receives about the environment while hiding his own influence intentions. Examples of information control include cue control, information filtering, and, in some conditions, warnings and mendations.

Ingratiation. According to Jones (1964), the deliberate use of strategies for the purpose of increasing one's attractiveness in the eyes of others with the eventual goal of acquiring gains and avoiding costs.

Integrative Bargaining. A bargaining situation that contains some areas of mutual concern and complementary interests between the interactive participants.

Interaction. According to Thibaut and Kelley (1959), that state of affairs in which people emit behaviors in each other's presence. These behaviors usually have associated with them some positive or negative consequences for the interacting parties.

Interdependence, Social. The degree to which one actor's behaviors, acts, or goals are dependent for their occurrence or change on the behaviors, actions, or goals of one or a set of other actors. See also *interaction*.

Internal Validity. Reflects whether a difference between experimental conditions can be attributed to some real effect or whether the difference is an artifact of the measurement process or uncontrolled factors.

Intraorganizational Bargaining. A situation in which one or a few individuals within an organization represent their fellows at the bargaining table. It involves the negotiators' efforts to bring their own constituents' expectations into alignment with their bargaining objectives.

Level Of Aspiration. The utility a bargainer would like to receive from a bargaining interaction.

Manipulation. Influence attempts in which the source tries to disguise or hide from the target the influence nature of the relationship. Reinforcement control and information control are examples of modes of manipulatory influence.

Man–Machine Simulation. A research situation in which a partial model of some real-world phenomena is used as a backdrop, and subjects make decisions and behave within the confines of the model.

Mediation. The intervention of a third party who is accepted by both negotiators and whose function is to help bargainers reach a fair and peaceful settlement to their bargaining dispute.

Mendation. An influence communication that predicts that some rewarding state of affairs may befall a target as a result of existing or future social and/or environmental contingencies. The source does not control the rewarding stimuli. Mendations may be contingent or noncontingent and request- and consequences-specific or nonspecific in much the same manner as promises.

Methodological Experiment. An experiment designed to explore, standardize, or perfect apparatus or measuring equipment.

Minimal Social Situation. An experimental situation in which each of two participants has fate control over the other but in which neither person is aware of the interdependence of their outcomes or of the social nature of the situation.

Minimax Strategy. A strategy by which a person attempts to secure his best outcome in the worst conditions another person can mete out.

Minimum Disposition. The minimum utility a bargainer will accept as a bargaining solution.

Mixed-Motive Situations. According to Schelling (1960), a situation in which the interests of interacting parties are partially coincident and partially in conflict; that is, the outcomes each receives for each set of behaviors are not perfectly correlated. See also pure conflict and pure coordination situations.

Model. A closed verbal, pictorial, or mathematical system based on an analogy and proposed as a simple but inclusive representation of the structural and dynamic components of some real-world phenomenon.

Mundane Realism. According to Aronson and Carlsmith (1968), the degree to which events that occur in an experiment resemble events that occur in the real world. The situation need not have an impact on the subject; it need only be similar to real-world experiences. See also *experimental realism*.

Mutual Contingency. According to Jones and Gerard (1967), an interaction pattern in which each individual's responses are determined partly by internal stimuli (e.g., plans, attitudes) and partly by the responses of the other in the ongoing situation.

Negotiation. A generic term designed to include all forms of bargaining between parties, especially in those conditions in which the experimental environment approximates real-world conditions. For example, bargainers might serve as representatives of some larger group, or a mediator might be present.

Nomological Experiment. See *hypothetico-deductive experiment*.

Nonzero-Sum Games. Games in which the outcomes found in each of the cells of the payoff matrix do not sum to zero. Pure coordination and mixed-motive situations can be described as nonzero-sum games.

Norm. A rule that prevails in a social group and that governs acceptable behaviors and prohibits unacceptable behaviors. Violation of the rule may bring about the imposition of sanctions by the prevailing group.

Normative Theory. A theory that offers advice about what an actor should do if he wants to maximize certain objectives. It describes what an individual should do rather than what individuals actually do. Also called prescriptive theory.

Open Influence. Influence attempts that do not attempt to hide the source's efforts to modify a target's behavior. Threats, promises, and some types of warnings and mendations are modes of open influence.

Operational Definition. An attempt to assign meaning to a concept by specifying in its definition the activities or operations used to measure it.

Outcome. A consequence of engaging in behavior that has some utility (positive, negative, or neutral) to the individual. Outcomes can be viewed in terms of those rewards and punishments that actually accrue to a person after behavior, or as those rewards and punishments that the person anticipates when considering his possible behavioral alternatives.

Perfect Information. An assumption of classical economic decision theory that presumes that the decision maker knows all of his available choice alternatives as well as the outcomes associated with each choice before he makes a decision.

Power Inversion Effect. The tendency of weaker group members to form coalitions against stronger group members, thereby causing the stronger players to lose and the weaker players to win; hence strength is weakness and weakness is strength.

Power, Social. Most generally the degree to which a source can gain compliance to his wishes, requests, demands, or offers from one or a set of other actors through the use of various influence modes (e.g., threats, promises, warnings, mendations) and the attendant provision or prediction of various reinforcing or punishing states of affairs for the target.

Prescriptive Theory. See *normative theory.*

Prestige. The perception of the material or physical resources of another person and of that person's intent to use such resources for purposes of influence.

Prisoner's Dilemma Game (PDG). A mixed-motive game used in the investigation of interpersonal conflict. It is a two-person, two-choice, nonzero-sum game that permits no participant communication and that meets certain rules on the structure of the payoffs.

Profit. According to Homans (1961), the total gains minus the total costs associated with a given behavior.

Promise, Contingent. An if–then implicative statement of the form, "If you do (or don't do) Y, I will do X," where X is some rewarding state of affairs and can be so discriminated by the target.

Promise, Noncontingent. A self-prediction on the part of a source of the form, "I will do X," where X is an action, the withholding of an action, the production of a rewarding stimulus, or the removal of a punishing stimulus that can be discriminated and evaluated by a target as rewarding or pleasurable. The source does not specify any actions by which the target can increase the probability of attaining the stipulated reward.

Pseudocontingency. According to Jones and Gerard (1967), a prototype of more complex social interactions in which each individual responds primarily on the basis of his own previous responses or carries out some preestablished plan.

Pure Conflict. A situation in which the outcomes associated with interaction are perfectly and negatively correlated for the participants. For example, according to Schelling, whenever one person gains his maximal amount, the other loses his maximal amount. See also pure coordination and mixed-motive situations.

Pure Coordination. According to Schelling (1960), a situation in which the interconnected outcomes associated with interaction are perfectly and positively correlated. For example, whenever one person gains his maximal amount, so does the other. See also *pure conflict situations* and *mixed-motive situations*.

Rational Behavior. The ability to demonstrate transitivity of preferences and then make choices between alternatives that maximize something—for example, profits, expected value, or subjective expected utility.

Reactive Contingency. According to Jones and Gerard (1967), an interaction in which each individual's response is almost solely determined by the preceding response of his partner.

Reinforcement Control. A manipulatory influence mode in which the source directly mediates rewards or punishments to the target in an effort to secure some desirable objective from the target.

Reliability. Reflects whether, if the same set of objects is measured repeatedly with the same or comparable measuring instruments, the same results will be obtained. Although it is necessary that results be reliable to be internally valid, it is not sufficient.

Risk, Choice Under. The decision situation that occurs when the connection between acts and outcomes is not certain but only probabilistic, and in which the decision maker is aware of the relevant probabilities.

238 *Glossary*

Saddle Point. A payoff matrix cell that represents the interaction of the two participants' dominant strategies. It is the cell that corresponds to the outcome each participant receives when both make choices that would yield them the best outcome they could attain in the worst possible conditions the other person can mete out. Only some games contain a saddle point.

Simulation. Any experiment, demonstration, or test situation that uses a model and attempts to provide an inclusive replica of both structural and dynamic characteristics of the phenomenon under consideration. See *all-computer simulation* and *man–machine simulation*.

Simulation Experiment. An experiment performed on a model.

Source-Based Costs. A type of cost, associated with the use of influence, that the source voluntarily incurs. The two types of source-based costs are those that are dependent on the target's behavior and those that are not. The independent type is typified by such fixed costs as securing communication opportunities, securing resources, and maintaining surveillance over the target. Source-based, target-dependent costs are still voluntarily incurred by the source but are contingent on the target's behavior; for example, a source must fulfill a threat only when the target noncomplies. See also *target-based costs*.

Status. The perception of another person's role position in a social hierarchy. Perceived status implies the need to show deference to an occupant of the role position.

Status Quo Point. The utility to an actor of not reaching an agreement during bargaining. The status quo solution leaves the bargainers at about the same position they occupied at the start of the bargaining, minus the time, energy, and other costs expended during the interaction.

Strategy. A set of directions or contingencies that can guide a person's responding in all of the potential conditions he can foresee.

Subjective Expected Utility. A decision criterion determined as the sum of the products of the subjective probabilities of occurrence of events and their associated utilities related to the choice of a particular behavioral alternative.

Subjective Expected Value. A decision criterion determined as the sum of the products of the subjective probabilities of occurrence of events and the associated objective values of the events related to the choice of a particular behavioral alternative.

Target-Based Costs. A type of cost associated with the use of influence that is not under the source's direct control—for example, the costs associated with retaliation or counterinfluence. See also *source-based costs*.

Theory. Generally a set of relationships between variables from which explanations of natural phenomena may be deduced and coherent hypotheses about novel phenomena may be generated.

Threat, Compellent. A contingent threat message that specifies that the target instigate or complete some action in order to avoid punishment.

Threat, Contingent. An if–then implicative statement of the form, "If you do (or don't do) Y, I will do X," where X is some punishing stimulus and can be evaluated as such by the target.

Threat Credibility. The truth value of a threat. Operationally the proportion of times that a source backs up his threats by punishing target's noncompliant acts over all those occasions when such noncompliance occurs.

Threat, Deterrent. A contingent threat message that specifies that the target refrain from some act in order to avoid punishment.

Threat, Noncontingent. A self-prediction on the part of a source of influence of the form, "I will do X," where X is an action, the withholding of an action, the production of a noxious stimulus, or the removal of a positive reinforcer that can be discriminated and evaluated by the target as detrimental or punishing. The source does not specify any actions by which the target can avoid the stipulated punishment.

Transitivity Of Preferences. The ability to so order preferences that if A is preferred to B, and B is preferred to C, A will be preferred to C.

Trucking Game. An experimental situation developed by Deutsch and Krauss (1960) for investigating the dynamics of conflict in an enriched environmental setting. In the trucking game each of two players is given the role of the owner of a trucking company and is assigned the task of transporting fictitious commodities from a starting place to a destination. The only route that can be used to obtain profits on any one trip (trial) contains a one-lane section through which only one of the trucks can pass at a time, and therein lies the conflict. Gates can be provided the bargainers to threaten the other person and deny him access to the one-lane path.

Trust. A reliance on information received from another person about uncertain environmental states and their accompanying outcomes in a risky situation.

Trustworthiness. A target perception that the communicator is accommodative in his intent and is motivated to communicate valid statements about the causal structure of the social or physical environment to the target.

Uncertainty, Choice Under. The decision situation that occurs when the connection between acts and outcomes is probabilistic and such probabilities are unknown or difficult to objectively determine from the actor's perspective.

Utility. The subjective value of a commodity or outcome for a particular individual.

Utility Function. The set of utilities a bargainer assigns to those outcomes that can accrue to him during a bargaining interaction.

Warning. An influence communication that predicts that some punishing state of affairs may befall a target as a result of existing or future social and/or environmental contingencies. The source does not control the punishing stimuli. Warnings may be contingent or noncontingent and request- and consequences-specific or nonspecific in much the same manner as threats.

Zero-Sum Games. Games in which the payoffs that accrue to each of the participants sum to zero; that is, whenever one person wins, the other loses. Zero-sum games are also pure conflict situations.

References

Abelson, R. P. Simulation of social behavior. In G. Lindzey & E. Aronson, eds., *Handbook of social psychology.* 2nd ed. Vol. II. Reading, Mass.: Addison-Wesley, 1968. Pp. 274–356.

Abelson, R. P., & Miller, J. Negative persuasion via personal insult. *Journal of Experimental Social Psychology,* 1967, *3,* 321–33.

Adams, H. *The education of Henry Adams.* New York: Modern Library, 1931.

Adams, J. S. Inequity in social exchange. In L. Berkowitz, ed., *Advances in experimental social psychology.* Vol. 2. New York: Academic Press, 1965. Pp. 267–99.

Albert, S., & Dabbs, J. M., Jr. Physical distance and persuasion. *Journal of Personality and Social Psychology,* 1970, *15,* 265–70.

Alexander, C. N., Jr., & Weil, H. G. Players, persons, and purposes: Situational meaning and the Prisoner's Dilemma game. *Sociometry,* 1969, *32,* 121–44.

Allen, V. L. Situational factors in conformity. In L. Berkowitz, ed., *Advances in experimental social psychology.* Vol. 2. New York: Academic Press, 1965. Pp. 133–75.

Amidjaja, I. R., & Vinacke, W. E. Achievement, nurturance, and competition in male and female triads. *Journal of Personality and Social Psychology,* 1965, 2, 447–50.

Anderson, A. J., & Smith, W. P. Threat, communication, and bargaining. Paper presented at the Eastern Psychological Association meeting, Atlantic City, New Jersey, 1970.

Anderson, R. E. Status structures in coalition bargaining games. *Sociometry,* 1967, *30,* 393–403.

Argyle, M. Social pressures in public and private situations. *Journal of Abnormal and Social Psychology,* 1957, *54,* 172–75.

Argyle, M., & Kendon, A. The experimental analysis of social performance. In L. Berkowitz, ed., *Advances in experimental social psychology.* Vol. 3. New York: Academic Press, 1967. Pp. 55–98.

Aronfreed, J., & Paskel, V. Altruism, empathy, and the conditioning of positive affect. Reported in J. Aronfreed, ed., *Conduct and conscience.* New York: Academic Press, 1968.

241

Aronson, E., & Carlsmith, J. M. Experimentation in social psychology. In G. Lindzey & E. Aronson, eds., *The handbook of social psychology*. Vol. 2. Reading, Mass.: Addison-Wesley, 1968. Pp. 1–79.

Aronson, E., & Golden, B. The effect of relevant and irrelevant aspects of communicator credibility on opinion change. *Journal of Personality*, 1962, *30*, 135–46.

Asch, S. E. The doctrine of suggestion, prestige and imitation in social psychology. *Psychological Review*, 1948, *55*, 250–76.

Asch, S. E. Effects of group pressure upon the modification and distortion of judgment. In H. Guetzkow, ed., *Groups, leadership and men*. Pittsburgh, Pennsylvania: Carnegie Press, 1951. Pp. 177–90.

Asch, S. E. *Social psychology*. Englewood Cliffs, N.J.: Prentice-Hall, 1952.

Atkinson, J. W. *An introduction to motivation*. New York: Van Nostrand, 1964.

Bachrach, P., & Baratz, M. S. Decisions and nondecisions: An analytical framework. *American Political Science Review*, 1963, *57*, 632–42.

Baldwin, D. Thinking about threats. *Journal of Conflict Resolution*, 1971, *15*, 71–78.

Bandura, A. Vicarious processes: A case of no-trial learning. In L. Berkowitz, ed., *Advances in experimental social psychology*. Vol. II. New York: Academic Press, 1965. Pp. 1–55.

Bandura, A. *Principles of behavior modification*. New York: Holt, 1969.

Bandura, A.; Ross, D.; & Ross, S. Transmission of aggression through imitation of aggressive models. *Journal of Abnormal and Social Psychology*, 1961, *63*, 575–82.

Bandura, A.; Ross, D.; & Ross, S. A comparative test of the status envy, social power, and the secondary-reinforcement theories of identificatory learning. *Journal of Abnormal and Social Psychology*, 1963, *67*, 527–34.

Bandura, A., & Walters, R. H. *Social learning and personality development*. New York: Holt, Rinehart, 1963.

Baron, R. A. Attraction toward the model and model's competence as determinants of adult imitative behavior. *Journal of Personality and Social Psychology*, 1970, *14*, 345–51.

Barton, R. E. *A primer on simulation and gaming*. Englewood Cliffs, N.J.: Prentice-Hall, 1970.

Bartos, O. J. Concession-making in experimental conditions. *General Systems*, 1966, SSRI Reprint No. 6, 145–56.

Bartos, O. J. Determinants and consequences of toughness. In P. Swingle, ed., *The structure of conflict*. New York: Academic Press, 1970. Pp. 45–68.

Bass, B. M. Amount of participation, coalescence, and profitability of decision making discussions. *Journal of Abnormal and Social Psychology*, 1963, *67*, 92–94.

Bass, B. M., & Wurster, C. R. Effects of company rank on LGD performance of oil refinery supervisors. *Journal of Applied Psychology*, 1953, *37*, 96–104. (a)

Bass, B. M., & Wurster, C. R. Effects of the nature of the problem on LGD performance. *Journal of Applied Psychology*, 1953, *37*, 96–99. (b)

Bennis, W. G.; Berkowitz, M.; Affinito, M.; & Malone, M. Authority, power, and the ability to influence. *Human Relations*, 1958, *11*, 143–55.

Berkowitz, L. The frustration-aggression hypothesis revisited. In L. Berkowitz, ed., *Roots of aggression: A re-examination of the frustration-aggression hypothesis*. New York: Atherton Press, 1969. Pp. 1–28.

Berkowitz, L., & Geen, R. G. Film violence and the cue preparation of available targets. *Journal of Personality and Social Psychology*, 1966, *3*, 525–30.

Berkowitz, W. Prisoner's Dilemma with a payoff-adjusting option. *The Psychological Record*, 1969, *19*, 479–90.

Berlo, D. K.; Lemert, J. B.; & Mertz, R. Dimensions of evaluations of sources. Unpublished manuscript. Department of Communication, Michigan State University, 1966.

Berne, E. *Games People Play*. New York: Grove Press, 1964.

Bickman, L. The effect of social status on the honesty of others. *Journal of Social Psychology*, 1971, *85*, 87–92.

Bixenstine, V. E., & O'Reilly, F. F., Jr. Money versus electric shock as payoff in a Prisoner's Dilemma game. *Psychological Record*, 1966, *16*, 251–64.

Bjorkman, M. On the ecological relevance of psychological research. *Scandinavian Journal of Psychology*, 1969, *10*, 145–57.

Blau, P. M. *Exchange and power in social life*. New York: Wiley, 1964.

Bond, J. R., & Vinacke, W. E. Coalitions in mixed-sex triads. *Sociometry*, 1961, *24*, 61–75.

Bonoma, T. V., & Monteverde, F. Extending the GRIT proposal: Some effects of target response on conflict resolution. Paper presented at the 43rd Annual Meeting of the Eastern Psychological Association, Boston, Mass., April 1972.

Bonoma, T. V., & Tedeschi, J. T. Compliance as a function of the threatener's exploitativeness. Mimeographed manuscript. State University of New York at Albany, 1971. (a)

Bonoma, T. V., & Tedeschi, J. T. Some effects of source behavior on target's compliance to threats. *Behavioral Science*, 1973, *18*, 34–41.

Boulding, K. R. *Conflict and defense*. New York: Harper, 1962.

Boulding, K. R. Reality testing and value orientation. *International Social Science Journal*, 1965, *17*, 404–16.

Bramel, D. Interpersonal attraction, hostility, and perception. In J. Mills, ed., *Experimental social psychology*. New York: Macmillan, 1969. Pp. 1–120.

Brinton, C. *The anatomy of revolution*. Rev. ed. Englewood Cliffs, N.J.: Prentice-Hall, 1952.

Brock, T. C. Communicator-recipient similarity and decision change. *Journal of Personality and Social Psychology*, 1965, *1*, 650–54.

Brock, T. C., & Becker, L. A. Volition and attraction in everyday life. *Journal of Social Psychology*, 1965, *72*, 89–97.

Brown, B. R. The effects of need to maintain face in interpersonal bargaining. *Journal of Experimental Social Psychology*, 1968, *4*, 107–22.

Brown, B. R. Face saving following experimentally induced embarrassment. *Journal of Experimental Social Psychology*, 1970, *6*, 255–71.

Brown, R. *Social psychology*. New York. Free Press, 1965.

Brown, R. C.; Helm, B.; & Tedeschi, J. T. Attraction, verbal conditioning, and social influence. *Journal of Social Psychology*, 1972.

Bugental, D. E.; Kaswan, J. W.; & Love, L. R. Perception of contradictory meanings conveyed by verbal and nonverbal channels. *Journal of Personality and Social Psychology*, 1970, *16*, 647–55.

Bugental, D. E.; Love, L. R.; & Gianetto, J. M. Perfidious feminine faces. *Journal of Personality and Social Psychology*, 1971, *17*, 319–24.

Burnstein, E.; Stotland, E.; & Zander, A. Similarity to a model and self-evaluation. *Journal of Abnormal and Social Psychology*, 1961, *62*, 257–64.

Butler, D. C., & Miller, N. Power to reward and punish in social interaction. *Journal of Experimental Social Psychology*, 1965, *1*, 311–22.

Bryne, D. Attitudes and attraction. In L. Berkowitz, ed., *Advances in experimental social psychology*. Vol. 4. New York: Academic Press, 1969. Pp. 35–89.

Caldwell, M. Coalitions in the triad: Introducing the element of chance into the game structure. *Journal of Personality and Social Psychology,* 1972, *20,* 271–80.

Campbell, D. T. Reforms as experiments. *American Psychologist,* 1969, *24,* 409–29.

Caplow, T. A theory of coalitions in the triad. *American Sociological Review,* 1956, *21,* 489–93.

Caplow, T. Further development of a theory of coalitions in the triad. *American Journal of Sociology,* 1959, *64,* 488–93.

Carson, R. C. *Interaction concepts of personality.* Chicago: Aldine, 1969.

Carter, L. F. Evaluating the performance of individuals as members of small groups. *Personnel Psychology,* 1954, *7,* 477–84.

Cartwright, D. Power: A neglected variable in social psychology. In D. Cartwright, ed., *Studies in social power.* Ann Arbor: Institute of Social Research, 1959. Pp. 183–220.

Cartwright, D., & Harary, F. Structural balance: A generalization of Heider's theory. *Psychological Record,* 1956, *63,* 277–93.

Cartwright, D., & Zander, A. *Group dynamics.* 3rd ed. New York: Harper & Row, 1968.

Chambliss, W. J. The deterrent influence of punishment. *Crime and Deliquency,* 1966, *12,* 70–75.

Chaney, M. V., & Vinacke, W. E. Achievement and nurturance in triads varying in power distribution. *Journal of Abnormal and Social Psychology,* 1960, *60,* 175–81.

Chapanis, A. Men, machines, and models. *American Psychologist,* 1961, *16,* 113–131.

Chapanis, A. Prelude to 2001: Explorations in human communication. *American Psychologist,* 1971, *26,* 949–61.

Chein, I. On the concept of power. Paper presented at the annual meeting of the American Psychological Association, Washington, D.C., September 3, 1967.

Cherryholmes, C. H. Some current research on effectiveness of educational simulations: Implications for alternative strategies. *American Behavioral Scientist,* 1966, *10,* 4–5.

Chertkoff, J. M. The effects of probability of future success on coalition formation. *Journal of Experimental Social Psychology,* 1966, 2, 265–77.

Chertkoff, J. M. A revision of Caplow's coalition theory. *Journal of Experimental Social Psychology,* 1967, *3,* 172–77.

Chertkoff, J. M. Coalition formation as a function of differences in resources. *Journal of Conflict Resolution,* 1971, *15,* 371–84.

Chertkoff, J. M., & Conley, M. Opening offer and frequency of concession as bargaining strategies. *Journal of Personality and Social Psychology,* 1967, *7,* 181–85.

Christie, R., & Geis, F. L. *Studies in Machiavellianism.* New York: Academic Press, 1970.

Chu, G. C. Fear arousal, efficacy, and imminency. *Journal of Personality and Social Psychology,* 1966, *4,* 517–24.

Clark, R. D. III, & Word, L. E. A case where the bystander did help. Paper presented at the 42nd annual meeting of the Eastern Psychological Association, April 1971.

Cohen, A. R. *Attitude change and social influence.* New York: Basic Books, 1964.

Coleman, J. S. Comments on "On the concept of influence." *Public Opinion Quarterly,* 1964, *27,* 63–82.

Coleman, J. S. Games as vehicles for social theory. *American Behavioral Scientist,* 1969, *12,* 2–6.

Conant, J. B. *Modern science and modern men.* Garden City, N.J.: Doubleday, 1952.

Coombs, C. H.; Dawes, R. M.; & Tversky, A. *Mathematical psychology: An elementary introduction.* Englewood Cliffs: Prentice-Hall, 1970.

Coopersmith, S. *The antecedents of self-esteem.* San Francisco: W. H. Freeman, 1967.

Crano, W. D. Effects of sex, response order, and expertise in conformity: A dispositional approach. *Sociometry,* 1970, *33,* 239–52.

Crockett, W. H. Emergent leadership in small, decision-making groups. *Journal of Abnormal and Social Psychology,* 1955, *51,* 378–83.

Croner, M. D., & Willis, R. H. Perceived differences in task competence and assymmetry of dyadic influence. *Journal of Abnormal and Social Psychology,* 1961, *62,* 705–8.

Cummings, L. L., & Harnett, D. L. Bargaining behaviour in a symmetric bargaining triad. *The Review of Economic Studies,* 1969, *36,* 485–501.

Dabbs, J. M., Jr. Self-esteem, communicator characteristics, and attitude change. *Journal of Abnormal and Social Psychology,* 1964, *69,* 173–81.

Dabbs, J. M., Jr., & Leventhal, H. Effects of varying the recommendations in a fear-arousing communication. *Journal of Personality and Social Psychology,* 1966, *4,* 525–31.

Dahl, R. A. The concept of power. *Behavioral Science,* 1957, *2,* 201–18.

Dahl, R. A. *Who governs?* New Haven, Conn.: Yale University Press, 1961.

Daniels, V. Communication, incentive, and structural variables in interpersonal exchange and negotiation. *Journal of Experimental Social Psychology,* 1967, *3,* 47–74.

Darley, J. M., & Latané, B. Bystander intervention in emergencies: Diffusion of responsibility. *Journal of Personality and Social Psychology,* 1968, *8,* 377–83.

Davis, K. E., & Florquist, C. C. Perceived threat and dependence as determinants of the tactical usage of opinion conformity. *Journal of Experimental Social Psychology,* 1965, *1,* 219–36.

Dawson, R. E. Simulation in the social sciences. In H. Guetzkow, ed., *Simulation in social science: Readings.* Englewood Cliffs, N.J.: Prentice-Hall, 1962. Pp. 1–15.

Deutsch, K. *The nerves of government.* New York: Free Press, 1966.

Deutsch, M. Trust and suspicion. *Journal of Conflict Resolution,* 1958, *2,* 265–79.

Deutsch, M. Trust, truthworthiness, and the F-scale. *Journal of Abnormal and Social Psychology,* 1960, *61,* 138–40.

Deutsch, M. Socially relevant science: Reflections on some studies of interpersonal conflict. *American Psychologist,* 1969, *24,* 1076–92.

Deutsch, M.; Canavan, D.; & Rubin, J. The effects of size of conflict and sex of experimenter upon interpersonal bargaining. *Journal of Experimental Social Psychology,* 1971, *7,* 258–67.

Deutsch, M., & Gerard, H. G. A study of normative and informational influence upon individual judgment. *Journal of Abnormal and Social Psychology,* 1955, *51,* 629–36.

Deutsch, M., & Krauss, R. M. The effect of threat upon interpersonal bargaining. *Journal of Abnormal and Social Psychology,* 1960, *61,* 181–89.

Deutsch, M., & Krauss, R. M. Studies of interpersonal bargaining. *Journal of Conflict Resolution,* 1962, *6,* 52–76.

Deutsch, M., & Lewicki, R. J. The effects of "locking oneself in" during a game of "chicken." *Journal of Conflict Resolution,* 1970, *14,* 367–78.

Druckman, D. Dogmatism, prenegotiation experience, and simulated group representation as determinants of dyadic behavior in a bargaining situation. *Journal of Personality and Social Psychology*, 1967, *6*, 279–90.

Druckman, D. Prenegotiation experience and dyadic conflict resolution in a bargaining situation. *Journal of Experimental Social Psychology*, 1968, *4*, 367–83.

Edwards, W., & Tversky, A., eds. *Decision-making.* Baltimore: Penguin Books, 1967.

Ellsworth, P. C., & Carlsmith, J. M. Effects of eye contact and verbal content on affective response to a dyadic interaction. *Journal of Personality and Social Psychology*, 1968, *10*, 15–20.

Emerson, R. M. Power-dependence relations. *American Sociological Review*, 1962, *27*, 31–41.

Emerson, R. M. Power-dependence relations: Two experiments. *Sociometry*, 1964, *27*, 282–98.

Endler, N. S. Conformity as a function of different reinforcement schedules. *Journal of Personality and Social Psychology*, 1966, *4*, 175–80.

Endler, N. S., & Hoy, E. Conformity as related to reinforcement and social pressure. *Journal of Personality and Social Psychology*, 1967, *7*, 197–201.

Epstein, Y. M., & Hornstein, H. A. Penalty and interpersonal attraction as factors influencing the decision to help another person. *Journal of Experimental Social Psychology*, 1969, *5*, 272–82.

Eron, L. D.; Walden, L. O.; & Lefkowitz, M. M. *Learning of aggression in children.* Boston: Little, Brown, 1971.

Evan, W. M., & Zelditch, M., Jr. A laboratory experiment on bureaucratic authority. *American Sociological Review*, 1961, *26*, 883–93.

Evans, G. Effect of unilateral promise and value of rewards upon cooperation and trust. *Journal of Abnormal and Social Psychology*, 1964, *69*, 587–90.

Evans, G., & Crumbaugh, C. M. Effects of Prisoner's Dilemma format on cooperative behavior. *Journal of Personality and Social Psychology*, 1966, *3*, 486–88.

Faley, T., & Tedeschi, J. T. Status and reactions to threats. *Journal of Personality and Social Psychology*, 1971, *17*, 192–99.

Feshbach, S., & Singer, R. D. *Television and aggression.* San Francisco: Jossey-Bass, 1971.

Festinger, L.; Pepitone, A.; & Newcomb, T. Some consequences of de-individuation in a group. *Journal of Abnormal and Social Psychology*, 1952, *47*, 382–89.

Fiedler, F. E. A contingency model of leadership effectiveness. In L. Berkowitz, ed., *Advances in experimental social psychology.* Vol. 1. New York: Academic Press, 1964. Pp. 149–90.

Fiedler, F. E. *A theory of leadership effectiveness.* New York: McGraw-Hill, 1967.

Fischer, C. S. The effect of threats in an incomplete information game. *Sociometry*, 1969, *32*, 301–14.

Fisher, R. Fractionating conflict. In R. Fisher, ed., *International conflict and behavioral science: The Craigville Papers.* New York: Basic Books, 1964.

Fisher, R. *International conflict for beginners.* New York: Harper & Row, 1969.

Fouraker, L. E., & Siegel, S. *Bargaining behavior.* New York: McGraw-Hill, 1963.

Frank, P. *Modern science and its philosophy.* New York: Collier, 1961.

Frank, J. *Sanity and survival: Psychological aspects of war and peace.* New York: Vintage Books, 1967.

Freidrich, C. J. *Man and his government.* New York: McGraw-Hill, 1963.

French, J. R. P., Jr., & Raven, B. The bases of social power. In D. Cartwright, ed., *Studies in social power.* Ann Arbor: Institute of Social Research, 1959. Pp. 150–67.

French, J. R. P., Jr., & Snyder, R. Leadership and interpersonal power. In D. Cartwright, ed., *Studies in social power.* Ann Arbor: Institute of Social Research, 1959. Pp. 118–49.

Friedman, J. W. On experimental research in oligopoly. *The Review of Economics,* 1969, *36,* 399–415.

Gahagan, J. P.; Horai, J.; Berger, S.; & Tedeschi, J. T. Status and authoritarianism in the Prisoner's Dilemma game. Paper read at the meetings of the Southeastern Psychological Association, Atlanta, Georgia, 1967.

Gahagan, J. P., & Tedeschi, J. T. Effects of promise credibility, outside options, and social contact on interpersonal conflict. Mimeographed manuscript. State University of New York at Albany, 1970.

Gallo, P. S. The effects of increased incentives upon the use of threat in bargaining. *Journal of Personality and Social Psychology,* 1966, *4,* 14–20. (a)

Gallo, P. S. The effects of mode of presentation and large rewards on a Prisoner's Dilemma game. ONR Tech. Report, no. 18, Contract no. 233 (54). 1966. (b)

Gallo, P. The effect of strategy of the "other player" on personality impression formation and cooperative behavior in a maximizing difference game. Paper read at the meeting of the Western Psychological Association, San Francisco, May 1967.

Gallo, P. Prisoners of our own dilemma? Paper presented at the annual meeting of the Western Psychological Association, Los Angeles, March 1968.

Gallo, P.; Funk, S. G.; & Levine, J. R. Reward size, method of presentation, and number of alternatives in a Prisoner's Dilemma game. *Journal of Personality and Social Psychology,* 1969, *13,* 239–44.

Gallo, P., & McClintock, C. G. Cooperative and competitive behavior in mixed-motive games. *Journal of Conflict Resolution,* 1965, *9,* 68–78.

Gamson, W. A. A theory of coalition formation. *American Sociological Review,* 1961, *26,* 373–82. (a)

Gamson, W. A. An experimental test of a theory of coalition formation. *American Sociological Review,* 1961, *26,* 565–73. (b)

Gamson, W. A. Experimental studies of coalition formation. In L. Berkowitz, ed., *Advances in experimental social psychology.* Vol. 1. New York: Academic Press, 1964. Pp. 81–110.

Gamson, W. A. *Power and discontent.* Homewood, Ill.: Dorsey Press, 1968.

Gelfand, D. M. The influence of self-esteem on rate of verbal conditioning and social matching behavior. *Journal of Abnormal and Social Psychology,* 1962, *65,* 259–65.

Gerard, H. B. Deviation, conformity, and commitment. In I. D. Steiner & M. Fishbein, eds., *Current studies in social psychology.* New York: Holt, Rinehart & Winston, 1965. Pp. 263–77.

Gibbs, J. P. Crime, punishment, and deterrence. *Southwestern Social Science Quarterly,* 1968, *48,* 515–30.

Giffin, K. The contribution of studies of source credibility to a theory of interpersonal trust in the communication process. *Psychological Bulletin,* 1967, *68,* 104–20.

Goffman, E. *The presentation of self in everyday life.* New York: Doubleday Anchor, 1959.

Goffman, E. *Encounters*. Indianapolis: Bobbs-Merrill, 1961.

Goffman, E. *Interaction ritual*. New York: Anchor, 1967.

Gouldner, A. W. The norm of reciprocity: A preliminary statement. *American Sociological Review*, 1960, *25*, 161–79.

Graen, G.; Alvares, K.; Orris, J. B.; & Martella, J. A. Contingency model of leadership effectiveness: Antecedent and evidential results. *Psychological Bulletin*, 1970, *74*, 285–96.

Gray, L. N., & Martin, J. D. Punishments and deterrence: Another analysis of Gibbs' data. *Social Science Quarterly*, 1969, *50*, 389–95.

Grusec, J., & Mischel, W. The model's characteristics as determinants of social learning. *Journal of Personality and Social Psychology*, 1966, *4*, 211–15.

Guetzkow, H. Some correspondences between simulations and 'realities' in international relations. In M. A. Kaplan, ed., *New approaches to international relations*. New York: St. Martin's Press, 1968. Pp. 202–69.

Gumpert, P.; Deutsch, M.; & Epstein, Y. Effects of incentive magnitude on cooperation in the Prisoner's Dilemma game. *Journal of Personality and Social Psychology*, 1969, *11*, 66–69.

Haley, J. *Strategies of psychotherapy*. New York: Grune & Stratton, 1963.

Hall, E. T. *The silent language*. New York: Doubleday, 1959.

Hall, E. T. A system for the notation of proxemic behavior. *American Anthropologist*, 1963, *65*, 1003–26.

Hammond, K. R., ed. *The psychology of Egon Brunswick*. New York: Holt, Rinehart & Winston, 1966.

Harnett, D. L., & Cummings, L. L. Bargaining behavior in an asymmetric triad: The role of information, communication, and risk-taking propensity. Mimeographed manuscript. Indiana University, 1968.

Harnett, D. L.; Hughes, G. D.; & Cummings, L. L. Bilateral monopolistic bargaining through an intermediary. *Journal of Business of the University of Chicago*, 1968, *41*, 1–9.

Harris, R. J. A geometric classification system for 2 x 2 interval-symmetric games. *Behavioral Science*, 1969, *14*, 138–46.

Harsanyi, J. C. Bargaining in ignorance of the opponent's utility function. *Journal of Conflict Resolution*, 1962, *6*, 29–38. (a)

Harsanyi, J. C. Measurement of social power, opportunity costs, and the theory of two-person bargaining games. *Behavioral Science*, 1962, *7*, 67–80. (b)

Harsanyi, J. C. A simplified bargaining model for the n-person cooperative games. *International Economic Review*, 1963, *4*, 194–220.

Heider, F. *The psychology of interpersonal relations*. New York: Wiley, 1958.

Helm, B.; Bonoma, T. V.; & Tedeschi, J. T. Reciprocity for harm done. *Journal of Social Psychology*, 1972, *87*, 89–98.

Helm, B.; Brown, R. C.; Jr.; & Tedeschi, J. T. Esteem and the effectiveness of a verbal reinforcer. *Journal of Social Psychology*, 1972, *87*, 293–300.

Helm, B.; Nacci, P.; & Tedeschi, J. T. Attraction, esteem, and coalition behavior. Mimeographed manuscript. State University of New York at Albany, 1972.

Helson, H. Adaptation level as a basis for a quantitative theory of frames of reference. *Psychological Review*, 1948, *55*, 297–313.

Hemphill, J. K. Why people attempt to lead. In L. Petrullo & B. M. Bass, eds., *Leadership and interpersonal behavior*. New York: Holt, 1961. Pp. 201–15.

Hermann, C. *Crises in foreign policy*. Indianapolis: Bobbs-Merrill, 1970.

Higbee, K. L. Fifteen years of fear arousal: Research on threat appeals: 1953–1968. *Psychological Bulletin*, 1969, *72*, 426–44.

Hoffman, P. J.; Festinger, L.; & Lawrence, D. H. Tendencies toward group comparability in competitive bargaining. *Human Relations,* 1954, *7,* 141–59.

Hogatt, A. C. Response of paid student subjects to differential behavior of robots in bifurcated duopoly games. *Review of Economic Studies,* 1969, *36,* 417–32.

Hollander, E. P. *Leaders, groups, and influence.* New York: Oxford, 1964.

Hollander, E. P., & Julian, J. W. Studies in leader legitimacy, influence, and innovation. In L. Berkowitz, ed., *Advances in experimental social psychology.* Vol. 5. New York: Academic Press, 1970. Pp. 33–69.

Homans, G. C. Social behavior as exchange. *American Journal of Sociology,* 1958, *63,* 597–606.

Homans, G. C. *Social behavior: Its elementary forms.* New York: Harcourt, Brace & World, 1961.

Homans, G. C. *The nature of social science.* New York: Harcourt, Brace & World, 1967.

Horai, J.; Haber, I.; Tedeschi, J. T.; & Smith, R. B., III. It's not what you say, it's how you do it. *Proceedings* of the 78th annual convention of the American Psychological Association, Miami Beach, Florida, 1970.

Horai, J., & Tedeschi, J. T. The effects of threat credibility and magnitude of punishment upon compliance. *Journal of Personality and Social Psychology,* 1969, *12,* 164–69.

Horai, J., & Tedeschi, J. T. Attribution of intent and the norm of reciprocity in dyadic conflict. Mimeographed manuscript. State University of New York at Albany, 1970.

Hornstein, H. A. The effects of different magnitudes of threat upon interpersonal bargaining. *Journal of Experimental Social Psychology,* 1965, *1,* 282–93.

Horwitz, M. Hostility and its management in classroom groups. In W. W. Charters & N. L. Gage, eds., *Readings in the social psychology of education.* Boston: Allyn & Bacon, 1963. Pp. 196–211.

Hovland, C. I.; Janis, I. L.; & Kelley, H. H. *Communication and persuasion.* New Haven: Yale University Press, 1953.

Huizinga, J. *Homo ludens.* London: Roy, 1950.

Hurwitz, J. I.; Zander, A. F.; & Hymovitch, B. Some effects of power on the relations among group members. In D. Cartwright & A. F. Zander, eds., *Group dynamics.* 3rd ed. New York: Harper & Row, 1968. Pp. 291–300.

Iklé, F. C., & Leites, N. Political negotiation as a process of modifying utilities. *Journal of Conflict Resolution,* 1962, *6,* 19–28.

Isen, A. M. Success, failure, attention, and reaction to others: The warm glow of success. *Journal of Personality and Social Psychology,* 1970, *15,* 294–301.

Janda, K. F. Towards the explication of the concept of leadership in terms of the concept of power. *Human Relations,* 1960, *13,* 345–63.

Janis, I. L., & Feshbach, S. Effects of fear-arousing communications. *Journal of Abnormal and Social Psychology,* 1953, *48,* 78–92.

Janis, I. L., & Field, P. B. A behavior assessment of consistency of individual differences. In C. I. Hovland & I. L. Janis, eds., *Personality and Persuasibility.* New Haven, Conn.: Yale University Press, 1959. Pp. 29–54.

Janis, I. L.; Mahl, G. F.; Kagan, J.; & Holt, R. R. *Personality: Dynamics, development, and assessment.* New York: Harcourt, Brace & World, 1969.

Johnson, H. H., & Izzett, R. R. Relationship between authoritarianism and attitude change as a function of source credibility and type of communication. *Journal of Personality and Social Psychology,* 1969, *13,* 317–21.

Jones, B.; Steele, M.; Gahagan, J.; & Tedeschi, J. Matrix values and cooperative behavior in the Prisoner's Dilemma game. *Journal of Personality and Social Psychology*, 1968, *8*, 148–53.

Jones, E. E. *Ingratiation: A social psychological analysis.* New York: Wiley, 1964.

Jones, E. E., & Gerard, H. B. *Foundations of social psychology.* New York: Wiley, 1967.

Jones, E. E.; Gergen, M. J.; & Jones, R. G. Tactics of ingratiation among leaders and subordinates in a status hierarchy. *Psychological Monographs*, 1963, *77* (Whole no. 566) .

Jones, E. E.; Wells, H. H.; & Torrey, R. Some effects of feedback from the experimenter on conformity behavior. *Journal of Abnormal and Social Psychology*, 1958, *58*, 207–13.

Kahn, A.; Hottes, J.; & Davis, W. L. Cooperation and optimal responding in the Prisoner's Dilemma game: Effects of sex and physical attractiveness. *Journal of Personality and Social Psychology*, 1971, *17*, 267–79.

Kahn, H. *On thermonuclear war.* Princeton, N.J.: Princeton University Press, 1960.

Kahn, H. *On escalation: Metaphors and scenarios.* New York: Praeger, 1965.

Kaplan, A. *Conduct of inquiry.* San Francisco: Chandler, 1964.

Kaufmann, H. Similarity and cooperation received as determinants of cooperation rendered. *Psychonomic Science*, 1967, *9*, 73–74.

Kazdin, A. E., & Bryan, J. H. Competence and volunteering. *Journal of Experimental Social Psychology*, 1971, *7*, 87–97.

Kelley, E. W. Bargaining in coalition situations. In S. Groennings, E. W. Kelley, & M. Leiserson, eds., *The study of coalition behavior.* New York: Holt, 1970. Pp. 273–96.

Kelley, H. H. Experimental studies of threats in interpersonal negotiations. *Journal of Conflict Resolution*, 1965, *9*, 79–105.

Kelley, H. H. A classroom study of the dilemmas in interpersonal negotiations. In K. Archibald, ed., *Strategic interaction and conflict.* Berkeley: University of California Institute of International Studies, 1966.

Kelley, H. H., & Arrowood, A. J. Coalitions in the triad: Critique and experiment. *Sociometry*, 1960, *23*, 231–44.

Kelley, H. H.; Beckman, L. L.; & Fischer, C. S. Negotiating the division of a reward under incomplete information. *Journal of Experimental Social Psychology*, 1967, *3*, 361–98.

Kelley, H. H., Deutsch, M., Lanzetta, J. T., Nuttin, J. M., Jr., Shure, G. H., Faucheux, C., Moscovici, S., Rabbie, J. M., & Thibaut, J. W. A comparative experimental study of negotiation behavior. *Journal of Personality and Social Psychology*, 1970, *16*, 411–438.

Kelley, H. H., & Ring, K. Some effects of "suspicious" versus "trusting" training schedules. *Journal of Abnormal Social Psychology*, 1961, *63*, 294–301.

Kelley, H. H., & Stahelski, A. J. The social interaction basis of cooperators' and competitors' beliefs about others. *Journal of Personality and Social Psychology*, 1970, *16*, 66–91. (a)

Kelley, H. H., & Stahelski, A. J. Errors in perception of intentions in a mixed-motive game. *Journal of Experimental Social Psychology*, 1970, *6*, 379–400. (b)

Kelley, H. H., & Stahelski, A. J. The inference of intentions from moves in the Prisoner's Dilemma game. *Journal of Experimental Social Psychology*, 1970, *6*, 401–19. (c)

Kelley, H. H., & Thibaut, J. W. Group problem solving. In G. Lindzey & E. Aronson, eds., *The handbook of social psychology.* 2nd ed. Vol. 4. Reading, Mass.: Addison-Wesley, 1969. Pp. 1–101.

Kelley, H. H.; Thibaut, J. W.; Radloff, R.; & Mundy, D. The development of cooperation in the "minimal social situation." *Psychological Monographs,* 1962, *76,* no. 19 (Whole no. 538).

Kemeny, J. *A philosopher looks at science.* New York: Van Nostrand, 1959.

Kerlinger, F. N. *Foundations of behavioral research.* New York: Holt, Rinehart, 1964.

Kerr, C. Industrial conflict and its mediation. *American Journal of Sociology* 1954, *60,* 230–45.

Kiesler, C. A., & Kiesler, S. B. *Conformity.* Reading, Mass.: Addison-Wesley, 1969.

Kipnis, D., & Vanderveer, R. Ingratiation and the use of power. *Journal of Personality and Social Psychology,* 1971, *17,* 280–86.

Knox, R. E., & Douglas, R. Low payoffs and marginal comprehension: Two possible constraints upon behavior in the Prisoner's Dilemma. Paper presented at the meeting of the Western Psychological Association, San Diego, April 1968.

Kogan, N., & Wallach, M. A. *Risk taking.* New York: Holt, Rinehart & Winston, 1964.

Köhler, W. *The place of value in a world of facts.* New York: Liveright, 1938.

Komorita, S. S. Cooperative choice in a Prisoner's Dilemma game. *Journal of Personality and Social Psychology,* 1965, *2,* 741–45.

Komorita, S. S., & Brenner, A. R. Bargaining and concession-making under bilateral monopoly. *Journal of Personality and Social Psychology,* 1968, *5,* 15–20.

Krauss, R. M. Structural and attitudinal factors in interpersonal bargaining. *Journal of Experimental Social Psychology,* 1966, *2,* 42–55.

Krebs, D. L. Altruism—an examination of the concept and a review of the literature. *Psychological Bulletin,* 1970, *73,* 258–302.

Kuhn, A. *The study of society: A unified approach.* Homewood, Ill.: Dorsey Press, 1963.

Kuhn, T. S. *The structure of scientific revolutions.* Chicago: University of Chicago Press, 1962.

Lake, D. G. Impression formation, Machiavellianism, and interpersonal bargaining. Unpublished doctoral dissertation. Teachers College, Columbia University, 1967.

Lanzetta, J. T., & Kanareff, V. T. The effects of a monetary reward on the acquisition of an imitiative response. *Journal of Abnormal and Social Psychology,* 1959, *59,* 120–27.

Lasswell, H. D. Conflict and leadership: The process of decision and the nature of authority. In A. S. deReuck & J. Knight, eds., *Ciba Foundation Symposium on Conflict in Society.* London: Churchill, 1966. Pp. 210–28.

Lasswell, H. D., & Kaplan, A. *Power and Society.* New Haven, Conn.: Yale University Press, 1950.

Latané, B., & Darley, J. M. Bystander "apathy." *American Scientist,* 1969, *57,* 244–68.

Latané, B., & Rodin, J. A lady in distress: inhibiting effects of friends and strangers on bystander intervention. *Journal of Experimental Social Psychology,* 1969, *5,* 272–82.

Leary, T. *Interpersonal diagnosis of personality.* New York: Ronald, 1957.

Lee, W. F. *Decision theory and human behavior.* New York: Wiley, 1971.

Lefkowitz, M.; Blake, R. R.; & Mouton, J. S. Status factors in pedestrian violations of traffic signals. *Journal of Abnormal and Social Psychology*, 1955, *51*, 704–6.

Lemert, J. B. Dimensions of source credibility. Paper presented at the meeting of the Association for Education in Journalism, August 1963.

Lemert, J. B. Status conferral and topic scope. *Journal of Communication*, 1969, *19*, 4–13.

Lewin, K.; Dembo, T.; Festinger, L.; & Sears, P. S. Level of aspiration. In J. McV. Hunt, ed., *Personality and the behavior disorders*. New York: Ronald Press, 1944. Pp. 333–78.

Lieberman, B. Experimental studies of conflict in some two-person and three-person games. In J. Criswell, H. Solomon, & P. Suppes, eds., *Mathematical methods in small group processes*. Stanford, Calif.: Stanford University Press, 1962.

Lieberman, B. i-trust: A notion of trust in three-person games and international affairs. *Journal of Conflict Resolution*, 1964, *8*, 271–80.

Liebert, R. M.; Smith, W. P.; Hill, J. H.; & Kieffer, M. The effects of information and magnitude of initial offer on interpersonal negotiation. *Journal of Experimental Social Psychology*, 1968, *4*, 431–41.

Lindskold, S.; Bonoma, T. V.; Schlenker, B. R.; & Tedeschi, J. T. Some factors affecting the effectiveness of reward power. *Psychonomic Science*, 1972, *26*, 68–70.

Lindskold, S., & Tedeschi, J. T. Reward power and attraction in interpersonal conflict. *Psychonomic Science*, 1971, *22*, 211–13. (a)

Lindskold, S., & Tedeschi, J. T. Self-esteem and sex as factors affecting influenceability. *British Journal of Social and Clinical Psychology*, 1971, *10*, 114–22. (b)

Lippitt, R.; Polansky, N.; Redl, F.; & Rosen, S. The dynamics of power. *Human Relations*, 1953, *5*, 37–64.

Lott, A. J., & Lott, B. E. A learning theory approach to interpersonal attitudes. In A. G. Greenwalt, T. C. Brock, & T. M. Ostrom, eds., *Psychological foundations of attitudes*. New York: Academic Press, 1968. Pp. 67–88.

Lott, D. F., & Sommer, R. Seating arrangements and status. *Journal of Personality and Social Psychology*, 1967, *7*, 90–94.

Luce, R. D., & Raiffa, H. *Games and decisions*. New York: Wiley, 1957.

Lutzker, D. R. Internationalism as a predictor of cooperative behavior. *Journal of Conflict Resolution*, 1960, *4*, 426–30.

Macaulay, J., & Berkowitz, L. *Altruism and helping behavior*. New York: Academic Press, 1970.

McClintock, C. G.; Gallo, P. S.; & Harrison, A. Some effects of variations in other strategy upon game behavior. *Journal of Personality and Social Psychology*, 1965, *1*, 319–25.

McClintock, C. G.; Harrison, A. A.; Strand, S.; & Gallo, P.; Internationalism-isolationism, strategy of the other player, and two-person game behavior. *Journal of Abnormal and Social Psychology*, 1963, *67*, 631–36.

McClintock, C. G., & McNeel, S. P. Reward and score feedback as determinants of cooperative and competitive game behavior. *Journal of Personality and Social Psychology*, 1966, *6*, 606–13.

McClintock, C. G., & McNeel, S. P. Prior dyadic experience and monetary reward as determinants of cooperative and competitive game behavior. *Journal of Personality and Social Psychology*, 1967, *5*, 282–94.

McCroskey, J. C. Scales for the measurement of ethos. *Speech Monographs,* 1966, *33,* 65–72.

McDermott, W. B. Thinking about Herman Kahn. *Journal of Conflict Resolution,* 1971, *15,* 55–70.

McGrath, J. E. A social psychological approach to the study of negotiation. In R. V. Bowers, ed., *Studies on behavior in organizations: A symposium.* Athens: University of Georgia Press, 1966.

McGuire, W. J. The nature of attitudes and attitude change. In G. Lindzey & E. Aronson, eds., *Handbook of social psychology.* Vol. 3. 2nd ed. Reading, Mass.: Addison-Wesley, 1969. Pp. 136–314.

MacIver, R. M. *Power transformed.* New York: MacMillan, 1964.

March, J. G. An introduction to the theory and measurement of influence. *American Political Science Review,* 1955, *49,* 431–51.

March, J. G. Some observations on political theory. In L. K. Caldwell, ed., *Politics and public affairs.* Bloomington: Indiana University Press, 1962.

March, J. G. Power. *International Encyclopedia of the Social Sciences,* 1968, Pp. 405–15.

Markham, D. The dimensions of source credibility of television newcasters. Unpublished doctoral dissertation. University of Oklahoma, 1965.

Marlowe, D.; Gergen, K. J.; & Doob, A. N. Opponent's personality, expectation of social interaction, and interpersonal bargaining. *Journal of Personality and Social Psychology,* 1966, *3,* 206–13.

Marwell, G., & Schmitt, D. R. Dimensions of compliance-gaining behavior. *Sociometry,* 1967, *30,* 350–64.

Marx, M. H., & Hillix, W. A. *Systems and theories in psychology.* New York: McGraw-Hill, 1963.

Matthews, G., & Dixon, T. R. Differential reinforcement in verbal conditioning as a function of preference for the experimenter's voice. *Journal of Experimental Psychology,* 1968, *76,* 84–88.

Mausner, B. Studies in social interaction: III. Effect of variation in one partner's prestige on the interaction of observer pairs. *Journal of Applied Psychology,* 1953, *37,* 391–93.

Mausner, B. The effect of one partner's success or failure in a relevant task on the interaction of observed pairs. *Journal of Abnormal and Social Psychology,* 1954, *49,* 557–60.

Mead, G. H. *Mind, self and society.* Chicago: University of Chicago Press, 1934.

Mehrabian, A. *Tactics of social influence.* New York: Prentice-Hall, 1970.

Mehrabian, A., & Williams, M. Nonverbal concomitants of intended and perceived persuasiveness. *Journal of Personality and Social Psychology,* 1969, *13,* 37–58.

Messé, L. A. The concept of equity in bargaining. Paper presented at the meeting of the *International Peace Research Society,* Ann Arbor, November 1969.

Messé, L. A. Equity in bilateral bargaining. *Journal of Personality and Social Psychology,* 1971, *17,* 287–91.

Messé, A. M., & Sawyer, J. Unexpected cooperation: The Prisoner's Dilemma resolved? Unpublished manuscript. University of Chicago, 1967.

Michener, H. A., & Lyons, M. Perceived support, mobility, and equity as determinants of revolutionary coalition behavior. Unpublished manuscript. University of Wisconsin, 1970.

Michener, H. A., & Suchner, R. W. The tactical use of social power. J. T.

Tedeschi, ed., *The social influence processes.* Chicago: Aldine-Atherton, 1972. Pp. 239–85.

Midlarsky, E., & Bryan, J. H. Training charity in children. *Journal of Personality and Social Psychology,* 1967, *5,* 408–18.

Milgram, B. Some conditions of obedience and disobedience to authority. *Human Relations,* 1965, *18,* 57–75.

Miller, A. H. Decision-theoretic models in personality and social psychology. Unpublished doctoral dissertation. University of Michigan, 1971.

Miller, N., & Butler, D. Social power and communication in small groups. *Behavioral Science,* 1969, *14,* 11–18.

Miller, N.; Butler, D.; & McMartin, J. A. The ineffectiveness of punishment power in group interaction. *Sociometry,* 1969, *32,* 24–42.

Mills, J., & Aronson, E. Opinion change as a function of the communicator's attractiveness and desire to influence. *Journal of Personality and Social Psychology,* 1965, *1,* 173–77.

Mills, J., & Jellison, J. M. Effect on opinion change of how desirable the communication is to the audience the communicator addressed. *Journal of Personality and Social Psychology,* 1967, *6,* 98–101.

Mills, J., & Jellison, J. M. Effect on opinion change of similarity between the communicator and the audience he addressed. *Journal of Personality and Social Psychology,* 1968, *9,* 153–56.

Mills, T. M. Power relations in three-person groups. *American Sociological Review,* 1953, *18,* 351–57.

Mischel, W. *Introduction to personality.* New York: Holt, 1971.

Mischel, W., & Grusec, J. Determinants of the rehearsal and transmission of neutral and aversive behavior. *Journal of Personality and Social Psychology,* 1966, *3,* 197–205.

Modelski, G. Simulations, "realities," and international relations theory. *Simulations and Games,* 1970, *1,* 111–34.

Modigliani, A. Embarrassment, facework, and eye contact: Testing a theory of embarrassment. *Journal of Personality and Social Psychology,* 1971, *17,* 1–10.

Morgan, W. R., & Sawyer, J. Bargaining, expectations, and the preference for equality over equity. *Journal of Personality and Social Psychology,* 1967, *6,* 139–49.

Morgenthau, H. *Politics among nations.* 5th ed. New York: Knopf, 1969.

Moscovici, S. Communication processes and the properties of language. In L. Berkowitz, ed., *Advances in experimental social psychology.* Vol. 3. New York: Academic Press, 1967. Pp. 225–70.

Murdoch, P. Development of contractual norms in a dyad. *Journal of Personality and Social Psychology,* 1967, *6,* 206–11.

Murdoch, P., & Rosen, D. Norm formation in an interdependent dyad. *Sociometry,* 1970, *33,* 264–75.

Mussen, P., & Rutherford, E. Effects of aggressive cartoons on children's aggressive play. *Journal of Abnormal and Social Psychology,* 1961, *62,* 461–64.

Nardin, T. Communication and the effects of threats in strategic interaction. *Peace Research Society Papers,* IX, Cambridge Conference, 1968.

Nash, J. F. The bargaining problem. *Econometrics,* 1950, *21,* 128–40.

Nemeth, C. Bargaining and reciprocity. *Psychological Bulletin,* 1970, *74,* 297–308.

Newcomb, T. M. An approach to the study of communicative acts. *Psychological Review,* 1953, *60,* 394–404.

Nord, W. R. Social exchange theory: An integrative approach to social conflict. *Psychological Bulletin*, 1969, *71*, 174–208.

Ofshe, R., & Ofshe, L. Social choice and utility in coalition formation. *Sociometry*, 1969, *32*, 330–47.

Ofshe, R., & Ofshe, S. L. Choice behavior in coalition games. *Behavioral Science*, 1970, *15*, 337–49. (a)

Ofshe, L., & Ofshe, R. *Utility and choice in social interaction*. Englewood Cliffs, N.J.: Prentice-Hall, 1970. (b)

Orne, M. T. On the social psychology of the psychological experiment: With particular reference to demand characteristics and their implications. *American Psychologist*, 1962, *17*, 776–83.

Osgood, C. E. *An alternative to war or surrender*. Urbana: University of Illinois Press, 1962.

Osgood, C. E., & Tannenbaum, P. H. The principle of congruity in the predictions of attitude change. *Psychological Review*, 1955, *62*, 42–55.

Oskamp, S., & Kleinke, C. Amount of reward as a variable in the Prisoner's Dilemma game. *Journal of Personality and Social Psychology*, 1970, *16*, 133–40.

Oskamp, S., & Perlman, D. Effects of friendship and disliking on cooperation in a mixed-motive game. *Journal of Conflict Resolution*, 1965, *10*, 221–26.

Parsons, T. On the concept of influence. *Public Opinion Quarterly*, 1963, *27*, 37–62.

Patterson, M. Spatial factors in social interactions. *Human Relations*, 1968, *21*, 351–61.

Pepitone, A. Motivational effects in social perception. *Human Relations*, 1949, *3*, 57–76.

Pepitone, A. *Attraction and hostility*. New York: Atherton, 1964.

Phillips, J. L., & Nitz, L. Social contacts in a three-person "political convention" situation. *Journal of Conflict Resolution*, 1968, *12*, 206–14.

Pilisuk, M.; Potter, P.; Rapoport, A.; & Winter, J. A. War hawks and peace doves: Alternate resolutions of experimental conflicts. *Journal of Conflict Resolution*, 1965, *9*, 491–508.

Podell, J. E., & Knapp, W. M. The effect of mediation on the perceived firmness of the opponent. *Journal of Conflict Resolution*, 1969, *13*, 511–20.

Powell, F. A., & Miller, G. R. Social approval and disapproval cues in anxiety-arousing communications. *Speech Monographs*, 1967, *34*, 152–59.

Pruitt, D. G. An analysis of responsiveness between nations. *Journal of Conflict Resolution*, 1962, *6*, 5–18.

Pruitt, D. G. Definition of the situation as a determinant of international action. In H. C. Kelman, ed., *International behavior: A social psychological analysis*. New York: Holt, Rinehart & Winston, 1965. Pp. 393–432.

Pruitt, D. G. Reward structure and cooperation in the decomposed Prisoner's Dilemma game. *Journal of Personality and Social Psychology*, 1967, 7, 21–27.

Pruitt, D. G. Reciprocity and credit building in a laboratory dyad. *Journal of Personality and Social Psychology*, 1968, *8*, 143–47.

Pruitt, D. G. Stability and sudden change in interpersonal and international affairs. *Journal of Conflict Resolution*, 1969, *12*, 18–38.

Pruitt, D. G., & Drews, J. L. The effect of time pressure, time elapsed, and the opponent's concession rate on behavior in negotiation. *Journal of Experimental Social Psychology*, 1969, *5*, 43–60.

Pruitt, D. G., & Johnson, D. F. Mediation as an aid to face saving in negotiation. *Journal of Personality and Social Psychology,* 1970, *14,* 239–46.

Radlow, A.; Weidner, M. F.; & Hurst, P. M. The effect of incentive magnitude and "motivational orientation" upon choice behavior in a two-person non-zero-sum game. *Journal of Social Psychology,* 1968, *74,* 199–208.

Rapoport, A. *Fights, games, and debates.* Ann Arbor: University of Michigan Press, 1960.

Rapoport, A. The use and misuse of game theory. *Scientific American,* 1962, *207,* 108–18.

Rapoport, A. *Strategy and conscience.* New York: Schocken Books, 1964.

Rapoport, A. *Two-person game theory: the essential ideas.* Ann Arbor: University of Michigan Press, 1966.

Rapoport, A. Prospects for experimental games. *Journal of Conflict Resolution,* 1968, *12,* 461–70.

Rapoport, A., & Chammah, M. *Prisoner's Dilemma.* Ann Arbor: University of Michigan Press, 1965.

Rapoport, A., & Guyer, M. J. A taxonomy of 2 x 2 games. *General Systems,* 1966, *11,* 203–14.

Raser, J. R. *Simulation and society: An exploration of scientific gaming.* Boston: Allyn & Bacon, 1969.

Raven, B. H. Social influence on opinions and the communication of related content. *Journal of Abnormal and Social Psychology,* 1959, *58,* 119–28.

Raven, B. H. Social influence and power. In I. D. Steiner & M. Fishbein, eds., *Current studies in social psychology.* New York: Holt, 1965. Pp. 371–382.

Riker, W. H. *The theory of political coalitions.* New Haven, Conn.: Yale University Press, 1962.

Ring, K., & Kelley, H. H. A comparison of augmentation and reduction as modes of influence. *Journal of Abnormal Psychology,* 1963, *66,* 95–102.

Rosen, S.; Levinger, G.; & Lippitt, R. Perceived sources of social power. *Journal of Abnormal and Social Psychology,* 1961, *62,* 439–41.

Rosnow, R. L., & Robinson, E. J. *Experiments in persuasion.* New York: Academic Press, 1967.

Rotter, J. B. Generalized expectancies for internal versus external control of reinforcement. *Psychological Monographs,* 1966, *80,* no. 1 (Whole no. 609).

Rotter, J. B. A new scale for the measurement of interpersonal trust. *Journal of Personality,* 1967, *35,* 651–65.

Rotter, J. B. Generalized expectancies for interpersonal trust. *American Psychologist,* 1971, *26,* 443–52.

Rudraswamy, V. An investigation of the relationships between perceptions of status and leadership attempts. *Journal of the Indian Academy of Applied Psychology,* 1964, *1,* 12–19.

Russell, B. *Has man a future?* New York: Penguin, 1961.

Sampson, E. E., & Insko, C. A. Cognitive consistency and performance in the autokinetic situation. *Journal of Abnormal and Social Psychology,* 1964, *68,* 184–92.

Sampson, E. E., & Kardush, M. Age, sex, class and race differences in response to a two-person nonzero-sum game. *Journal of Conflict Resolution,* 1965, *9,* 212–20.

Sapolsky, A. Effect of interpersonal relationships upon verbal conditioning. *Journal of Abnormal and Social Psychology,* 1960, *60,* 241–46.

Sawyer, J., & Friedell, M. F. The interaction screen: An operational model for experimentation on interpersonal behavior. *Behavioral Science,* 1965, *10,* 446–60.

Sawyer, J., & Guetzkow, H. Bargaining and negotiation in international relations. In H. C. Kelman, ed., *International behavior: A social psychological analysis.* New York: Holt, 1965. Pp. 433–63.

Schelling, T. C. *The strategy of conflict.* New York: Oxford University Press, 1960.

Schelling, T. C. *Arms and influence.* New Haven, Conn.: Yale University Press, 1966.

Schenitzki, D. Bargaining, group decision making, and the attainment of maximum joint outcome. Unpublished manuscript, 1962.

Schlenker, B. R.; Bonoma, T. V.; Tedeschi, J. T.; Lindskold, S.; & Horai, J. The effects of referent and reward power upon social conflict. *Psychonomic Science,* 1971, *24,* 268–70.

Schlenker, B. R.; Bonoma, T. V.; Tedeschi, J. T.; Lindskold, S.; & Horai, J. Induced interpersonal attraction as a determinant of reactions to threats. Unpublished manuscript. State University of New York at Albany, 1972.

Schlenker, B. R.; Bonoma, T. V.; Tedeschi, J. T.; & Pivnick, W. P. Compliance to threats as a function of the wording of the threat and the exploitativeness of the threatener. *Sociometry,* 1970, *33,* 394–408.

Schlenker, B. R.; Helm, B.; & Tedeschi, J. T. The effects of personality and situational variables on behavioral trust. *Journal of Personality and Social Psychology,* In press.

Schlenker, B. R.; Schlenker, P.; & Tedeschi, J. T. Impressions of the prestige of an influencer. Mimeographed manuscript. State University of New York at Albany, 1972.

Schlenker, B. R., & Tedeschi, J. T. The exercise of social influence. Paper presented to the XVIIth International Congress of Applied Psychology, Liege, Belgium, 25 July, 1971.

Schlenker, B. R., & Tedeschi, J. T. Interpersonal attraction and the exercise of reward and coercive power. *Human Relations,* 1972, *25,* 427–439.

Schur, E. M. *Law and society.* New York: Random House, 1969.

Scodel, A. Induced collaboration in some non-zero-sum games. *Journal of Conflict Resolution,* 1962, *6,* 335–40.

Shapley, L. S. A value theory for *n*-person games. In H. W. Kuhn & A. W. Tucker, eds., *Contributions to the theory of games.* Vol. 2. Princeton, N.J.: Princeton University Press, 1953. Pp. 307–18.

Shaw, M. E., & Constanzo, P. R. *Theories of social psychology.* New York: McGraw-Hill, 1970.

Sherif, M., & Hovland, C. I. *Social judgment: Assimilation and contrast effects in communication and attitude change.* New Haven, Conn.: Yale University Press, 1961.

Shomer, R. W.; Davis, A. H.; & Kelley, H. H. Threats and the development of coordination: Further studies of the Deutsch and Krauss trucking game. *Journal of Personality and Social Psychology,* 1966, *4,* 119–26.

Shubik, M. On the study of disarmament and escalation. *Journal of Conflict Resolution,* 1968, *12,* 83–101.

Shure, G. H., & Meeker, R. J. Bargaining and negotiation behavior. Quarterly Technical Progress Report, System Development Corporation, Santa Monica, California, 1967.

Sidowski, J. B.; Wycoff, L. B.; & Tabory, L. The influence of reinforcement and punishment in a minimal social situation. *Journal of Abnormal and Social Psychology,* 1956, *52,* 115–19.

Siegel, S., & Fouraker, L. E. *Bargaining and group decision making.* New York: McGraw-Hill, 1960.

Simmel, G. The number of members as determining the sociological form of the group. *American Journal of Sociology*, 1902, *8*, 158–96.

Simon, H. A., & Stedry, A. C. Psychology and economics. In G. Lindzey & E. Aronson, eds., *Handbook of social psychology*. 2nd ed. Vol. 5. Reading, Mass.: Addison-Wesley, 1969. Pp. 269–314.

Singer, J. D. Threat-perception and the armament-tension dilemma. *Journal of Conflict Resolution*, 1958, *2*, 90–105.

Singer, J. D. International influence: A formal model. *American Political Science Review*, 1963, *57*, 420–30.

Skinner, B. F. A case history in scientific method. *American Psychologist*, 1956, *11*, 221–33.

Small, W. S. An experimental study of the mental processes of the rat. *American Journal of Psychology*, 1899–1900, *11*, 133–64.

Smith, W. P. Reward structure and information in the development of cooperation. *Journal of Experimental Social Psychology*, 1968, *4*, 199–223.

Smith, W. P., & Leginski, W. A. Magnitude and precision of punitive power in bargaining strategy. *Journal of Experimental Social Psychology*, 1970, *6*, 57–76.

Steele, M. W., & Tedeschi, J. T. Matrix indices and strategy choices in mixed-motive games. *Journal of Conflict Resolution*, 1967, *11*, 198–205.

Stevens, C. M. *Strategy and collective bargaining negotiation*. New York: McGraw-Hill, 1963.

Stoll, C. S. Review of simulation and society by John Raser. *Simulation and Games*, 1970, *1*, 93–95.

Swingle, P. *The structure of conflict*. New York: Academic Press, 1970.

Tedeschi, J. T. Threats and promises. In P. Swingle, ed., *The structure of conflict*. New York: Academic Press, 1970. Pp. 155–192.

Tedeschi, J. T. Compliance as a function of source esteem and threat credibility. Unpublished manuscript. State University of New York at Albany, 1971.

Tedeschi, J. T., & Bonoma, T. V. Power and influence: An introduction. In J. T. Tedeschi, ed., *The social influence processes*. Chicago: Aldine-Atherton, 1972. Pp. 1–49.

Tedeschi, J. T.; Bonoma, T. V.; & Brown, R. C., Jr. A paradigm for the study of coercive power. *Journal of Conflict Resolution*, 1971, *15*, 197–224.

Tedeschi, J. T.; Bonoma, T. V.; & Lindskold, S. Threateners' reactions to prior announcement of behavioral compliance or defiance. *Behavioral Science*, 1970, *15*, 131–39.

Tedeschi, J. T.; Bonoma, T. V.; & Novinson, N. Behavior of a threatener: Retaliation vs. fixed opportunity costs. *Journal of Conflict Resolution*, 1970, *14*, 69–76.

Tedeschi, J. T.; Bonoma, T. V.; & Schlenker, B. R. Influence, decision, and compliance. In J. T. Tedeschi, ed., *The social influence processes*. Chicago: Aldine-Atherton, 1972. Pp. 346–418.

Tedeschi, J. T.; Bonoma, T. V.; Schlenker, B. R.; & Lindskold, S. Power, influence, and behavioral compliance. *Law and Society Review*, 1970, *4*, 521–44.

Tedeschi, J. T.; Horai, J.; Lindskold, S.; & Faley, T. The effects of opportunity costs and target compliance on the behavior of a threatening source. *Journal of Experimental Social Psychology*, 1970, *6*, 205–13.

Tedeschi, J. T.; Horai, J.; Lindskold, S.; & Gahagan, J. P. The effects of threat upon prevarication and compliance and social conflict. *Proceedings* of the 76th annual American Psychological Association Convention, 1968. Pp. 399–400.

Tedeschi, J. T., & O'Donovan, D. Social power and the psychologist. *Professional Psychology*, 1971, *2*, 59–64.

Tedeschi, J. T.; Schlenker, B. R.; & Bonoma, T. V. Cognitive dissonance: Private ratiocination or public spectacle? *American Psychologist*, 1971, *26*, 685–95.

Tedeschi, J. T., Schlenker, B. R., & Lindskold, S. The exercise of power and influence: The source of influence. In J. T. Tedeschi, ed., *The social influence processes*. Chicago: Aldine-Atherton, 1972. Pp. 287–345.

Tedeschi, J. T.; Smith, R. B., III; & Brown, R. C., Jr. A reappraisal of the concept of aggression. Unpublished manuscript. State University of New York at Albany, 1972.

Teger, A. I. The effect of early cooperation on the escalation of conflict. *Journal of Experimental Social Psychology*, 1970, *6*, 187–204.

Terhune, K. W. Motives, situation, and interpersonal conflict within Prisoner's Dilemma. *Journal of Personality and Social Psychology Monograph Supplement*, 1968, *8*, (3, pt. 2).

Terhune, K. W. The effects of personality in cooperation and conflict. In P. Swingle, ed., *The structure of conflict*. New York: Academic Press, 1970. Pp. 193–234.

Thibaut, J. The development of contractual norms in bargaining: Replication and variation. *Journal of Conflict Resolution*, 1968, *12*, 102–12.

Thibaut, J., & Faucheux, C. The development of contractual norms in a bargaining situation under two types of stress. *Journal of Experimental Social Psychology*, 1965, *1*, 89–102.

Thibaut, J., & Kelley, H. H. *The social psychology of groups*. New York: Wiley, 1959.

Thibaut, J., & Reicken, H. W. Authoritarianism, status, and the communication of aggression. *Human Relations*, 1955, *8*, 95–120.

Tittle, C. R. Crime rates and legal sanctions. *Social Problems*, 1969, *16*, 409–23.

Tornatzky, L., & Geiwitz, P. J. The effects of threat and attraction on interpersonal bargaining. *Psychonomic Science*, 1968, *13*, 125–26.

Torrance, E. P. Some consequences of power differences on decision making in permanent and temporary three-man groups. *Research Studies*, State College of Washington, 1954, *22*, 130–40.

Townsend, R. *Up the organization*. New York: Knopf, 1970.

Triandis, H. C.; Vassiliou, V.; & Thomanek, E. K. Social status as a determinant of respect and friendship acceptance. *Sociometry*, 1966, *29*, 396–405.

Trost, J. Coalitions in triads. *Acta Sociologica*, 1965, *8*, 226–43.

Tuchman, B. *The guns of August*. New York: Macmillan, 1962.

Turner, J. L.; Foa, E. B.; & Foa, U. G. Interpersonal reinforcers: classification, interrelationship, and some differential properties. *Journal of Personality and Social Psychology*, 1971, *19*, 168–80.

Uejio, C. K., & Wrightsman, L. S. Ethnic-group differences in the relationship of trusting attitudes to cooperative behavior. *Psychological Reports*, 1967, *20*, 563–71.

Uesugi, T. T., & Vinacke, W. E. Strategy in a feminine game. *Sociometry*, 1963, *26*, 75–88.

Vinacke, W. E. Sex roles in a three-person game. *Sociometry*, 1959, *22*, 343–60.

Vinacke, W. E. Power, strategy, and the formation of coalitions under four incentive conditions. Technical Report 1, University of Hawaii, 1962.

Vinacke, W. E. Variables in experimental games: Toward a field theory. *Psychological Bulletin*, 1969, *71*, 293–318.

Vinacke, W. E., & Arkoff, A. Experimental study of coalitions in the triad. *American Sociological Review,* 1957, *22,* 406–15.

Vinacke, W. E.; Crowell, D. C.; Dien, D.; & Young, V. The effect of information about strategy on a three-person game. *Behavioral Science,* 1966, *11,* 180–89.

Vinacke, W. E.; Lichtman, C. M.; Cherulnik, P. D. Coalition formation under different conditions of play in a three-person competitive game. *Journal of General Psychology,* 1967, *77,* 165–76.

Von Neumann, J., & Morgenstern, O. *Theory of games and economic behavior.* New York: Wiley, 1944.

Wallace, D., & Rothaus, P. Communication, group loyalty, and trust in the PD game. *Journal of Conflict Resolution,* 1969, *13,* 370–80.

Walster, E.; Aronson, E.; & Abrahams, D. On increasing the persuasiveness of a low prestige communicator. *Journal of Experimental Social Psychology,* 1966, *2,* 325–42.

Walster, E., & Festinger, L. The effectiveness of "overheard" persuasive communications. *Journal of Abnormal and Social Psychology,* 1962, *65,* 395–402.

Walters, R. H. Implications of laboratory studies of aggression for the control and regulation of violence. *Annals of the American Academy of Political and Social Science,* 1966, *364,* 60–72.

Walters, R. H. Some conditions facilitating the occurrence of imitative behavior. Paper presented at the Miami University Symposium on Social Behavior, Oxford, Ohio, 1967.

Walton, R. E., & McKersie, R. B. *A behavioral theory of labor negotiations.* New York: McGraw-Hill, 1965.

Weber, M. *The theory of social and economic organization.* New York: Oxford University Press, 1947.

Weiss, R. F.; Buchanan, W.; & Pasamanick, B. Social consensus in persuasive communication. *Psychological Reports,* 1964, *14,* 95–98.

Weiss, R. F.; Weiss, J. J.; & Chalupa, L. M. Classical conditioning of attitudes as a function of source consensus. *Psychonomic Science,* 1967, *9,* 465–66.

Weiss, W. A. A "sleeper" effect in opinion change. *Journal of Abnormal and Social Psychology,* 1953, *48,* 173–80.

Weiss, W. A. Opinion congruence with a negative source of one issue as a factor influencing agreement on another issue. *Journal of Abnormal and Social Psychology,* 1957, *54,* 180–86.

Wertheimer, M. Some problems in the theory of ethics. *Social Research,* 1935, *2,* 353–67.

Whiting, J. W. M. Resource mediation and learning by identification. In I. Iscoe & H. W. Stevenson, eds., *Personality development in children.* Austin: University of Texas Press, 1960. Pp. 112–26.

Whiting, J. W. M., & Child, I. L. *Child training and personality: A cross-cultural study.* New Haven, Conn.: Yale University Press, 1953.

Willis, R. H., & Long, N.J. An experimental simulation of an internation truel. *Behavioral Science,* 1967, *12,* 24–32.

Wilson, A. *The bomb and the computer.* New York: Delta Books, 1968.

Withey, S. B. Sequential accommodations to threat. In G. H. Grosser, H. Wechsler, & M. Greenblatt, eds., *The threat of impending disaster: Contributions to the psychology of stress.* Cambridge, Mass.: The MIT Press, 1964. Pp. 105–14.

Wright, P. Attitude change under direct and indirect interpersonal influence. *Human Relations,* 1966, *19,* 199–211.

Wrightsman, L. S. Personality and attitudinal correlates of trusting and trustworthy behaviors in a two-person game. *Journal of Personality and Social Psychology,* 1966, *4,* 328–32.

Ziller, R. C.; Zeigler, H.; Gregor, G. L.; Styskal, R. A.; & Peak, W. The neutral in a communication network under conditions of conflict. *American Behavioral Scientist,* 1969, *13,* 265–282.

Zinnes, D. A. Coalition theories and the balance of power. In S. Groennings, E. W. Kelley, & M. Leiserson, eds., *The study of coalition behavior: Theoretical perspectives and cases from four continents.* New York: Holt, 1970. Pp. 351–68.

Zipf, S. G. Resistance and conformity under reward and punishment. *Journal of Abnormal and Social Psychology,* 1960, *61,* 102–9.

Index

Abelson, R. P., 68, 188, 208
Abrahams, D., 92
Activation of commitments, 50
Adams, H., 107
Adams, J. S., 144, 162
Aggression, 217, 218, 226
Albert, S., 113
Alexander, C. N., Jr., 197, 205
All-computer simulation, 230
Allen, V. L., 104
Altruism, 219
Alvares, K., 86
Amidjaja, I. R., 169
Anderson, A. J., 112, 137, 140
Anderson, R. E., 171
Argyle, M., 113, 213
Arkoff, A., 159, 160–63, 165–68
Aronfreed, J., 216
Aronson, E., 68, 92, 209, 232, 234
Arrowood, A. J., 165, 169
Asch, S. E., 47, 80, 212
Asymmetrical contingency, 26, 230
Atkinson, J. W., 97
Attitudes, 80, 147, 181, 208
Attitudinal structuring, 230
Attraction, 42, 48, 50–52, 66, 68, 105, 106, 181, 208, 211, 213, 220, 225, 230
Authentication, 66, 70, 76, 211, 230
Authority, 47

Bachrach, P., 30, 31, 38, 232
Baldwin, D., 34
Bandura, A., 74, 91, 214, 217, 218, 226
Baratz, M. S., 30, 31, 38, 232

Bargaining, 230
  definitions, 117–19, 153
  distributive, 110, 125, 126, 231
  essential features, 117, 125
  free bargaining behavior, 119
  integrative, 125, 233
  intraorganizational, 125, 233
  problems, 117, 128–30
Bargaining games, 123, 129
Bargaining outcomes,
  bargaining dilemma, 131
  break-off points, 126, 127
  comparison level for alternatives, 126, 129
  concession point, 126, 127
  equilibrium point, 126, 127
  fall back position, 126, 127
  goals, 126, 127, 128
  level of aspiration, 126, 127, 129, 132, 135, 142, 233
  minimum disposition, 126, 127, 131, 135
  minimum necessary settlement (MNS), 101, 102
  range, 126, 135, 230
Bargaining strategies,
  bids, 129
  coercive power, 36, 47, 49, 135, 139
  commitment, 133, 137
  concessions, 129, 142
  escalation, 136
  toughness, 131, 133
Baron, R. A., 216
Barton, R. E., 188
Bartos, O. J., 131, 132

263